An Accidental T

A Caribbean Misa

Jason Smart

First English edition published in 2017 by Smart Travel Publishing

Cover design by Ace Graphics

ASIN: 9781520328256
ISBN-13: 978-1542415637
ISBN-10: 1542415632

Smart, Jason J
An Accidental Tourist

ALSO BY JASON SMART

The Red Quest

Flashpacking through Africa

The Balkan Odyssey

Panama City to Rio de Janeiro

Temples, Tuk-tuks & Fried Fish Lips

Bite Size North America

Rapid Fire Europe

Crowds, Colour, Chaos

Meeting the Middle East

From Here to Anywhere

Africa to Asia

Take Your Wings and Fly

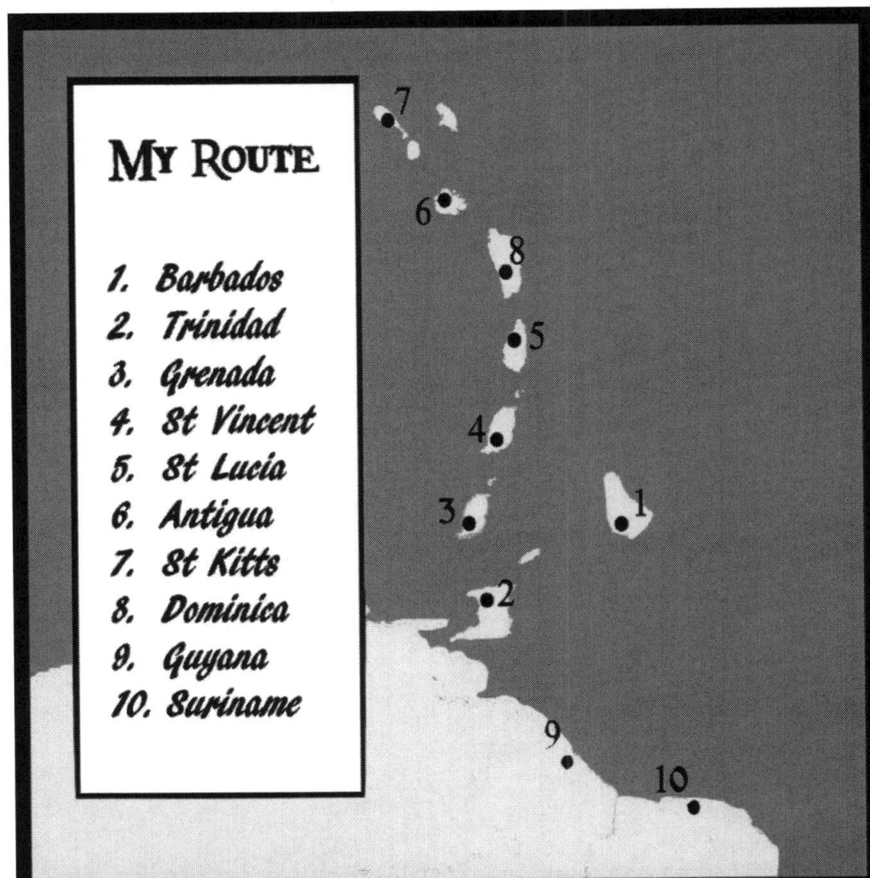
MY ROUTE
1. Barbados
2. Trinidad
3. Grenada
4. St Vincent
5. St Lucia
6. Antigua
7. St Kitts
8. Dominica
9. Guyana
10. Suriname
7
6
8
5
4
3
1
2
9
10

For Andrew Billington. He knows why, though I think he'd prefer a cake.

Contents:

Jason Smart

An Accidental Tourist

A Caribbean Misadventure

SMART TRAVEL PUBLISHING
MANCHESTER

Chapter 1. Beginning in Barbados

The Caribbean has always interested me. Maybe it was because I knew next to nothing about most of the palm-fringed islands that dotted this tropical part of the ocean. Take St Kitts and Nevis for starters. This pair of islands is an independent sovereign nation and yet the only thing I knew about it was that cruise ships sometimes stopped there. And I only knew that because my parents-in-law had been. Beyond that, I knew nothing. Zilch. I couldn't even place St Kitts on a map. And it was the same with Grenada and St Vincent and the Grenadines. The latter didn't even sound like a real place and more like a 1960s skiffle band. As for Grenada, the only things I knew about this tiny teardrop island was that the United States had invaded in the 1980s, and that someone invented the hand grenade there, though I probably made up this last fact.

I knew more about Barbados and Trinidad, of course, and Jamaica and Cuba to the north. I had also heard of the Dominican Republic. These five were the big hitters of the Caribbean league. But what about Dominica? It sounded like the same place as the Dominican Republic, but when I looked into this, I could not have been further from the truth. The Dominican Republic was a large country that shared the island of Hispaniola with Haiti, whereas Dominica was a block of volcanic rock a thousand miles away. They were both separate nations as different as France is to the Canary Islands. And then there were places such as Antigua and St Lucia, islands whose names dripped with delicious *exoticness.* From brochures and TV programs, I knew they had pristine beaches and tropical palms, but was there anything else to see? What were their capital cities like? What about their wildlife? What did their citizens do for fun? I needed answers for these questions. So, with that decided, I set aside three weeks so I could visit as many of these Caribbean nations as I could, soon discovering there were four options available to me.

Option one was to spend half a million dollars chartering a yacht, a skipper and a ton of skimpily-dressed bikini girls. Together, we would tour the islands in a rum punch haze of utter hedonism. This was my favoured option: apart from the fact I didn't have a spare briefcase full of used banknotes.

Option two was my least favourite. I could book myself on a package tour to Barbados, Jamaica or St Lucia and laze about on the same beach for two weeks, seeing a bit of the island, but little else. If I had been going with my wife, this might have been the only option but, as it stood, I discounted it as a nonstarter.

Option three was probably the most popular way of seeing the Caribbean: the cruise. I could board a ridiculously oversized vessel and visit seven or eight islands without having to repack my luggage every other day. But the thought of sitting aboard a ship with three thousand retirees and a man hollering over a loudspeaker that the Captain's Special included a free pre-dinner cocktail filled me with shuddering dread. This left option four.

2

Option four was a bold one, audacious even. It involved flying between the islands, thereby maximising the speed at which I could travel around them. I would choose a hotel in each capital and then, after a day or two, move on to somewhere new. Of course, there was no way I could cover the entire Caribbean this way – I would need about two months for that – no, I had to be selective; so, after poring over a map, I decided upon the southern part of the Caribbean for the simple fact that many independent nations were close together there. When I discovered that a small company called Liat Airlines existed, I sketched out an itinerary that seemed ridiculous on paper, but might actually work. Utilising a series of cheap Liat Airlines flights, I could fly as far as Antigua in the North and Trinidad in the South, with Barbados, Grenada, St Vincent, St Lucia, St Kitts and Dominica in between. And then, simply because I could not resist, I could fly to South America and take in the beauty of Guyana and Suriname, countries entrenched with enough Caribbean flavour to warrant their inclusion in the trip. The thought of visiting all these different places excited me and so, before I could back out, I booked the flights. Click, click, click: nine separate Liat flights, plus another with Trinidad's national carrier, Caribbean Airlines, and one more with Suriname Airways. The trip was on. All I needed to do was book my return flights from Europe. That done, I delved a little deeper at Liat Airlines.

What I discovered was not good, especially since the lion's share of my trip was depending upon them. Liat Airlines were infamous for their delays, cancellations, non-existent customer service and lost luggage. One website had a page dedicated to a constant stream of bad online reviews. Words and phrases such as 'anxiety', 'frustration', 'never again', 'shocking' and the simple but effective 'horror airlines' peppered almost every review. I looked up from the screen and felt stirrings of alarm. Then I looked down again.

Liat stands for Leeward Islands Air Transport, but some mockers had changed it to Luggage In Another Terminal or Leave Island Any Time. One reviewer, a passenger called Arthur Hicks, wrote a letter of complaint about Liat Airlines that went viral. Hicks describes a nightmarish day of flying on six separate Liat flights, when all he wanted was to fly from A to B. He had to change planes each time, getting frisked by security every time, and then, to add insult to injury, when he arrived at his destination, weary and embittered, the last ferry home had already gone. Needless to say, Liat Airlines lost his luggage, too.

I read another damning review and actually laughed. Liat had cancelled one woman's flight, which was bad in itself, but it was the Liat Airline customer service agent who was the source of the writer's ire. When the woman complained about the cancellation, inquiring about how to get home, the Liat employee told her to swim.

To swim!

I closed my laptop and sighed heavily. It looked like a cancelled or heavily-delayed flight might well upset my densely packed Caribbean adventure trip. If Liat Airlines cancelled my flight from Trinidad to Grenada – my first hop with them – then the dominoes would fall; I would not be able to catch my connecting flight to St Lucia, and then would not be able to fly onto Antigua. I would be trapped on a Caribbean island. Why hadn't I checked all this before booking the damned flights?

But what could I do?

Nothing. There was no point fretting about things now – if Liat Airlines cancelled one of my flights, then I would deal with it in situ as best I could. Worrying about it for the next two months would only cause my hair to fall out.

3

Packing for my trip was easy with just hand luggage. I threw in a few T-shirts, a couple of pairs of shorts, some underwear, a pair of flip-flops (should I decide to lurk by a swimming pool) and a hat. There was still enough room for a bag of toiletries, which included some Zika-repelling mosquito spray and some strong suntan spray. After slipping in a laptop and some spare chargers, I was ready to rock.

My wife agreed to drive me to Manchester Airport. We set off on a warm, sunny July morning. My Virgin Atlantic flight was not due to depart until 1.15pm, which was plenty of time, since it was only 10am.

"I wish I was going to Barbados," Angela lamented for the tenth time. "Sitting on a beach with a cocktail, enjoying the sunset: it sounds idyllic. Not staying at home and building a shed. It should be the other way around."

"You should've come with me. You had the chance."

This was true, but we both knew it was never going to happen. Ten countries in three weeks meant airport after airport and lots of stress.

"I know. But I quite fancy the idea of Barbados now…" Angela's words trailed off because in front of us was a monumental traffic jam. Red brake lights and flashing motorway signs told us there was an accident ahead. We joined the back of the queue and stopped. Then we stayed put for ages. While we waited, I switched on the radio and searched for a traffic update. It came fifteen minutes later, informing us that a seven-car pile-up had closed both sides of the M62. The traffic announcer said he didn't know how long it would be closed.

"What shall we do?" Angela asked.

I said nothing, feeling the first edges of unease. I looked at my watch. It was ten thirty, which left under three hours until the flight. No need to worry unnecessarily, quite yet. Besides, there was nothing much we could do anyway. "Just sit tight and hope it clears."

It didn't.

Two hours later, I had to face facts: there was no chance I would reach the airport in time for my flight. I'd already rung Manchester Airport on the off chance that the flight was delayed, but it was not. It was due to take off in one hour with or without me. Liat Airlines had not scuppered my plans: the British traffic had. While I fumed and panicked, Angela had an idea. She was looking at Google Maps and had noticed a thin, country road running parallel to the motorway. "Why don't you grab your luggage and find this road," she said, pointing at the map. "You might be able to flag down a car or something. You can explain about your flight, offer the driver some money. You might just make it."

I laughed despite myself. "Look at where we are?" I gestured to the rolling hills of moorland on both sides of the motorway. A sturdy fence was blocking falling rocks from rolling onto the road. "Can you seriously imagine me climbing over that fence with my luggage, dragging it up that hill? If a farmer doesn't shoot me for sheep worrying, then I'll probably break an ankle in a ditch. And even if I do make it to the other side – which is about half a mile away, by the way – I'll still have to wait for someone to roll past with a tractor? I might as well walk to the airport."

"Well, why don't you, then?" Angela snapped. "I was only trying to help."

After a fraught phone call to the Virgin office at Manchester Airport, a kindly woman offered a solution. She could book me on another Virgin flight leaving the next afternoon. The problem was that it left from Gatwick Airport, which would mean a journey down to London. "Oh, and something else," the woman said. "The only seat remaining is in upper class. Are you happy to pay the difference?"

"How much?

"Let me check." The woman tapped away on her keyboard. I could hear the keys clicking. "Because of the situation you're in, and the fact that you've already paid for an economy ticket, the price is only £750."

Jesus!

I conferred with Angela. £750 was a lot of money, but at least it would mean I would get to the Caribbean. If I didn't board the Gatwick flight, then that would be that: everything gone, and all the money I'd spent on hotels and flights down the drain. But another thing bothered me, too. Flying the next afternoon would mean a day less in Barbados, cutting my time there by half. But if I stayed in England, I would be helping Angela build a shed in the back garden. That was it, I decided. I told the Virgin Atlantic woman that, yes, I did want the seat. She tapped something on her far-away keyboard, then asked for my credit card details. All I had to do now was get off the motorway and find a route down to Gatwick airport.

Seven hours and three trains later, I was there, checking into an airport hotel. My trip to the Caribbean was still on.

4

Upper class (why it wasn't called business class, I have no idea) in Virgin was nice; it was certainly better than the cramped cabin to my rear. With eight hours until we reached Barbados, I stretched out and tried not to think about how much money it had cost me to sip on complimentary champagne.

An hour later, I spied a teenage girl across from me playing on her iPad. The name of the game was something like *Wedding Day*. The basic premise was simple: to prepare a young, cartoon woman for her special day. First, the face was cleansed of spots and unsightly blemishes by using a control option that brought up a little tray of pretend foundation cream. The teenager deftly applied some electronic foundation and, when the program deemed the pretend face clear enough, she was rewarded with a pleasing array of stars, and a progression to the next level. The new stage, I noted with interest, involved hair, eyes and lipstick. The teenager was clearly an expert because she propelled through these levels, receiving a dizzying number of stars in the process, before moving onto the confusing task of picking out shoes, necklaces and fingernails. I watched, rapt, as the teenager flicked through the options, then exchanged some of her new stars for hairstyles. When it was time for the wedding dress option, I realised I was getting addicted and so I tore myself away, thankful there was no Wi-Fi or I might have downloaded the game myself. As it was, for the next couple of hours I watched the latest Star Wars film.

When the pilot came over the intercom a while later and told us we were about to land, I was so surprised that I actually looked at my watch. Where had the time gone? I must have dozed, that was the only explanation. I looked out of the window. All I could see was sea.

And then, like a Caribbean privateer, I spied land ahoy. My first sighting of the West Indies! Barbados' south-western coastline was a pleasing dollop of tropical green, edged by a thin sliver of cream-coloured sand. Gorgeous ocean surrounded it – the sun's rays reflecting off sand beneath the surface to create a kaleidoscope of turquoise, cobalt, azure and cyan. And then we were down on the runway with barely a squeak of the main undercarriage. I had arrived in country number one of my Caribbean adventure and I could almost taste the rum.

5

I was one of the first passengers out of the aircraft and rushed headlong to reach immigration before anyone else. With time at a premium, I wanted to get to my hotel as soon as possible to see as much as I could before I flew to Trinidad the next morning. The only problem was the stout woman in uniform blocking my path through the empty zigzag course leading to the immigration desks.

The woman wasn't even aware I was behind her. She was sauntering along without a care in the world, her considerable booty swinging from side to side as I tried to get past. I huffed, which made her turn around. As she moved to the side, she drawled, "Slow down, Mister. You're in the Caribbean now."

I was the first person to reach the desk and the man behind it questioned me why I was only staying in paradise, as he put it, for one night.

"I have to fly to Trinidad tomorrow."

"Why?"

"Because I am a lunatic who thrives on short connections and hurried airport runs. I'm going to Trinidad so I can catch a flight to Grenada, so that later the same day I can fly to St Vincent and the Grenadines. Does that answer your question?" Except, I didn't say any of that and simply said I was a tourist with a lack of time.

With just hand luggage, I was through the whole airport in just twelve minutes. That was a record even for me. Even so, it was 4.45pm and, with sundown about two hours away, I had to get to the hotel before then. I jumped in the back of a taxi and asked the driver how long it would take to get to the Radisson.

"Maybe thirty minutes, man. Why? You in a hurry?" The driver was a twenty-something man who spoke with a thick Caribbean accent. Thirty minutes was *tirty* minutes.

"As it happens, yes."

The man nodded. "Okay then, hang on. I'll take some shortcuts that people don't normally see."

With that, we were off, roaring away from the airport with me gripping on for dear life. The man was a certified lunatic, relishing overtaking on blind bends, tearing around roundabouts and throwing his head back and guffawing like a crazy person. Actually, I made up the last bit, but it may well have been true; his driving certainly belied the common misconception that people in the Caribbean never rushed. While I considered how fast we were going, we careened along a thin strip of a road, edged by quaint pastel blue and green wooden bungalows, all with tin roofs. I might have taken a photo if it weren't for a bus heading straight for us. A second later, it was upon us and I could see the whites of the bus driver's eyes as we roared past his wing mirror by a hair's width.

"You can slow down a bit, if you want," I whispered breathlessly.

"Nah, man. Goin' for the record. I think I might do it this time."

I spied a row of palm trees passing in a flash, then some fruit stalls. They were all gone in a multi-coloured blur. Finally, we slowed as we drove past a large building that declared itself the Deighton Griffiths Secondary School, but the respite was brief, for as soon as we cleared some speed humps, we were off again like a pea fired from an elastic band. At one point, I saw an elderly woman wearing a wide-brimmed straw hat about to cross the road. A blast of the horn and she scurried for cover, almost losing her hat. It was as thrilling as a roller coaster, except with more danger. Then we stopped. Traffic lights thwarted forward momentum. The madman next to me had his gear and accelerator primed and ready. I used the lull to ask him what he thought about Liat Airlines.

"What do you wanna know?"

"Are they reliable?"

The man shrugged. "Some days they are good, some days they are bad. But what can you do?"

With that, we catapulted off, hugging a road that offered occasional glimpses of the ocean but, more often than not, beach resorts and cafés called BBQ Beach Grill, Chicken George and Yankee Joe's. And then, I was thrust forward in my seat as we came to a dramatic halt. The driver checked his watch. "Eighteen minutes, twenty seconds: my new world record. Enjoy Barbados, man."

6

My arrival in the Caribbean had coincided with the beginning of the hurricane season. Thankfully (and I had checked diligently), there were no storms brewing over the Atlantic, at least not yet. That said, the late afternoon was muggy and hot: the perfect temperature for sweating and stickiness. I dumped my things in the room, grabbed a map of Bridgetown, Barbados' compact capital city, and started walking. More or less as soon as I left the hotel, I spotted a small brown monkey springing across the road to reach the safety of some trees. Before I could do a second take, it was gone, hidden in deep foliage. Originally imported from Senegal and The Gambia during the height of the slave trade, these mischievous imps were now in their seventy-fifth generation and thriving in the Caribbean.

I turned left along Bay Street, occasionally trying to stifle a yawn. Although my watch said it was 5.30pm, my body thought it was 11.30 at night. I was ready for bed, but couldn't – not with things to see. On my left, appearing behind a set of nondescript, warehouse-type buildings was the Caribbean Sea – a delicious slice of blue, lapping against a palm-fringed beach. Out in the surf, a few heads bobbed up and down. When I had imagined the Caribbean, this was it. This was *exactly* it.

A man wearing a beanie hat was walking towards me on the same side of the road. His hand was up to his ear and I thought he was listening to his phone. Then I saw he was carrying a small, handheld speaker. As he breezed past, he nodded. From his miniature speaker, some tinny reggae music played. Further along, I stopped opposite some dignified government buildings. Standing proudly in front of one was a large statue of Grantley Adams, the man for whom the airport was named.

Adams' pose was serious and wistful, a healthy mix for the first premier of Barbados, I felt. The grounds where he stood belonged to the government of Barbados – a collection of colonial-era buildings that looked closed for the day. I snapped off a quick photo and then was on the move again, itching to see the centre of Bridgetown before it was too late.

"Hey man," said a grey-haired gent passing the time of day by reclining on a wall. Just along from him was a row of tiny wooden houses, all painted in pleasingly summer hues: greens, oranges and pinks.

I said hello but didn't stop.

"You wanna party?" he added.

It seemed an unusual question. I turned in his direction. The man could see I was confused. He said, "I mean, do you want something?" The man looked along the street in both directions; then glanced over his shoulder, even though there was nothing there apart from a few shrubs and then the sea. "Something to party with, man."

I shook my head, brushing off his potential drug peddling. In fact, all I could think about was finding a shop so I could buy some water. I was ridiculously hot and bothered, my forehead was already dripping and I could taste salt on my upper lip.

"Suit yourself," the man said, already looking for other people walking along in my wake. As for me, I picked up the pace along Bay Street, stopping only to purchase a bottle of water from a small convenience store. I drank it in ten seconds flat. Ten minutes later, I arrived at my destination: Independence Square.

7

Barbados actually means *the bearded ones*. When Portuguese explorers first sighted the land we now know as Barbados, they did not see men with beards, but saw plenty of fig trees with dangling, beard-like leaves. The Portuguese didn't linger, though; they were more interested in the great continental landmass to the south, and so it was left to the British, who arrived in 1625, to settle on the island.

The British pioneers found things hard at first. The constant buzzing of insects, the poor quality of their meagre food rations and the relentless heat all took their toll. When some of them couldn't face working the fields, they asked their friends back home for help. And so, Irish peasants were plucked – against their will – from the countryside and put aboard ships bound for the Caribbean. They weren't the only ones: a fair few Scots ended up toiling in the hateful fields of the Caribbean, working for British landowners who were too lazy to do the work themselves. In fact, by the mid-1600s, there were so many Irish and Scottish workers that the majority of the Barbadian population were white.

Things changed a century later with the introduction of sugar cane. Almost overnight, the plantation owners needed hardier workers than the emaciated, disease-ravaged Europeans they currently had, and so African slaves were shipped across the Atlantic. They came in such quantities that, within just a few decades, black people outnumbered whites by a colossal margin. And yet they kept on coming, working so hard that Barbados was soon outperforming all the other Caribbean islands put together. At the height of the sugar rush, almost every plot of arable land in Barbados was growing sugar cane, so much so that food had to be imported. The Brits of Barbados didn't care; their capital, Bridgetown, was growing into one of the largest cities in the Americas. For them, everything was hunky-dory. Then, quite suddenly, it wasn't.

The black slaves rebelled. After contributing to one of the greatest money-spinners of the British Empire, they had little to show, apart from whipping wounds, empty stomachs and exhaustion. One slave, a man who went by the name of Bussa, led the rebellion of 1816. Using his natural intelligence, he gathered a large group of slaves and led them on a march across some plantations, burning the sugar crop as they went. When the British landowners didn't do anything apart from running away, more slaves threw down their tools and joined Bussa's marauding band. Eventually, twenty thousand slaves were with him and, between them, they controlled over seventy plantations. It was one of the biggest slave rebellions the Caribbean had ever seen.

The British decided to do something. They sent some ships full of soldiers and weapons to Barbados. As soon as they stepped foot onto the island with their advanced weaponry, the troops chased the slaves down, killing hundreds of them. That was the end of their slave rebellion and the plantations carried on churning out their sugar crop.

Sugar remained the top Barbadian export until the 1970s. Around this time, some progressive individuals realised that to have all their eggs in one sweet basket was asking for trouble, especially when a hurricane could wreak havoc with the crop. So the Government of Barbados diversified into making medicines, establishing offshore banking and building a new tourist infrastructure. Nowadays, Barbados is one of the richest countries in the Caribbean and has produced one of music's biggest selling artists of all time, namely pop star Rihanna. So it's safe to say that after a few false starts, Barbados is doing quite well for itself.

8

Independence Square is small but distinguished. It has a few arches, a pleasing little water feature and a statue of someone called Errol Walton Barrow, twice prime minister of Barbados. His likeness overlooks a small inlet of the Caribbean Sea called the Constitution River, a thin line of water that splits the capital in two. A couple of elderly ladies were sitting chatting, enjoying the fading afternoon sun, facing the river. Suddenly, one of them erupted into a raucous throaty guffaw, which she finished with a terrific thigh slap. When her pal sniggered in appreciation, I decided I liked Barbados.

Across a small bridge, I caught sight of my first Caribbean Burger King. It looked like it was doing good business, but I ignored it in favour of an obelisk in memory of Barbados's war heroes. I read a few names while trying to ignore the stares from the assembled taxi drivers. Another statue caught my eye. It was of a man I instantly recognised – Horatio Nelson, who had visited Barbados in June 1805. His statue was controversial. A few Barbadians wonder why a man so vehemently in favour of the slave trade should be honoured in Barbados, especially in a part of Bridgetown dedicated to national heroes. Nelson was no hero of Barbados, they argue. Others claim he didn't even like Barbados. Some have even suggested that his statue be pulled up and dumped in the wharf.

I looked at the famous admiral. A couple of local seagulls were using his head as a perch. One wobbled and then flapped its wings, launching itself in the direction of Bridgetown's most prominent landmarks, a trio of structures known collectively as the Parliament Buildings. I decided to take its cue and head towards them myself.

The Parliament Buildings could have happily graced any English city's historical centre. The main building featured a grand and turreted clock tower, a plethora of wide arches and a huge blue and yellow Barbadian flag rippling on the top. During a spectacularly fearsome storm in 2010, the flag was ripped off the roof, and the clock hands below it pummelled, twisted and bent so much that they never worked again. Thankfully, everything looked in working order now.

Behind the Parliament Buildings was a busy shopping precinct of souvenir shops. Bags, sunglasses and huge quantities of clothes spilled out onto the street, trying to tempt last-minute shoppers before the shops closed for the evening. I walked past stores with names like The Shoppers Paradise, Souvenir Gifts or Two Dollar Store, finding that Bridgetown was no beauty, but nonetheless perfectly safe and altogether walkable. There were no dramatic hills and no chugging highways to cross; the only thing slowing me down was the humidity and my fatigue.

I found a small outdoor bar. It stood in the middle of a market square and looked an ideal spot in which to enjoy my first Caribbean beer. I wandered over to a small hatch and ordered a Banks Beer. It came in a dinky quarter of a pint bottle that hit the spot as soon as it touched the back of my throat. The drink gave me a chance to take stock. It was almost six-thirty, which meant twelve-thirty in England. I suddenly felt exceptionally weary. I drained my beer and decided to head back in the direction of the hotel, stopping en route at just two more things.

9

The first was the Garrison: to give it its full title, St. Ann's Garrison. It is a little plot of Barbados that is home to a large racetrack, an even larger parade ground known as the Savannah, and, best of all, a selection of historical buildings (including a guardhouse, clock tower, drill hall and old military hospital). When the British army used the area as their headquarters during the sugar cane rush, they levelled some of the rough ground near the buildings in order to build a racecourse. Many a fun-filled weekend was filled with racing competitions between their army thoroughbreds and the plantation owners' horses. Nowadays, whenever cruise ship passengers spend the day in Barbados, many of them wander the Garrison, nodding their elderly heads appreciatively at the sights.

I walked up a slight hill towards it, wishing I could escape the humidity. If I had an extra day on the island, I'd have saved the Garrison until the next day. As it was, unless I wished to ignore Barbados' most 'historically pleasing' attraction, I had to go today.

Halfway up, I stopped near a fancy yellow building brimming with green shutters and white columns. A sign informed me it was the George Washington House, and, had I arrived a few hours previously, I would have been able to see its interior. It was closed now, but, as consolation, I read the information sign that told me that a nineteen-year-old man called George Washington had once stayed in the house in order to look after his sick brother, Lawrence. Both had sailed from Virginia under doctors' advice. The warm tropical air of the Caribbean might help Lawrence's ailing condition, their physician told them. Unfortunately, not long after they arrived, they both caught smallpox. George recovered enough to help his brother for a short while before realising that Barbados was not for him. He returned to Virginia, where he became the first president of the United States. As for Lawrence Washington, he eventually regained enough strength to follow his brother back to America, where he promptly dropped dead of tuberculosis, aged 33.

At the top of the hill was a wide plateau, home to the horse track and old Garrison buildings. The former was busy with people taking shortcuts, and, more bizarrely, teenage girls in glittery costumes practising cheerleading. A woman, presumably their trainer, watched a short distance away. I decided to talk to her in order to find out what the girls were up to.

The woman sized me up and decided to answer my query. "You asking what dese girls are doin'?"

I nodded.

"In't it obvious? Dese girls are practising for the weekend race. Dey are de cream of the crop." She looked proud and I was not surprised. The girls were dancing a tight choreographed routine that would attract plenty of attention, not least because of their bright pompoms.

"So there are lots of races held here?"

The woman looked at me as if I was an idiot straight off the boat. "Course dey do! We have almost two hundred a year. Come race day this weekend, where we are standing right now will be full of stalls selling food and drink. Brass bands will be playing and my cheerleaders will be dancing their asses off. You should come and see for yourself. The stands over there will be full of thousands of people."

I gazed out, imagining it all. With the sun sinking over to the west, it was hard to conjure visions of ladies in floppy hats standing arm-in-arm with well-turned out gentlemen. But it clearly did happen, and often. I thanked her and went off to explore the rest of the Garrison.

10

Behind me were the old military buildings. The red and white clock tower of the old sentry station stood proud and remarkably well kept. Beneath it was a small museum (formerly a prison) which was, rather predictably, closed for the evening. But something was going on. From a side building, a troop of old men emerged, marching in tight formation with old wooden pretend rifles. None was in uniform, not even the man in charge – a wizened old gent wearing a yellow T-shirt. He barked at them to about turn, stand to attention and march. The pensioner platoon did this with seasoned accomplishment.

A couple of gents were watching the spectacle from a distance. Both were leaning against a car bonnet. I walked up to them and introduced myself, asking what was going on.

'Dey practicing for the Changing of the Sentry," one of the men said, a gap-toothed old grizzler with a stubbly chin. "Tourists like to watch 'em, so dat's why they practicing. Come back on Thursday and see for yourself." His pal nodded.

"So the men are former soldiers?" I asked. The small troop was marching again, back and forth, keeping their steps in perfect rhythm.

"Dat's correct," said the toothless man. "They've retired from the Barbados Legion, just like Charlie and me. We come out and watch dem practise; sometime holler when they make a mistake." He looked at Charlie to confirm this. Silent Charlie nodded.

With nothing much to say to that, I threaded my way downhill towards something called Needham's Point. Once a naval dockyard, not much remains apart from a lighthouse, and it was this that I was interested in seeing. I followed a leafy lane that brought me out along an area of woodland bordered by sand and sea. As I crunched along, I could hear the swish of the ocean on my left and, from somewhere up ahead, music. I presumed the jolly calypso was emanating from a hotel, which turned out to be true, because instead of a lonely, possibly windswept area of the coast, Needham's Point was now the grounds of the Hilton Hotel. To emerge from the woods into a complex of sunbathing, barbequing and people throwing balls around a swimming pool, all to the accompaniment of a live band, was disconcerting to say the least. Even the lighthouse, I noted with keen disappointment, was squashed into a courtyard in front of some balconies. As a lighthouse, it was utterly useless.

A waiter came over and, with a servile smile, asked whether I wanted a drink. I politely declined. The sun was going down and my eyes were drooping. I decided to call it a night on my first day in the Caribbean.

Back in my room, I repacked my hand luggage in preparation for my flight to Trinidad the next morning. It would have been nice with more time in Barbados, but I couldn't complain too much – at least I'd made it. By the time I zipped my bag closed, I was dog-tired. I think I was asleep before my head even hit the pillow.

Clockwise from top left: Needham's Point Lighthouse; Downtown Bridgetown; War Memorial monument; One of the Bridgetown's Parliament Buildings; Part of the Garrison complex; Chillin' in Bridgetown; Banks Beer: The Beer of Barbados.

Chapter 2. Hummingbirds, gangs and the Magnificent Seven

The next morning, I awoke at the ungodly hour of 4.30am. Except my body thought it was 9.30am, so it wasn't too bad. I got up and watched the sunrise from the balcony. Glorious shades of auburn and buttery yellow were reaching across a cloud-streaked sky and yet, despite the hour, people were already on the beach, wandering or jogging up and down on the sand.

At 7am, with the sun fully up, I was in a taxi to the airport. Instead of a youthful hothead at the wheel, it was a grey-haired man driving so sedately – and with his face so close to the windscreen – that I wondered whether he was half-blind. Even with hardly any other cars in sight, he drove at a snail's pace, barely getting out of second gear. When we ponderously pulled up outside the departure terminal, I noted that the journey had taken thirty-five minutes: almost double the length of the octane-fuelled rollercoaster journey I'd endured on the way in.

There was an incident at the Caribbean Airlines check-in desks. Thankfully, it didn't concern me, it involved a party of six Jamaicans at the next desk. The three couples had just been informed that they would not be permitted to travel to Trinidad because none of them had yellow fever vaccinations.

"But we did not know," one of the party exclaimed, an ageing gent in a suit and tie. "When did this rule begin?"

The check-in agent was a young man who didn't seem troubled that he had just delivered some unpleasant news. He sighed and addressed the man in the suit. "Look, Caribbean Airlines is not stopping you from flying today; it's the government of Trinidad and Tobago. Anyone with a Jamaican passport must have a valid yellow fever certificate – that's what they say. Unless you show me one, you will not get past immigration in Trinidad. They will send you back here and probably fine us."

"But I say this to you," the man countered. "Why didn't Caribbean Airlines inform us of this rule? All it takes is an email.

Then we would have brought our yellow fever certificates with us from Kingston. And everyone would be happy. So why did we not receive this notification?"

It seemed a valid question to ask.

The young check-in agent sighed again. "Please listen. I'm not in charge of emails, but I do know this: no one from Jamaica is allowed to travel to Trinidad without a yellow fever certificate. It's not our rule; it's the rule of Trinidad."

The old man was getting angry. "Young man, I am not a dimwit. I understand what you are saying, but *you* are not listening to me. All of us possess yellow fever certificates. Mine is inside our bureau at home, with my wife's. They are safe and sound. Had we known to bring them, they would be with us now, but the simple fact of the matter is that we did not know to bring them because your airline did not tell us. You happily took our money, though. So, again, tell me why we were not informed."

And so the sorry dance went on. When I received my boarding card and walked toward departures, they were still arguing about it.

2

After security, I found a duty-free shop and picked up a small bottle of wine for later that evening. When I plopped it on the counter and told the man I didn't need a bag, he recognised my accent as British. "So why did you leave Europe?" he asked in a thick Caribbean accent.

It took me a moment to figure out what he meant. He was referring to the recent referendum on the United Kingdom leaving the European Union. "I don't know," I answered. "Some people were deceived by the Leave campaign; others just wanted to see what would happen."

The shop man considered this. "But I just don't understand why you would want to leave. It's like a shopkeeper in Bridgetown closing his doors on anyone from St Lucia. It makes no sense at all."

I nodded absently, looking at the price of the wine. Ever since the vote to leave the EU had become official, the British pound had nosedived against the US dollar. With the Barbadian currency linked to the US dollar, everything was about fifteen percent more expensive.

I stuffed my bottle into my already over-packed luggage and found a seat with a panoramic view of outside. A squadron of Liat turboprops was parked near my gate, their paint scheme a fruity cocktail of orange, yellow and blue, mixed with a healthy dose of pure white for the main body. A pilot was walking around one of the turboprops, doing his pre-flight checks. The next day he might be flying me to Grenada. When I thought of Liat Airlines, I could not help but feel the tender but rapid beat of butterfly wings in the pit of my stomach.

Boarding for my Caribbean Airlines flight was dead on time and I had a whole row to myself. Taking off from Barbados was just as breathtakingly beautiful as landing had been, but soon we were over open sea, heading southwest. Forty minutes into the journey, a deep and crackly voice came over the intercom.

"Hi, this is the captain speakin'." The man's accent drizzled with prime Caribbean flavour, especially with his curled vowels. "We will be landin' in Piarco International Airport in about ten minutes, where the weather is hazy. Very hazy, in fact. We might have a bit of chop on approach, too. Nottin' to worry about, though. Thanks for flyin' Caribbean Airlines."

He was right. As we descended over Trinidad's sister Island, Tobago, all I could see was cloud. Trinidad wasn't much better, enveloped in a blanket of grey and murk. Down we went into the thick of it, buffeting in the turbulent air. Then we cleared the cloud and I caught my first real glimpse of the wealthiest of all the Caribbean nations: an expanse of deep green, bisected by a thin, meandering brown river. In the distance was a range of high ground. Then, as rain streaked the window, Port of Spain came into view:

factories, roads, small parks and tiny specks of houses and, finally, the airport. Country number two awaited.

3

According to the British Foreign Office, '*There are high levels of violent crime in Trinidad, including murder, especially in parts of the capital, Port of Spain. Robbery and other crimes targeting tourist have occurred.*'

The advice also mentioned an incident involving a British national called Adrian St John, 22, murdered in the capital seven weeks prior to my arrival. The young Londoner had been holidaying on the island, visiting relatives and generally enjoying himself by watching cricket until, one day, everything changed. Mr St John was minding his own business, driving around Port of Spain with a couple of female relatives, when he pulled over. The place he chose for his stop could not have been any worse, because it happened to be the lurking place of two young hoodlums. When they saw the car stop, they seized the opportunity and pointed a gun inside the driver's door. After demanding everyone hand over their phones and money, the gunmen told the driver to go, which should have been that.

Except it wasn't.

According to witnesses, the hoodlums watched the departing car for a moment and then decided to shoot it. One shot shattered the rear window and hit Adrian St John in the back of the head. As blood splattered the interior of the vehicle, one of his passengers managed to bring the car to a shuddering halt. But it was already too late: Adrian St John was dead. Life was that cheap in Trinidad.

Thinking of this tragedy made me a little wary about being in Trinidad. Plus my own father had given me a warning, too. Before his retirement, he had worked in the oil industry, which sometimes had taken him to places as far afield as Argentina, Australia and Trinidad. When he found out I was off to Trinidad as part of my adventure, he had solemnly advised me to be on guard at all times. When he'd visited in the 1990s, the petroleum company had whisked him from the airport under armed escort. They had not allowed him to see anything of the city, apart from their oil refinery.

Because of all these warnings, I arranged for my hotel to pick me up from the airport. While I waited for this transport to arrive, I regarded the portion of Trinidad I could see from the pick-up zone. It looked tropical and leafy. In the distance, beyond the fence, were tropical palms and dramatic hills. And then, as I regarded them, the sun finally broke through the gloom, bathing the landscape in a warming radiance. Under such tropical conviviality, it was hard to imagine anything bad happening in Trinidad.

My car arrived, and we began a long drive along Churchill-Roosevelt Highway, a six-lane road flanked by lush greenery and electricity pylons named after not one, but two wartime leaders. As we coasted along, I spied a large shopping mall called the TruValue Grand Market, followed by a series of sleek commercial buildings. Further back, well away from the highway, were some fetching townhouses. On our left, a cricket pavilion came into view. Cricket is big business in Trinidad, I knew, easily outflanking football as the national sport. There was no cricket going on today; a herd of goats was tending to the grass, nibbling at the periphery.

"You are lucky with the traffic today," the driver commented. We were passing large billboards advertising familiar products such as Coca Cola, M & Ms and Subway, and less familiar ones such as Choco Moo, which ran with the tagline, *Real Milk, Real Chocolate, Real Delicious.* Bolder ads were for Stag Lager, nobly pointing out that *Real Men Don't Drink and Drive*. "Today is Eid, which means a national holiday. Normally this journey would take an hour. Today, it will be thirty minutes."

"Eid? So, is there a large Muslim population in Trinidad?" I asked.

"Not really. But there is enough for a national holiday. You know something? We get all the religious holidays here. Muslim,

Christian, Hindu – all of them mean a day off in Trinidad. It's a wonder any work is done."

We came to the heart of the capital, an area of tightly-packed streets embellished with a fair smattering of modern skyscrapers. Compared to Bridgetown, Port of Spain looked like a real city, a place of wealth. Later, I would see more of it, but, for now, I was happy to be deposited outside my hotel, an establishment whose location was within a whisker of Brian Lara's mansion, the driver told me. I thanked him, grabbed my luggage and headed for the door.

4

Despite being in one of the most dangerous Caribbean countries, I wanted to see a few things before my afternoon tour began. Outside, the road running alongside my hotel seemed safe enough, and so, after a quick look in both directions, I was across the other side, staring at the fetching Ministry of Agriculture, a green and white two-storey colonial-era structure guarded by a line of palm tree sentries. It looked closed.

Around the corner was a huge recreation ground known locally as Queen's Park Savannah, once a sugar plantation and now a place of open grassland where games of cricket, football and rugby were played in and around leafy nature trails. The park was so large that the locals described it as the largest roundabout in the world. Apart from a few men lounging asleep under trees and a sprinkling of people ambling through, the park was empty. If I came back the following February, the park would have been awash with vivid feathers, bright costumes and steel drumming bands. February in Trinidad and Tobago meant carnival time!

The park hasn't always been an area of joviality. In 1783, Queen's Park Savannah was in the hands of the Peschiers, a family of wealthy European sugar caners. After three decades of hard plantation farming, Henri Peschier and his sons decided to sell the land to the British government for the princely sum of six thousand dollars. With the deal done, the Peschiers moved on, leaving the new owners of Queen's Park Savannah to scratch their heads and wonder what to do with the land, until some bright spark suggested getting rid of the sugar cane and planting some grass.

The grass began growing so thickly that another bright spark brought in a herd of cows. The beasts would, he said, keep the grass down to manageable levels while providing the odd tasty steak. And so, the cattle (plus a few horses) roamed the former plantation until, at the turn of the century, things took a turn for the more exciting when a crowd gathered in Queen's Park Savannah to watch a pair of daredevils sitting inside a hot air balloon. To their amazement the balloon rose into the air, and, just when they thought it couldn't go any higher, one man jumped out. As the onlookers screamed and averted their eyes, the man descended safely with his rudimentary parachute.

This escapade brought about a rush of new daredevil antics in the park, including one man who, with a sizeable audience watching, suspended a long stretch of rope from a couple of tall structures and then proceeded to tightrope walk across. In the sky above their heads, pioneer aviators looped the loop and wowed people with their hair-raising landings. All of this meant that the livestock were cleared and the park set aside for public gatherings, most notably the carnival, which arrived in the park in 1922 and has stayed ever since.

I walked along the eastern edge of the park, wondering whether to amble through it, but realised I didn't have time. Besides, the buildings across the road had already caught my attention. Seven individual mansions lined the leafy street. After a quick check that no lurking youths awaited me, I went over to investigate.

5

Each of the Magnificent Seven, the collective name for the beautiful structures, looked – as their name suggests – utterly magnificent.

The first one, chock full of round towers, pointed gables and fancy columns, is known as Stollmeyer's Castle. To me, it looked like it belonged in Bavaria or the highlands of Scotland or, at the very least, a fairy-tale theme park.

Stollmeyer's Castle is named after its original owner, a German landowner called Conrad Frederick Stollmeyer. Sixty years prior to its construction, Conrad's father, a 32-year-old with a wife and six kids in tow, had somehow ended up stranded in Port of Spain with only five dollars to his name. Undaunted, Conrad senior found some cheap accommodation for his family and then bought an axe. With it, he started to chop firewood to sell. While he did this, his wife and kids washed uniforms belonging to soldiers over at the local barracks. When he had saved enough money, Stollmeyer put a deposit down for a loan and then bought some land.

After poking around his plot of overgrown land for a while, Stollmeyer cleared the jungle and planted some coconut trees. When they were ripe, he employed a few people to load them onto carts to sell around town for a penny apiece. They sold like hotcakes. When the money started rolling in, he bought some more land and planted more coconut trees. Then, in a piece of extraordinary good luck, he discovered that one large parcel of his newly bought land contained a rich seam of asphalt, a prized commodity in the burgeoning road construction business. It wasn't exactly a gold mine, but it wasn't far off, and Stollmeyer ended up making a fortune. When he died, he left it all to his son, Charles, who decided to build the mansion I was now staring at, styling it on a Scottish castle he'd once seen.

A voice sounded. Appropriately enough, it was a man selling coconuts from a cart. His sign proclaimed *100% Coconut Water for all events*. The man was gesturing to his wares. "You want a coconut, man?"

"How much?"

"Five dollar, TT."

Five-dollar TT meant five Trinidad & Tobago dollars, about 60p. I wondered what Conrad Stollmeyer would think of the new, inflation-led, price. He would approve, I thought. “Maybe later,” I said, preferring instead to savour the fabulousness of the remaining six marvels, with names such as Whitehall, the Archbishop’s House, Roomor, Mille Fleurs, Hayes Court and Queen’s Royal College. Each one was as different as the next, coated in chocolate box prettiness.

6

Fort George sits atop a hill overlooking Port of Spain and the Gulf of Paria, an inlet of the Caribbean Sea. Full of cannons, battlements, park benches and a sturdy signal station (now a museum), the old fortification offered respite from the honking traffic and thick crowds below.

“It never saw any military action,” Ricardo, my guide for the afternoon, told me. He was a thickset, large man in his late twenties who, despite his size, possessed a quiet and intelligent voice. “And by 1846, the British stopped using it as a fort.”

Below us lay the sprawl of Port of Spain, a relatively low-rise city. It was only in the very central core that things changed: six or seven modern skyscrapers jutted for attention there. Away from them, by the water’s edge, a series of spindly shipping cranes were receiving machinery and chemicals to fuel Trinidad’s massive petroleum industry. They looked like oversized flamingos. Due to the nation’s reserves of oil and gas, Trinidad and Tobago is the third richest nation in the Americas.

I gazed down at a huge, deep green expanse that lay behind the city. Ricardo told me it was the Caroni Swamp, a protected mangrove region, home to over one hundred bird species, untold insects, molluscs, caimans and snakes. With more time, I could have enjoyed a boat ride through it, spotting scarlet ibises and boa constrictors. “If you look to the left of the swamp, up on that high ground, you will see a district of the city called Laventille. You heard of it?”

I nodded. Some earlier research on Port of Spain had revealed Laventille as a place to avoid. Made up of poor, tightly-packed shacks, perched on a hillside, it was crime central in Trinidad. Consider the following statistic: inside Laventille's compact little boundary, an astonishing 79 murders occurred in just the first two months of 2016. This doesn't sound too bad, except when you compare it to somewhere such as New York. In that same period, New York had fewer murders, with a population that is fifty times bigger than Laventille.

In one 24-hour period from January 2016, six people were killed in Port of Spain. The first involved a group of teenagers. As they were travelling home from school, a lone gunman stopped their car, ordered everyone out and, instead of robbing them, decided to shoot two boys with five bullets each.

Why the boys were shot is a mystery, since neither was part of the drug gangs in Laventille. Indeed, one of them, a young man who went by the name of Denelson Smith, was training to be a pilot in his spare time. With police seemingly indifferent to the murders, some locals took matters into their own hands and, a few hours later, turned up at the doorstep of the alleged murderer's father. When the man answered it, he was shot in the chest, left to die in his wife's arms.

Around the same time that the man's attackers were fleeing, police heard gunshots at a place called Clifton Hill. Upon investigation, they discovered a young man's body lying prone. He was dead, too. Later that night, a fifth person was shot to death, this one at home asleep with his family. No warning, just bullets: another statistic to add to the depressing tally.

The final death in the 24-hour period came in the early hours of the next morning. Further across town, as a young street vendor was setting up his stall for the day, a gunman approached and shot him dead. Six bodies in the city morgue and a new day began in Trinidad.

7

"Laventille is the most dangerous part of the city," Ricardo said soberly. "If you walked there, day or night, you would be robbed, no question. Probably murdered, too. Many bad guys with guns live there. Even I would not go into Laventille. A few weeks ago, my sister went there by mistake. She was in her car, following her GPS and, somehow, it ended up taking her through Laventille. She only realised as she was driving through. She told me she put her foot down and did not stop. How she escaped in her BMW, I will never know. She is one lucky girl."

"Why is it so bad there?"

"Gangs. Venezuela is only eleven kilometres away – a quick boat ride. That's how close the South American drugs trade is. High unemployment doesn't help; neither does easy access to guns. The police can't do much. There's too much for them to cope with. When it gets bad in Laventille, the government sends the army in to flush out the criminals, but the bad guys always come back. I'll tell you something, Jason. Crime is the main threat to any tourist visiting that part of the city. Not malaria, not Zika, not falling into the ocean or being run over, but crime. I think we have about one hundred gangs in operation. This is why the cruise ships won't come to Trinidad. Imagine the headline: Fifty tourists murdered by Trinidad gangs. And I can imagine this happening."

Ricardo paused, possibly seeing the worry etched across my face. "Look, I'm not trying to scare you, but I am trying to scare you about Laventille. Do not go there, not even for a minute."

I told him I did not intend to visit Laventille. I asked him, "Do you feel safe here? I mean, in Trinidad as a whole."

He gazed out over the ocean, almost invisible on the horizon. "Yeah, I do feel safe. For most people in the city, gun crime is not a problem. We can go about our business and not have to worry about it. But if I decided to walk through Laventille, I'd have something to worry about. And it's such a shame; it's where steel pan started.

Bands used to play on street corners. My grandmother used to live there and she told me that when she was a little girl, people left their doors unlocked. She used to go out and listen to the men playing the pans. She felt totally safe. Neighbours looked out for each other." He shook his head. "Not like now: it's all Rastas versus Muslims. I have heard stories that the Syrians are getting ready for something in Laventille. The rumour is that they are providing weapons to the gangs so that they will eventually kill each other. Then they will knock the cheap houses down and build hotels. Laventille has a good view, you know – it could be prime real estate one day."

"Syrians?" Had Syrian refugees arrived in Trinidad, I wondered?

"Yes. They are a large minority in my country. All of them are very rich. They own all the cement factories and breweries."

"So they're not refugees?

"Refugees? No, they've been here a long time."

Later I discovered that whenever anyone in the Caribbean mentioned Syrians, it was a generic term for someone from the Middle East.

At another vantage point, we could see the faintest shimmer of Venezuela. The narrow strait that separates it from the Western tip of Trinidad is named Bocas del Dragón, *Mouths of the Dragon*. Up until a few years ago, it was possible to take a ferry across the strait, but not anymore. Ever since the Venezuelan economy had nosedived due to falling oil prices, Trinidad did not want Venezuelans crossing freely to their country, buying up goods and then returning home to make a killing. The lack of commercial ferries, however, has not stopped all of them coming. Some arrive on fishing boats, setting down on windswept beaches away from any security checks. Others turn up to trade weapons and drugs in return for flour, baby food and toilet rolls.

"I don't blame them for coming," said Ricardo sadly, "but some who stay become thieves and prostitutes. They are a drain on our economy."

8

From Fort George, we drove into the heart of Port of Spain. Ricardo wanted to show me a part of the city called The Avenue, which was home to bars, restaurants, casinos and nightclubs. Even though it was still early afternoon, the place was thronging. It was a young person's paradise and I imagined that Ricardo was a frequent visitor.

"It's open 24-7," he told me, as we did a slow drive along the strip. Places with names such as Smokey & Bunty, Soho's, Elixir and the Mexican-themed El Pecos lined both sides of the street. "If you're ever bored, come down here and party. And it's safe too. You can walk along here at night, enjoy a few beers, eat a roti, and you'll be safe."

I noticed a young Chinese couple crossing the road. I wondered whether they were tourists. "No," Ricardo told me. "They look Chinese, but they are Trinidadians. If you could hear them speak, they would sound more Trinidadian than me. The Chinese came to Trinidad about one hundred and fifty years ago. They worked in the plantations when all the slaves were freed. Nowadays, I think we have about six thousand Chinese Trinidadians. They own a lot of shops and restaurants."

We passed another roti shop, and I wanted to know whether they were similar to the flatbreads found in Asian cuisine. Apparently they were. When Indian workers (like the Chinese) came to Trinidad in the mid-1800s to replace the newly freed slaves, they brought with them their curry and roti recipes. The latter caught on so much that it is now one of the most popular meals in the southern Caribbean.

Talk of rotis brought about a discussion of exotic food. The wackiest food Ricardo had tried was curried mango, which he deemed palatable but unworthy of a second portion. When I told him I'd once tried rabbit, he baulked.

"Man, I would never try rabbit. They are pets!" He pulled a face. "And I've heard the sound they make when they are killed. Have you?"

I told him I hadn't. We were driving further into the city away from The Avenue.

"They scream like babies. It's horrible. Rabbit is not for me. And neither is dog."

"Dog? Do people eat dogs in Trinidad?"

Ricardo paused, as if assessing whether to tell me or not. "Listen, last year, some guy lost his dog and when he couldn't find it, he looked over his neighbour's fence and caught them skinning it. They were Chinese and were about to cook the thing! He went ape-shit, as you can imagine."

I grimaced.

"But the uproar was because he filmed them at it and put it on YouTube. Well, people stopped going to Chinese restaurants. Some restaurants in Port of Spain were attacked. On the news, some politician said that the footage explained where all the stray dogs in the city had gone."

I didn't know whether to laugh or cry.

"Now, as you'd expect, Trinidad's Chinese restaurants all said they'd never served dog meat, and never would. They said the family who killed the dog were not part of any restaurant, and probably killed it because they were hungry and hadn't realised it was anyone's pet. But let me tell you this: I no longer eat at Chinese restaurants, and neither do my family and friends. I think soon, some restaurants and takeaways will go out of business."

We were now almost in the centre of Port of Spain, and pulled up next to a huge red building that looked like it was undergoing restoration work. With my mind full of dreadful thoughts about pet dogs, Ricardo and I left the car to look more closely at it.

9

The long red building turned out to be Trinidad and Tobago's parliament building, affectionately known as the Red House. It explained the presence of the police station opposite, a wonderful grey edifice of red and white that ought to be the domicile of clowns. The parliament building was more interesting, though, and Ricardo told me that it had been painted red in 1897 to celebrate Queen Victoria's diamond jubilee.

If I ignored the metal scaffolding that cloaked its expansive front facade, I could see that the Red House was a striking, majestic affair and, had Queen Victoria clapped eyes on it (she never did), I could imagine her nodding in royal approval. Mind you, if she had seen the Red House six years later, she might have fainted, for it was on fire. It all started because of water.

The year of the great fire coincided with the Port of Spain authorities wanting to increase the cost of water for its citizens. This was in response to the townsfolk's flagrant wastage of water. On average, each citizen of Trinidad and Tobago used twice the amount of water as citizens of London because, according to one report, Port of Spain was full of gushing fountains, heavily irrigated gardens, sloshing gutters and streets splashing with the sound of wasted water. One household, the report stated, regularly used 8000 gallons of water a day, with taps constantly running to fill its deep Roman baths. That is the same amount of water to fill one hundred modern bathtubs. So it seemed reasonable that the authorities wanted to curtail this needless usage.

Unsurprisingly, the resulting law didn't go down too well with the water wasters of Port of Spain. They were so incensed that some of them banded together and had a riot. At one point, a mob assembled outside the parliament building, not far from where I was currently standing. Following a period of shouting and baying (and perhaps some flagrant water guzzling), someone threw a rock. Then a few other rioters picked up projectiles and hurled them, too. Soon, ornate windows lay smashed and broken. For the politicians inside, their only course of action was to take cover under tables. Finally, the rock throwing stopped.

One of the rioters shuffled his feet and came up with a new plan. He set fire to a bottle and lobbed it through one of the broken windows. Seeing this, other rioters were soon throwing burning bottles towards the Red House, which soon had the lower levels flaming and smoking. Luckily, the police arrived and started shooting. None of the politicians were injured, but sixteen protestors were killed before the riot ended.

It was ironic, then, that in a city with so much water, none managed to douse the flames of the parliament building. By the time the last embers fizzled out, the Red House was a smouldering shell. Four years later, it was up and running again, with the government wisely deciding to leave the city's water alone.

10

We stopped at some traffic lights and were rewarded with the rich sound of steel drums. The music was coming from a small hall on our left. Through the windows, we could make out people playing them, perhaps in rehearsal for something. I asked Ricardo whether he had ever played the steel drums.

"Of course. Everyone in Trinidad can play the steel drums. We learn to play them at school. And as I said before, steel pan playing began in Laventille. They used bits of metal, dustbin lids, biscuit tins, anything they could find. They banged away until someone decided they needed to tune them. That's when people started using oil drums."

"Are they expensive to buy?"

Ricardo nodded. "A set of good quality drums will be about twenty thousand US."

I whistled. That was over a thousand dollars per drum.

"So when someone buys a set, they look after them."

We arrived at a long pedestrian-only boulevard known as the Brian Lara Promenade. A grove of trees lined the walkway and behind them stood the skyscrapers of the city. We parked near a statue of Trinidad's favourite cricketing son at the western end of the promenade, standing atop a giant cricket ball. Ricardo asked whether

I would be okay by myself for twenty minutes or so. “You can walk along the promenade and I can drive and meet you at the roundabout. It’s near KFC; you can’t miss it. Or I can stay here and you can walk along and then come back.”

“I prefer option one.”

Ricardo nodded and drove away, leaving me to stare at Mr Brian Lara. Born into a family of eleven children, Lara began his illustrious cricketing career aged six, which culminated in him achieving the highest score in first-class cricket history. His statue had captured the man in full cricketing pose with his bat pulled over his shoulder and his knee up high. I took a photo and then headed eastwards towards the noise and activity further along the promenade.

No one cared a jot I was walking among them. Nobody gave me a second glance. They were all too busy with their own lives and activities. The end of the promenade had opened out into a busy hotspot of fruit stands, CD hawkers and young Trinidadians wandering with slow lolloping gaits. I felt as safe as could be. The square, however, was not a place for peaceful contemplation and relaxing meditation, rather it was a place for eager viewing. I spun around, taking it all in – the man selling mangos, the Rasta nodding his head in time to some music, the gents playing backgammon, the honking traffic, the noble, double-towered cathedral in the distance, the pair of old women laughing heartily at something while they flagged down a taxi, and the shifty man sidling up to me.

Shifty men always sidled, I’d noticed. And most of them spoke from the side of their mouths, which was exactly what this gentleman did. “Ya lookin’ fa weed?” he asked, eyes moving at everything going on.

I shook my head. “Just waiting for a friend.”

The man was already gone before I’d finished the sentence.

By far the busiest part of the square was the aforementioned KFC restaurant. A constant stream of people was entering and leaving. I was not surprised to learn that for a short time in 2009, the Kentucky

Fried Chicken establishment I was staring at was the best-selling KFC outlet in the world. A honk brought me out of my Colonel Sanders musings. It was Ricardo gesturing that it was time to go and see some hummingbirds.

11

We passed a white lighthouse. It stood on a thin traffic island in the middle of a six-lane highway, an incongruous location for a nautical navigation aid, I felt. Old photos show the lighthouse standing on the edge of a busy jetty while burly men carrying sacks of supplies trod the boardwalks with gulls fluttered above their heads. Nowadays, the sea is not in sight. A mixture of tall buildings and an area of reclaimed land separate the lighthouse from the water's edge.

"I still can't believe you didn't know Trinidad has hummingbirds," smiled Ricardo as the lighthouse receded behind us. Earlier, when he'd mentioned that most tourists who visited Port of Spain only wanted to see the tiny birds and nothing much else, I admitted that I hadn't even known his country had them. After he had finished guffawing, he told me that there was a hummingbird sanctuary close by, and, even though it was closed due to Eid, we would still be able to see some birds, if I wanted. I wouldn't be able to feed any or see them fluttering around my head, he told me, but it was still worth a visit, which was why we were now heading there.

As we drove eastward, still within the city, Ricardo slowed and pointed to our left. "Laventille."

I stared at the small homes perched on the hillside. From a distance, they didn't look too bad, offering a hotchpotch of orange, white, green, red and pastel blue buildings. Behind the dwellings, at the very top of the hill were a couple of huge, cylindrical water tanks. Neither looked to have bullet holes in their casings. Everything looked perfectly normal. It certainly did not look like the hotbed of crime it was. I asked whether anyone had been killed recently.

“Not that I know of. Maybe Eid is keeping the Muslims busy. The Rastas probably know that if they do anything stupid on Eid, it will turn into a hate crime rather than a gang crime. Who knows?”

We drove along in silence for a while. “Have you ever flown on Liat Airlines?” I suddenly asked Ricardo.

“Have I flown Liat Airlines?” he said knowingly. “Yes, I have, but I will never use them again.”

He explained why.

Four months previously, Ricardo had booked himself a trip to Jamaica with Liat Airlines. After a short delay in Trinidad, the flight took off and then, a while later, landed again. “But I was not in Kingston,” Ricardo told me. “I was in Antigua. The pilot said we had to stop for fuel or something. That’s fine, I thought, fuel is good. I don’t want to be on a plane that runs out of fuel in the middle of the ocean. But then he comes over the intercom and tells us we all have to get off. Fine, I think, I’ll get off and have a drink. So while I was having a Coke, I looked outside and saw the plane moving. I thought I’d missed the call but then everyone started shouting. The plane was going without us. So we all went to the Liat desk and they just shrugged and told us to wait. Well, we ended up waiting in Antigua for the next eleven hours. Some people gave up and found a hotel. I stayed in the airport; I couldn’t afford a hotel. The next day, Liat told us to get on another plane, which we all did. When we landed, I thought we were in Jamaica, but we weren’t. We were in Barbados! And then we took off again and landed back in Trinidad where we started! When I asked the Liat desk about Jamaica, they said nothing. When I asked about my luggage, they said it was in Grenada! When I asked them what I should do, they told me to do whatever I wanted, so I went home. My luggage arrived a week later. That’s Liat for you.”

“So did you get to Jamaica?”

“No. I figured I was not meant to go there after all that.”

I noticed a huge Trinidad and Tobago flag. It was billowing above a line of commercial buildings. "Big flag," I said, stating the obvious.

"Biggest in the Caribbean. But it's at half-mast because of Patrick Manning, our former prime minister. He died last week and his funeral is in two days' time. The streets will be packed to see his coffin."

Patrick Manning is famous across the Caribbean. When he took over the leadership of Trinidad and Tobago in the early 90s, the country was in political turmoil. Oil prices were tumbling, crime was rising and, for five days in July 1990, some extremists had held Manning's predecessor (plus the rest of his cabinet) hostage inside the Red House. The siege ended peacefully, but it was against this backdrop that Manning assumed control. Luckily for the new prime minister, his background in geology helped rekindle the country's flagging petroleum flame. Suddenly people's wages were higher, the country's prospects higher and Manning was hailed a hero.

12

Ricardo and I turned off the main highway and began a ponderous ascent up a thin track. Dense jungle ran riot on both sides of the track, occasionally broken by heady and bustling villages. In these villages, chickens strutted amok under mango and breadfruit trees while children played in tiny gardens. On the outskirts of one tiny village, Ricardo stopped the car and pointed to a strange red fruit that looked a cross between a pepper and an apple. He asked me what it was; I shook my head in ignorance.

"It's a cashew nut. Can you see the nut growing out the bottom?"

I studied the hanging fruit and could indeed see the cashew nut protruding from the end. I'd never thought about where cashews came from, but now I knew "So that's why cashews are so expensive. Each one grows on a fruit like that."

"Exactly."

The hummingbird sanctuary was located almost at the top of the hill. The twisting track turned thinner as big floppy leaves brushed the wing mirrors. This was as close to the rainforest as you could get, I reckoned, without getting your feet wet. When we parked in a slight lay-by and climbed out, all I could hear was birdcall and insects. Above us was a vast cotton tree; tiny balls of white littered the ground.

We climbed the rest of the way up the hill and arrived at a small driveway. A large and sturdy gate blocked any further movement. Bushes and flowering shrubs edged both ends of the gate, and, beyond them, a driveway curled towards a distant building – the hummingbird sanctuary. And then I saw a hummingbird. It was a tiny green thing, almost metallic looking, with a long, needle-like bill. After fluttering like a miniature helicopter for a second or two, scoping out some blossom on a nearby tree, it was gone. I was delighted.

"That was a copper-rumped hummingbird," Ricardo told me. "And if this place was open, you would see lots more of them. The owner has trained them to listen for a bell. When they hear it, they all come to feed." He instructed me to stand quietly and more would appear.

And they did. Another miniature green bird landed on a branch near the gate and remained motionless long enough for me to get a photo. Then, in a flash, it was gone. "Do hummingbirds make nests?" I asked. I was wondering whether any were around.

"They do make nests, but their nests are tiny. I once saw some hummingbird eggs. They were about the size of an M&M. There won't be any around here, though; they like quiet places away from the roads."

After a quick look around for any other hummingbirds that might be nearby, but finding none close enough to study, we about-turned and headed back for the car.

13

Our final stop on the afternoon tour was Mount Saint Benedict Abbey, a hilltop complex that was over one hundred years old. Ricardo wanted to show me the abbey for two reasons: its views and its yoghurt.

The views were great, but similar to the ones I'd seen from the fort. The story of the yoghurt was more interesting. In 2003, the dozen or so Benedictine monks who lived in the abbey decided to make some yoghurt in order to supplement their meagre diet. They rustled up a batch in their kitchen and when it was ready, they served it. After deciding their yoghurt tasted mighty fine, they decided to make some more. Soon, they had enough spare pots in their fridge so that whenever a visitor turned up at the abbey, the monks would offer him or her some yoghurt. And soon word started to spread about the special abbey yoghurt up the hill.

Seeing an opportunity to make some extra cash, the monks set up a small stall and were soon taking orders for their yoghurt. To drum up more trade, the monks branched out with some snazzy flavours, which proved so popular that they quickly couldn't cope with demand. The people of Trinidad were going mad for their creamy stuff.

So they closed up their monastery and chanted for a while, hoping for inspiration. And then one of the monks came up with a splendid idea: they would invest the money they had made and buy some industrial-sized yoghurt-making equipment. And, instead of waiting for people to come to the abbey to buy it, they would deliver it in a refrigerated van. With this clever plan hatched, the monks went out and spent some money. Soon they were raking in the cash. When hotels and supermarkets found out about their dairy product, they asked the monks to think up a name so they could sell it for them. And so the Pax Yoghurt Company Limited (named after the Latin word for peace) was born.

Perhaps the yoghurt's success was down to its properties, which reportedly prolonged life, increased sexual potency, remedied baldness and calmed frazzled nerves. With a couple of Liat Airlines flights coming the next day, I decided to give it a whirl. Unfortunately, it was not to be: the yoghurt shop was closed because the monks had gone on holiday for ten days.

Back at the hotel, I thanked Ricardo for his services. "Tonight, I think I'll have a walk around Laventille. Maybe knock on a few doors, flash the cash, you know."

He laughed. "Well, make sure you pick your coffin before you go."

We shook hands and that was that.

An hour later, as evening drew in over this most southerly of the Caribbean islands, I packed my luggage in preparation for the next day. My first experience of Liat Airlines would be flying with them to Grenada, and then onto St Vincent, both on the same day. One Liat flight was enough to give me a cause for concern, but two . . . My trip was in the lap of the gods.

Clockwise from top left: One of the Magnificent Seven; The tallest skyscraper in Port of Spain; Brian Lara statue; Looking up towards Laventille – home of Trinidad's crime gangs; Looking down at Port of Spain from Fort George; My first sighting of a hummingbird!

Chapter 3. Grenada – The Spice Isle

I was up at 8am and printed off two boarding cards. Without them, I would need to visit a check-in desk at the airport, which would mean two things: one, time spent in a queue and two, the dreadful possibly that an eagle-eyed Liat employee might notice my heavily-overweight hand luggage.

At the airport, I nonchalantly bypassed the check-in decks, dragging my luggage behind me. Before I reached the conveyer belts of security, a uniformed official stopped me. He wanted to see my boarding card. I showed him the correct one and smiled.

"No, you must get a real boarding card," he said, handing back the printed piece of paper.

"This is a real boarding card," I countered.

The man looked at me sourly. "Is it made from card?"

I was about to argue the toss but realised it would be a pointless endeavour as no amount of pleading would sway him from his idiotic stance. With nerves on the edge, I traipsed to the Liat desk and explained to the woman behind the desk that the security officer was not happy with my paper boarding card.

The large woman took my boarding card and threw it in a litterbin. After looking at my passport, she asked, "Any luggage to check in?"

I shook my head.

"What about hand luggage?"

I thought about lying, but the woman had probably seen me wheeling it towards her desk. So, I nodded, trying to remain calm. Then she said something that made my blood run cold. "Please put it on the scales."

My eyes regarded the black luggage. It was swollen, distended, and clearly overweight. It even bulged in places. The limit on Liat Airlines was 15 pounds, which was about seven kilograms. When I hauled my bag up onto the machine, it tipped the scales at 23 pounds. The woman tutted. “Oh my, that’s too heavy. You’ll have to take something out.”

I removed the bag and did something I’d seen other people do but had never had cause to do myself. I took out vaguely heavy items and stuffed them into my pockets. That done, I plonked my bag on the scales again: 21 pounds. It had hardly made a difference.

The woman read the scale and shook her head. I repeated the process, filling every space in my trouser pockets, and then came up with a masterstroke. Tucking my socks over the bottom of my trousers so nothing would fall out, I loosened my belt and began filling the dead space with all sorts of things. In went a rolled up T-shirt, then two pairs of socks, followed by a battery charger, my camera and an assortment of toiletries. By the time I was finished, I looked like the Michelin Man, and could hardly walk. I shuffled to the weighing scales of judgment and plonked the case on. 15.5 pounds. The woman looked at the reading and then me. “This is okay. Where did you put your things?”

I pointed at my bugling legs. A tube of mosquito repellent and a packet of tissues had lodged itself in the best place possible. It gave my manhood a pleasingly *virulent* look. The woman appraised my ingenuity and actually nodded appreciatively as she put a little *Liat approved hand luggage* sticker on my bag. Then she handed me a boarding card for my flight to Grenada.

“Thanks. But can you also print off the boarding card for my flight to St Vincent too, please?”

The Liat Airlines check-in agent shook her head. “No can do, mister. You’ll have to go to a check-in desk again when you get to Grenada.”

I was about to walk away when I suddenly had another question to ask. “Are there any delays today with Liat?”

“I don’t know. There’s nothing showing on my screen, but that don’t mean nothin’.”

I thanked her anyway, ponderously walked to where she could not see me and repacked all my things in the luggage.

2

My plan for the day was brave. Upon landing in Grenada, I would grab some lunch at the airport; then meet my guide for an afternoon of sightseeing. Following this, he would deposit me at a hotel within walking distance of the airport, where I could grab a beer or two and then, when I was ready, amble to departures to catch my night flight to St Vincent & the Grenadines. On paper, it seemed a good plan, but now that I was sitting in the passenger terminal at Trinidad's Piarco International Airport, I was a nervous wreck. What if the flight to Grenada was delayed? What if it was cancelled? What if the cabin crew decided they didn't like the look of my bag and wanted to put it in the hold? What if? What if?

To take my mind off Liat Airlines, I found some free Wi-Fi in order to do some quick research about Grenada. A few minutes later, I discovered that six volcanic islands made up the state of Grenada, and that the national bird was the rare and elusive Grenada Dove. I also found out that the name, Grenada, probably came from the Spanish word for pomegranate.

Grenada, I also read, was famous for its nutmeg plantations, which explained its nickname: the Spice Isle. Nutmeg first arrived in Grenada in 1843 when a passing ship decided to stop and plant a few nutmeg seeds. The seeds germinated, grew and then thrived. In fact, they thrived so much that nowadays forty percent of the world's nutmeg originates from Grenada. After finding out these interesting titbits, I was eager for more.

The most famous thing to happen in Grenada occurred in 1983. That year saw the might of the United States invade the tiny island. As a twelve-year-old, I recalled the invasion being on the news. But I could not recall why it happened, or what the result was. Google came to my assistance.

In 1979, five years into independence from the British, a Marxist group staged a coup and took over Grenada, quickly aligning themselves with countries such as Cuba, Nicaragua and the Soviet

Union. Predictably, this unsettled the United States, who did not want another communist state on their doorstep. Their concern grew keener when the Marxist leader, a man called Maurice Bishop, was executed for not being Marxist enough. The final straw was when planes began landing in Grenada filled with Cuban workers. When they started building a new, longer runway, the Americans gnashed their teeth in bitterness. They believed that Soviet aircraft, filled to the brim with weapons, would soon be using the new runway as a refuelling point on their way to Central America. In response, Ronald Reagan ordered *Operation Urgent Fury,* citing the presence of a few American medical students as just cause. And so, despite condemnation by the United Nations, the Americans sent seven thousand military personnel to battle the Marxists amid the palm trees and sand of Grenada. The Marxists didn't stand a chance, and eight weeks later, gave up the fight. When the dust settled, the Americans organised some elections and then departed as quickly as they came. Since then, Grenada only makes the news when hurricanes are heading its way.

"Ladies and gentlemen," said a voice over the airport intercom system, making me look up from my phone. "We are sorry to announce the delay of Liat flight 772 to Grenada. Departure time will now be 11.45."

I looked at my watch. 11.45 was not too bad – only a twenty minute delay; I could live with that. And while I waited, some footage on a TV screen drew my attention. It was a news report from America and the grainy film playing out was horrifying. From what I could gather, a policeman had pointed a gun into a car and shot the driver. Whoever had filmed it had done so from the passenger seat. The driver, a black man, died as the footage played out.

The departure lounge turned silent as thirty or so passengers watch it play again. When a news anchorwoman came on the screen talking about the footage and asking why a police officer would shoot a seemingly unarmed member of the public, another announcement sounded across the airport.

"Ladies and gentlemen, we are pleased to announce the departure of Liat Airlines flight 772 to Grenada. Please have your boarding cards ready for inspection at Gate 8."

It was time to go.

3

My first flight with Liat Airlines went without incident. During the thirty minutes it took to fly north to Grenada, the crew were courteous and professional. True, there was no meal or even a glass of water, but, for the price I had paid, I did not expect such things.

When we landed, I was one of the few passengers making my way down the steps; the rest were remaining on board to fly the next leg to Barbados. At the bottom of the steps, I sniffed the air for a hint of spice. There was none, only a gush of warm tropical air infused with a hint of aviation fuel. Feeling quite excited, I dragged my luggage towards the terminal.

Maurice Bishop International Airport (named after their slain Marxist prime minister) wasn't exactly heaving and I was through security in record time, even quicker than my arrival into Barbados. After passing a large photo of the Grenadian prime minister, a man called Keith Mitchell (who bore an uncanny resemblance to former boxer, Chris Eubank), I was outside, sitting in an outdoor café.

I ordered a sandwich then stared up at the sunny and cloudless sky. If I had looked upwards in October 1983, I might have seen hundreds of US paratroopers. As it was, I finished my spicy chicken sandwich, thanking Liat Airlines for delivering me to my third Caribbean country in as many days.

"Mr Jason Smart?" said a deep Caribbean voice.

I turned to see a tall, thin man with a wispy grey beard adorning a deeply craggy face. From my seated position, he looked about seven feet tall. I nodded, stood up and shook his hand.

"My name's Sam. How r'tings, man?"

I told him I was fine. Now that I was standing, I could see he wasn't quite seven feet tall, but he wasn't far off. I felt like a child in his presence. "How did you know it was me?"

Sam gestured to all the other patrons of the café. "How many white faces do you see?"

I nodded at his observation.

Sam said, "Well, let me show you a few t'ings on the glorious island of Grenada. Come on, let's get cracking."

I smiled and followed him to his van, amused by Sam's gait plodding along in a most pleasing Caribbean way.

4

Something struck me as we drove from the airport. As beautiful as the Caribbean islands undoubtedly were, they all looked alike (at least the ones I had visited so far). Each featured the same variety of trees (a healthy mix of luxurious palms, red-blossomed Royal Poinciana trees and forests of mango and breadfruit trees), the same pastel coloured (but deliciously Caribbean-flavoured) homesteads and the same stretches of ocean bordered by long strips of powdery sand.

"So do you enjoy living in Grenada?" I asked Sam as we powered up a winding coastal road.

Sam grinned. "I love Grenada! I would not live anywhere else in the world. It's friendly, it doesn't have any corruption and the pace of life is nice and slow. Plus the weather's great. You're from England, right? Well, I've been to London five times – my brother lives over there – and each time I went it just rained. I don't know how you people stand it."

"Where does your brother live?"

Sam delayed answering as he was busy negotiating his way past a large tractor carrying a rusted and smashed-up car. The vehicle was swinging ponderously in the road, meaning we had to slip by on the verge. A scrap yard on the other side of the road was the tractor's destination. "He lives in Ilford. He owns a fruit and vegetable shop. You call them greengrocers, I think. We go to the Notting Hill Carnival. You been?"

I shook my head.

Sam looked incredulous. "Never been to Notting Hill Carnival? You should go, man."

The winding road veered onto a public beach called Grand Anse Bay. I climbed out of the car and looked at the collection of small boats bobbing around in the water as gentle waves lapped against them. The horseshoe bay was empty and I found myself the only person enjoying the view, until a dog came sniffing around from behind a palm tree. It stared at me briefly, cocked a leg up, peed against the palm tree and then scampered inland towards what looked like a closed beach bar. Behind the bar, on the other side of the road, a series of green hills formed a stunning backdrop.

Sam came to join me. Together, we gazed out across the bay. If we had possessed superhuman eyesight, perhaps we might have seen the next block of land across the sea: Nicaragua, some two and a half thousand miles distant.

"You see this every day," I stated.

Sam nodded. "I'm a lucky man."

5

Back on the road, I enjoyed the sights of Grenada as we passed them: an old man sitting on a barstool inside a dingy bar; a mother and son, both with floppy hats, ambling hand in hand by the side of the road; a bus stop painted with spices: nutmeg, cinnamon, cloves and allspice; roadside verges splashed in red, yellow and green, the colours of the Grenadian flag; churches in pastel blues and whites. Grenada was awash with colour.

"You tried a Carib yet?" asked Sam, referring to the local beer. We had just passed a sign for it.

"I tried one in Trinidad."

“Well ours it better than theirs. It’s all to do with the water. Mind you, they would probably say the same thing about theirs. I’m more of a rum man, myself. I do like a cold beer from time to time, but rum is my drink. Make sure you try some while you’re on the island. Clarke’s Court is our most famous brand.”

I asked about crime, which was turning into my favourite topic of the trip.

Sam pondered for a moment. “This island is one of the safest in the Caribbean. We don’t have the drug and gang problems like Trinidad and Guyana: we have them, but not on their scale. We don’t have many murders, but about six months ago, a tourist was attacked – an American woman. She was walking along a beach with her husband when someone jumped them. She got killed.”

“That’s horrible.”

“Yeah. But, the police caught the murderer – a young drifter who’d been hassling tourists for a while – straight away. He had ambushed them, held the woman hostage and told the husband to fetch money. While he was gone, he raped her and killed her with a cutlass. ”

“A cutlass?”

“Yeah, a cutlass, a large knife, you know? But that’s the only killin’ I can remember in a long time. Grenada is a safe country, especially with this man in prison.”

We were on our way to a waterfall. Not knowing what to expect, but not expecting much (no mention of the waterfall had come up on my earlier Google search of interesting things about Grenada), I was not disappointed when I saw it. The waterfall was a slight trickle flowing down a mossy cut in the rock before splashing pathetically into a pool of brown water. Even so, it still had a resident hawker – a middle-aged man who had a towel and some swimming trunks as equipment. He wasn’t selling them: he wanted to use them. For thirty East Caribbean dollars (about $10 US), he told me he would climb to a point overlooking the brown pool and dive in. “You can take a photo," he suggested. "Or maybe a video. People back home will love it."

"Maybe later," I said. "I'm going to see the nature trail first." I'd spotted the sign for it just before arriving at the waterfall.

"Okay, I'll do it for twenty dollars."

"I'll see."

"Fifteen?"

I walked away, following the trail that led me up and around where the waterfall lay. Small lizards scurried along the handrails while pretty flowers dangled at waist height. The jungle on one side abounded with mangos, coconuts and papayas. From somewhere I heard a splash, and when I stumbled upon a clearing that overlooked the waterfall pool, I spied the hawker pulling himself out of the water while a Japanese man filmed him. His wife stood watching, clapping her hands with glee. At least he had received some money, I thought. I carried on walking until the trail ended back where I started. With the diver still busy with his Japanese fans, I made my escape to Sam's car without feeling guilty.

6

"Do you want to visit a spice plantation?" Sam asked me. Dense swales of tubular – almost tree-like – bamboo bordered both sides of the thin road. Bamboo grew at an alarming rate, I knew, capable of sprouting six inches a day. If we stopped to watch a branch for a while, I reckoned we would actually see it growing. Sam agreed. "Sometimes you can hear it grow. It's a soft crackling sound, like paper being scrunched up."

I considered his idea of a spice plantation. It sounded historically and tropically interesting. I asked him how far away it was.

"Not far. It's along this road. You can learn about the spices that grow on the island. Maybe try some. If you like any, you can buy some."

My vision of an old plantation faded instantly. "So it's a shop?"

“No, man. Not a shop! A plantation! You’ll like it. And you don’t have to buy anything. No pressure or anything.”

Ten minutes later, we pulled over by a row of shops. Their location lay on a convenient bend in the road where traffic was forced to slow and regard their wares. One sold lampshades and wind chimes, another was a small café which also claimed it could digitally top me up if I so required. The third building – the largest of the trio – was the spice plantation, except it was no such thing. It was a large rectangular store full of aisles, tills and a man smiling at me. Sam, clearly a regular of the spice shop ruse, was heading off with the owner, perhaps to have a cup of coffee, leaving me as easy prey. Inwardly sighing, I followed Mr Smile to a corner of the room where a small table awaited us. On it, a collection of spices was laid out.

7

“First time in Grenada?” asked the man with the smile.

I told him it was, trying to make the best of the situation. “It’s a great island, and it’s a pity I didn’t bring more luggage. No room to buy any souvenirs, I’m afraid.” I thought I’d set out my own stall right from the onset.

The man considered this and then pointed to his table, his smile slightly more forced. And so, for the next ten minutes, I listened as he explained about the spices of Grenada. He made me smell a strip of cinnamon bark, then some pieces of ginger and turmeric, followed by a bay leaf, which he wafted under my nose. At one point, I stupidly misidentified a coco bean as a coconut, which made the man pity me. He told me a coconut was easy to recognize because it was fifty times bigger than a cocoa bean.

“Do you know what this is?” the man asked, holding a hard, beige, round thing about the size of a peach. When he pulled it apart, I saw it housed a red nut that resembled a miniature cycling helmet.

I shook my head.

"Nutmeg – the spice that Grenada is most famous for." He held it out for me to prod and smell. It felt lumpy and smelled of spice. "At one time, this would have been worth its weight in gold. Only the richest people could afford it – especially since it takes about eight years for one tree to produce its first harvest – and that was why European nations wanted to control its trade. Because of nutmeg, Grenada became one of the most strategically important islands in the Caribbean."

I nodded appropriately, finding his spiel unexpectedly interesting, especially when he told me about the medicinal properties of nutmeg. Apparently, it was a great sedative, a painkiller, a booster of immune systems and it could, allegedly, prevent leukaemia. It also had another, less well-known, side effect: if taken in sufficient quantities, nutmeg was a hallucinogenic.

I recalled a story a friend told me. Many years previously, as a wayward teenager in Glasgow, he and his brother decided they wanted to sample some drugs. Steering clear of more popular narcotic choices such as marijuana, LSD and cocaine, the siblings opted for nutmeg; one of them had read about its unusual effects. Wisely waiting for their parents to depart on a weekend break, they nipped down the local supermarket and purchased the biggest jar of nutmeg they could find. Back home, safe behind closed doors, they scratched their heads and thought about how to proceed. Discounting the snorting option and the time-consuming choice of baking a nutmeg infused cake, the brothers elected for the most straightforward choice, i.e. necking half a jar of the spice each, washing the powder down with copious gulps of water. That done, the pair waited for the fun to begin.

Nothing happened.

But then, something did. Like a tidal wave, the nutmeg hit began. My pal told me that the spicy hallucinations lasted for two days and, at one point, the brothers believed they were going to die. They were housebound, not daring to leave the kitchen, surviving on rations of pot noodles and digestive biscuits. When their parents returned from their weekend trip, they found their sons in a vegetative state and almost took them to hospital there and then. Luckily, the boys recovered fully and since then have not touched nutmeg.

"To produce nutmeg for sale, the nut is harvested, then opened by hand," the man told me. "The outer part of the nut is called mace." He pointed to the strange red layer around the actual nut. "It's used in cooking, and to make nutmeg oil. It's less sweet than the nutmeg." He removed the mace layer to reveal an actual nut of nutmeg. It looked like a small walnut. "This is nutmeg. It's crushed to make nutmeg powder. If it's okay with you, I'll show you a few products containing Grenadian nutmeg powder."

From a well-stocked shelf behind him, the man produced a tray of goodies that I knew he wanted me to buy. Nutmeg soap, nutmeg butter, nutmeg rum punch, nutmeg vinegar and even just the nutmeg itself were proudly shown to me. I looked and sniffed some of the items, nodding my head in all the right places, while at the same reminding the man about the lack of room in my luggage

Mr Smile showed me a chocolate bar with a hint of nutmeg. "Maybe this for your wife? Your daughter? Your mother? I'm sure they would appreciate such a fine gift."

Feeling like a cad, especially with all the effort he had put into his little presentation, I remained steadfast thinking that, come the cruise ship season, the man and his 'spice plantation' would make a killing. In the end, though, I bought a small bar of chocolate, vowing to avoid such situations for the remainder of my trip around the Caribbean.

8

"If we took that road," said Sam, pointing at a thin trail that led up to thick jungle, "we'd come to a place called Sauteurs. It was where forty Caribs – you know, the indigenous people of the Caribbean – jumped off a cliff so the French wouldn't take them as slaves. It's called Leapers' Hill. If we had more time, I could have taken you there."

Instead, our journey took us further through the highlands of Grenada. Almost at the top was a sturdy wooden lookout platform hugged by thick bamboo. Sam stopped so I could take a photo. After almost losing my left sandal in a sticky and almost unseen patch of gloopy mud, I stepped onto the platform and surveyed my domain. Rainforest, more rainforest and, then in the far distance, a hazy smattering of coastal villages lying at the edge of an almost indistinct ocean.

After taking a photo, I nimbly sidestepped the mud and then landed in an even deeper patch of wet soil. One moment my foot was there, the next it was gone, submerged in the gloop. Sam looked aghast. His clean car was no doubt on his mind. I looked on it as revenge for taking me to the spice plantation. I pulled my foot out, hearing the satisfying slurp of its release, and observed the mess. It looked like my foot was covered in chocolate. Wet dollops of mud dripped onto the grass. Sam looked at the mess.

"I've got an idea," I said, wiping my foot down on some thick grass. "I'll put a plastic bag around my foot. That should work. Have you got one?"

"No."

"Okay. I'll get rid of as much as I can on this grass, and let the rest of it dry up. Then I can brush it off."

Sam looked unconvinced, but short of a better idea, there was not much he could do. So, while I busied myself with rubbing my soiled foot against upturned roots, leaves and anything useful I could find, he told me about the monkeys of Grenada. He was referring to a nearby sign showing photos of black and white monkeys with Zorro-like eye patches. *Protect our Mona Monkeys*, the sign read, *Feed them fruits only and stop hunting them.*

"They first came to Grenada from West Africa aboard slave ships. We are not sure whether they were brought for food or as pets, but when they got here, they loved it and soon there were lots of them.

But now their numbers are getting dangerously low because of hunting and hurricanes. I think there are only a few hundred left. That's why you see signs like this in the hills."

"Why do people hunt them?" I asked Sam.

"Sometimes they kill the adult monkeys so they can sell the babies as pets, but usually they kill them for food. It's called bush meat. It's not so common nowadays, but it used to be. You'd see it in the local restaurants and markets for years."

"Have you tried it?"

Sam nodded. "When I was young I tried some. It was like smoky beef, Very chewy."

By now, I'd cleared the worst of the mud away. I rubbed a large leaf across my foot to remove even more. Sam deemed me clean enough for us to carry on our journey. Our next stop was the exciting and dramatic sounding Crater Lake.

9

A couple of shops selling tourist knickknacks and a grand house further up the hill signalled our stop for the lake. Sam parked by the side of the road and explained that, if I walked past the shops and house, and followed the trail that led behind them, I would come to a viewpoint overlooking the lake.

Grand Etang is only one a handful of crater lakes in the Caribbean. Legends about its dark depths abound. Some believe a mermaid lives in the lake, tempting passing men with her sensual calling. Others believe a monster lurks within its deepness, waiting to drag unsuspecting visitors to their doom. Another myth is that anyone who drowns in the lake will magically reappear in neighboring Trinidad. Some claim the lake is bottomless, a vague term for uncertainty, whereas others say the lake is precisely eighteen feet deep. The latter guess is about right.

I waited for Sam to lead the way but, evidently, I was on my own because he lowered his seat into a slumbering position. "Take as long you like," he said. "I'm going to catch a nap."

Grumbling to myself ever so slightly about paying a guide to go to sleep, I ambled past the gift shops, waving to the proprietors as I did so. They all waved back and then returned to their conversations. The sun above me was a furnace; instead of being cooler in the highlands of Grenada, it was even hotter, and more humid, too. I felt sweat dribbling down my back.

The house, a well-kept white structure, claimed it was a Visitor Information Centre. Predictably, it was closed, and so I followed Sam's verbal instructions and found the trail behind it, which led me past a toilet block. I decided to avail myself of its facilities before carrying onto the lake. Instead of the mosquito-ridden hellhole I'd expected, I was rewarded with a clean cubicle and running water.

There was even a mirror in which I regarded myself. I was red, sweating profusely and my eyes bulged like a chameleon. I splashed water over my face, hearing it fizz and evaporate into nothing, so repeated the splashing until I could at last feel a semblance of relief. Then I flung handfuls of water over my head, savouring the feeling of stark coldness running down by neck. Even the skulking lizard regarding me from the wall did not dampen my spirits, and so I flung even more, allowing a whimper of pleasure to escape my lips as I did so. Even to my own ears, I sounded like a dog about to be fed.

The trail took me between a line of trees (some of them abundant with bunches of green bananas) and then upwards across a boulder-strewn incline that resounded with the call of insects. Some of the critters were so loud that I stopped to find the source of the sound. It was impossible: the screeches were coming from everywhere. But one sound cut through all others. It sounded like a car alarm and was just as loud. Then it suddenly stopped. The other insects stopped too and the jungle was abruptly silent.

It was a little unnerving. What could be out there? What was lurking in the trees waiting to eat me? Maybe it was a monkey, or perhaps a pack of wild dogs? What about anacondas? Did serpentine monsters live in Grenada? I moved off, heading deeper into the trail, keeping a wary look out. After a few seconds, the jungle orchestra started up again, making me realise that it had been me who had startled the insects.

The crater lake was not that impressive. It looked just like a regular lake which, I supposed, was to be expected. Perhaps to temper visitors' disappointment, someone had placed a climbing frame near it, which offered another jungle lookout point. I climbed to the top and gazed upon pure, primeval rainforest spreading out in all directions: an artist's palette of every shade of green broken only by a volcanic caldera. With the sun at full power, I didn't stay for long, and was soon under the shade of the jungle trail one more.

The car alarm insect noise still cascaded though the forest. As it grew louder, it abruptly ceased. I stopped in my tracks, keeping as still as possible. Thirty seconds later, the alarm sounded again, and I moved my head an inch.

Silence.

It was as if the insects were observing me. After another minute of pretending to be a statue, they began their raucous call and I listened, keeping still, trying to triangulate the sound's source, but finding it impossible. The buzzing and shrilling was reverberating from all directions. Growing impatient, especially with the humidity, I moved off, finding that the sound didn't stop. It was as if the insects had deemed me harmless, their chirrups and shrillness growing ever more raucous. I looked this way and that, looking at trees, scoping out leaves and undergrowth until, finally, I gave up and found Sam.

10

At the other side of the island, we began a descent towards the town of Grenville, a small coastal settlement that boasted street names such as Gladstone Road, Salisbury Road and Victoria Street (which was home to the Anglican Church) – all indicators of its colonial past. Grenville was actually Grenada's second largest town, home to the principal nutmeg factory on the island, and was therefore a honking place of trading, of vegetable prodding, and of men sitting around doing nothing in particular.

"These men," said Sam, "are unemployed. That is one of the bad things about Grenada – not enough jobs. So these men will sit around and do nothing or sometimes drink beer. They are one of the reasons education is so important here on the island. If kids get good grades at school, they might get a job and not end up like these fellows. That is what I told my son and what he now tells my grandson." Sam paused to manoeuvre around a parked bus. Once safely around it, he continued. "I've heard that the kids in England have little respect for their teachers. Is this right?"

I nodded. "Not all, but a lot of them."

Sam contemplated this. "So when they leave school with bad grades, and then can't find a job, what happens to them? My brother says the state looks after them. Is this right?"

I nodded.

Sam shook his head. "So they are rewarded for doing nothing! Not in Grenada. No qualifications mean no job and that means no money."

"Would you prefer Grenada to be more like England and give money to people without jobs?"

Sam's eyes widened. "No! People should work. People should not be lazy. I do not agree with your methods in England."

As we threaded our way through the town, I noticed the absence of pedestrian pavements – the roads all ended abruptly at a ditch, presumably to allow water to run off. These ditches forced people, whether pensioner or a child, to walk along the road's edge. Thankfully, the endless traffic was moving too slowly to cause any of them serious harm, but it didn't seem right, somehow.

"Are the ditches for storm water?" I asked.

"Yeah."

"So Grenada gets some pretty bad storms?"

"Hurricane Ivan was the worst. It hit Grenada in 2004. I think it was the tenth worst hurricane to cross the Atlantic. When we got the warnings, my family went to my sister's house. We all bunkered down and waited for it to hit. I think it came about 1pm, and then lasted a couple of hours. The noise was terrifying, like nothing I've heard before or since. It was like the air was screaming. And even inside the house, we all got soaked. We were like drowned rats. Afterwards, when everyone went out to see the damage, we saw everyone's roof had gone – blown away by the hurricane. But do you know what? People pulled together. We helped each other out, fixed the roofs, cleared the trees and cleared the mess."

Ivan had wrought damage across the whole of Grenada, leaving over three quarters of the island in devastation. Schools, hospitals, banks, churches and office buildings: all shaken, pummelled and left in ruin. The capital, St George's, was particularly badly hit. In the aftermath, the prime minister's palace was left in such a perilous state that he had to relocate to a naval vessel. The city's prison was so badly damaged that most of the prisoners escaped (all were later recaptured). And while the convicts ran for the hills, looters stripped damaged shops bare. Not helping matters was the disarray of the Grenadian police force. With almost all their police stations in rubble, they could do nothing except wait for assistance from troops sent over by neighbouring islands. The damage from Hurricane Ivan ran to almost a billion US dollars.

11

Back inland, we passed a series of large, palatial homes. Each of them stood in its own extensive garden: homes of the very rich, I reckoned. Sam confirmed this, telling me that many of the houses belonged to wealthy Grenadians who, back in the fifties and sixties, had moved to the United Kingdom and made enough money to retire back to the island. "We call these houses JCBs."

"JCBs?"

"Just Come Backs. As soon as they arrive, they build a big house in this area. I think it's great. They made their money and now live like kings in their homeland. Sometimes we get younger guys, though. They have made a lot of money quickly and buy one of these houses as a holiday home. They think they are better than the people who stay on the island. I don't like these JCBs. They should be DCBs: Don't Come Backs."

Eventually we arrived at the capital of Grenada. St George's was a sprawling sweep of pastel-coloured dwellings perched on a hillside that formed a crescent around a pretty harbour. On top of the hill was Fort George, thoughtfully named by the British after mad King George III, who never once visited the Caribbean.

We trundled through the Sendall Tunnel, a narrow route that allowed only one car at a time to pass through. For pedestrians, it provided a handy shortcut between the outer and inner parts of the capital. One side was the peaceful outer harbour area we had just driven through, the other a tumult of noisy people and even noisier traffic. A platoon of blue-uniformed policemen wearing red and white caps controlled the traffic, blowing whistles and holding out their arms. Amid the chaos, street vendors, pedestrians and parked delivery vans filled the space.

Sam found a spot and pulled over. "Okay, do you want me to show you around, or do you prefer to be on your own?"

I pretended to mull this over. "I'll go and look around by myself."

Sam nodded. "Okay, then. How about one hour to do your own exploring? Go and see the fort. I'll be waiting right here."

I grabbed my hat, sunglasses and bottle of water. It was time to explore the capital of Grenada.

12

Outside was hot and muggy. I crossed a street and then, while I stood getting my bearings, a gaunt man approached, weaving and wobbling across the road to reach me. “You got some dollars to spare?” he muttered, forcing a grin that revealed more missing teeth than ones in place.

I hated situations like this. On the one hand, I often felt sorry for the individual in questions, but common sense dictated that to give any money would often bring other beggars, not to mention that the money would probably be wasted anyway. The man looked like a drunk or – more likely – a drug addict, but he looked desperately thin. I handed him a few coins and he gratefully took them, thanking me profusely. I left him standing there, making my escape before any other chancers made an unwelcome appearance. I headed uphill towards Fort George.

Unlike Trinidad’s Fort George, Grenada’s wasn’t much to look at. A combination of prime neglect and hurricane damage had left it in a sorry state. Blackened grime coated many of the bastions and pathways, with only a few cannons hinting that it was ever a fort. On the way up, I had passed a church that was missing its roof. Twelve years on from Hurricane Ivan, the damage was still clear to see.

Nowadays, instead of bright-uniformed troops, a branch of the Royal Grenadian Police Force occupies the fort, and one officer was watching me from his elevated position on some steps. I mimed whether it was okay to take some photos and the man nodded assent. Apart from us, there was nobody there. I found a spot that overlooked the town of St George’s. If I ignored the power cables that crisscrossed the hillside view, the harbour looked gorgeous: ripples, reflections and red-roofed buildings. All the grime, dust, flaking paintwork and hot car fumes were invisible from this height; I could have been in Croatia or perhaps Italy, it was so postcard pretty.

Behind me, in the old parade ground, I found a plaque. It read: *In everlasting memory of Prime Minister Maurice Bishop, killed at this fort, Oct 19 1983*. I took a photo, pondering the fact that I was standing on the very spot that kicked off the American invasion of Grenada. Despite Maurice Bishop campaigning for women’s rights, education and better healthcare, his Marxist underlings thought him weak. When he refused to step aside to allow a more extreme leader to take his place, he was arrested and shot by a firing squad.

I headed back down the hill to find Sam. When I found him, I asked him about the US invasion. By my reckoning, he would have been in his twenties. Sam seemed reticent to answer at first, but then told me he remembered the invasion well, and was glad the Americans came. "I was nineteen at the time, but I did not call it an invasion, I called it the expelling of the enemy."

I wanted to ask what else he remembered, but I got the impression he did not want to talk about it. Instead, we rode in silent contemplation to our final stop of the tour – an upmarket hotel close to the airport where I would while away a few hours before walking to the terminal to catch my second Liat Airlines flight of the day.

"Well, have a good flight to St Vincent," said Sam outside the Rex Hotel.

"Thanks." I shook his hand, and then entered the spacious lobby of the hotel, my temporary residence for the next couple of hours.

13

As the sun slipped towards the horizon, it turned the sky to honey as it cast lovely tinges upon the palms and sand. Sipping a beer, I was surprised to find I was the only person enjoying the view, apart from a flock of white egrets, who, for whatever reason, had decided to roost in the same tree. Then the battle cries of an arriving horde broke the ambience.

From some beachfront apartments, a mob of children spilled forth, perhaps twenty or thirty of them, their parents waddling behind in tight formation. When they swarmed upon the beach, upsetting the sand, birds and peace, I made my escape to the lounge bar to wait out my time. Even from a distance, though, the beach looked amazing. If a photographer wanted to capture the essence of a Caribbean sunset, then they would be hard pushed to find something better than my current view. I stared out over the water, following a line of wispy clouds sailing above the horizon like orange balloons. Half an hour later (now onto my second beer) as darkness stole the shadows, I realised it was time to go.

It took ten minutes to walk to Maurice Bishop International Airport, a journey undertaken in complete darkness. When I arrived, I stuffed my pockets, socks and trousers with the heaviest items from my luggage and shuffled to the check-in counter. This time, however, no one weighed my bags.

In the departure lounge, I began my regular period of angst as to whether Liat Airlines would turn up. If they cancelled the flight, then where would I stay the night? The beach hotel down the road would be a good choice, but I already knew it to be expensive. As I thought about this, an airport employee turned on a small TV. Twenty pairs of eyes swivelled towards the screen as it showed more news on the American shooting.

The report gave a name and a location. At about 9pm the previous evening, a 32-year old black man called Philando Castile had been returning home from a shopping trip with his girlfriend when a white police officer pulled them over. The officer mistakenly believed Mr Castile had been involved in a recent robbery. The footage I'd seen in Trinidad that morning (filmed by Castile's girlfriend) was showing again, this time with subtitles for the dialogue. The shaky video showed a police officer standing by the Philando Castile's window asking to see his driving licence. Castile tells the police officer that it's in his wallet, adding that he also has a licensed weapon. Upon hearing this, the officer says, "Don't move."

Things happen quickly after that.

As Philando Castile raises his hands in acquiescence, the police officer shoots him. No warning, no preamble, just four or five quick shots pumped into Castile's body. As he slumps in his seat, audibly moaning, the girlfriend says, "Please don't tell me he's dead." As the video plays out, Mr Castile dies.

Most of my fellow passengers were shaking their heads A few rows ahead, a fifty-something man turned to his companion, another man about the same age. “These white police think they’re above the law… an innocent black man just going about this business.”

The friend nodded, staring at the screen. “Racist Americans.”

What none of us knew was that by the next morning, protests would be breaking out across America. Some Caribbean nations would soon be offering travel advisories to their citizens about visiting America. I wondered what all this would mean for me. Suddenly, being a white man in the Caribbean had turned just a little bit edgy, especially if people thought I was an American white man. But there was nothing I could do about that now. With the footage on a constant loop, I waited for the Liat aircraft to arrive. It did, and was only thirty-five minutes late. By the time I landed in St Vincent, it was 11pm and I was tired and weary. All I wanted was to get to the hotel and sleep.

So that’s exactly what I did.

Clockwise from top left: Liat Airlines – the Caribbean Airline; Policeman in St George's looking like he means business; A panorama of St George's taken from the fort; Looking down over Grenada; A beautiful Caribbean sunset; A not so interesting waterfall in the middle of Grenada

Chapter 4. St Vincent and the Pirates of the Caribbean

Refreshed after an unbroken night's sleep, I pulled the curtains back and took in the splendour of St Vincent, an island named by Christopher Columbus in 1498 because he happened to sight it on the feast day of Valencia's patron saint. Beyond my balcony was a small but perfect harbour, busy with tall-masted yachts and white catamarans, each dipping and undulating in a most pleasing way.

I raised my gaze upwards. The sky was blue with a few clouds hanging limply in the almost non-existent breeze. So much for rain and wind (as predicted by the BBC online weather) – St Vincent was basking in gorgeous tropical sun.

I turned on the news. CNN was showing the same horrible footage of the man dying at the hands of a white police officer. The news was also reporting on the demonstrations. Things were looking bad for the United States in their race wars. Even President Barack Obama was saying that the US could do better.

My guide for the day was a local taxi driver called Brian. He was in his sixties and coughed like a man who smoked fifty a day, though I didn't see him smoke a single one. "Welcome to St Vincent and the Grenadines," he said, after recovering from a coughing fit. Whatever he had produced from his lungs was now on the grass by the side of the car. "Where yas from?"

"England."

"Ah, England. Dat's good. I thought you might be American. After what happened to that boy, I'm not a fan of Americans today. Tomorrow, maybe, but not today. That cop shot him like a dog."

I nodded in concurrence. "American is not right at the moment."

"Not right is a good description. America isn't right for a black man to be. Anyway, this is not about America, this is about your tour." He visibly cheered. "The first stop will be the capital, Kingstown, den the fort. And then after dat, we'll go up to where Pirates of the Caribbean was filmed. Alright?"

"Sounds good."

"Alright. But first, I need to make a stop at my house. My daughter made me some tea and in my rush to meet you, I left it behind. Don't worry, though; the house is on the way."

The roads in St Vincent are narrow and winding, often cracked and pitted with shallow potholes as they follow the contours of the island's many hills. Dense, tropical vegetation, dotted with sporadic Caribbean-style, homesteads passed in a blur. Occasionally, through gaps in the green, I caught glimpses of the ocean. "So, do you enjoy living in St Vincent?" I asked Brian.

"I love it! The weather, the beer, the life. I would not live anywhere else. The police are good, the politicians are okay. Yes, we have some drug issues, but this does not affect my family or me. So, yes, I enjoy life in St Vincent."

"Have you ever been to any of the Grenadines?" I asked, referring to the island chain that made up the rest of the country.

"Many times. I was in Bequia last month. That's the next biggest island to St Vincent. My brother lives over there. He works in Port Elizabeth's harbour. You should visit Bequia in Easter. That's when all the yachts come over for the regatta."

We turned off the hillside road and pulled up into a small lay-by. Hugging a wall was a small house. After Brian beeped his horn, a head popped out around a door, then disappeared again. "My daughter. She'll bring me my tea. She's a good girl."

I asked Brian whether it would be okay to have a look over the side of his wall at the view.

"Help yourself, man."

As I climbed out of the car, a squat dog came bounding out of the house and, after briefly sniffing in my direction, ran excitedly up to Brian. The old man reached down and petted his elated canine. "Alright," he said. The dog yapped and jumped even more.

Brian's daughter came out and delivered Brian a flask of tea and a Tupperware box, saying hello to me as she flitted back to the house. Brian's dog, finished with fussing over its owner, regarded me again, and decided it liked what it saw, for its spindly tail began to wag excitedly. When I murmured an inviting sound, it rushed over. It was a small dog but it galloped towards me like the clappers and then tried to paw at my Grenadines. I ruffled its head and it gazed up with gleeful eyes, tongue lolling. Brian watched from his driver's seat and smiled, too. Then he coughed and spat the resulting mixture onto his drive.

I looked over the wall. Nestled beneath a vista of green highland was the capital of St Vincent and the Grenadines: Kingstown. It looked attractive enough, but no more than St George's or Port of Spain had from afar. Clustered around a tight harbour of spindly jetties was a mishmash of multi-coloured buildings. A flotilla of service boats and small ferries flitted around them. There was not a single skyscraper in sight. From a distance, Kingstown looked like a place of light commerce rather than a place of tourism. I looked towards the higher ground. If my eyesight was powerful enough, I might have been able to see a dramatic peak called La Soufriere (The Sulphurer), a 4000-foot active volcano that in 1902 spewed enough lava and pyroclastic flow to kill 1680 people. Since then, it has erupted twice (with less devastating results), the last time in 1979.

I turned tail and, after rubbing the dog's chin, climbed back into the car.

2

The French founded Kingstown in the year 1722. Back then, it was a mosquito-infested settlement of rudimentary wooden dwellings with a small port to service transport ships. A few years later, the French grew weary of the heat and passed it over to the British. Then the British passed it back to the French, who scratched their heads and wondered what to do with their tropical slice of island. In the end, they decided to do what all the other islands were doing and planted some sugar cane, coffee and tobacco, then shipped over some African slaves to work the fields. The slaves did such a sterling job that the French ordered some more. When one of the arriving slave ships hit bad weather and started listing off the coast of St Vincent, the French watched for a while, but did little else. When it began sinking, they shook their heads and turned away, leaving the local Carib population to step in to save some of the drowning slaves. Not only that: they welcomed the soaked Africans into their villages and, over time, allowed them to integrate into their own communities.

Meanwhile, the English and French signed another treaty, which passed the nation between them again. A few years later, when the French took St Vincent and the Grenadines back on their colonial books, the Caribs looked on with dismay. Their homeland was passing forth between two colonial powers like a ball in a tennis match. When control passed back to the British, they decided enough was enough and staged a rebellion. With their strongest men, plus the freed African slaves, they took over half of the island. Instead of fighting back, the British handed the bothersome island chain back to the French.

The French reluctantly moved back in, reasonably allowing the Caribs to keep their half of the island, but when their troops kept dying of malaria, they finally decided St Vincent was not for them and left for good.

To fill the void, the British grudgingly moved back in and, still smarting from the Carib rebellion, staged a massive attack on the indigenous population, this time overpowering them. Instead of killing them, the British herded the Caribs aboard transport ships and exiled them to an island off the coast of Honduras. Today, many descendants of this exiled group still live there. As for St Vincent, under British rule, the island turned into a plantation factory, until a hurricane and then a volcanic eruption destroyed most of the arable land.

Today, instead of sugar cane or coffee, bananas are the country's biggest money-maker, closely followed by tourism. Being one of the latter who enjoyed eating the former, I was looking forward to seeing as much as I could in the one day at my disposal.

3

Brian threaded us down towards Kingstown. And then, at a sharp hairpin bend, he brought us to a standstill. A minibus was coming the opposite way and Brian recognised the driver. After the bus pulled alongside us, it stopped. Both drivers wound their windows down.

"Alright?" said Brian, nodding to the other driver, a man in a stripy beanie hat.

"Alright," said the man, smiling a Rasta grin worthy of a reggae album cover.

And that was it. Conversation over. Windows back up and on we went. "He's a friend of mine," explained Brian. "On his way to the airport to pick up some passengers."

The airport, ET Joshua International, the very one I'd arrived into the previous night, was below us, jutting out along a small ocean-flanked headland. Adjacent to it was a cricket ground. I wondered what happened when a ball went astray.

Down we drove until we hit the busy streets of Kingstown. The capital of St Vincent was not equipped for the sheer volume of traffic it was getting. To coin a phrase, it was in total gridlock. Even a man pulling a cart with a butane gas canister balanced on the back was stuck in it. In an effort to cope, the city planners had installed a one-way system, but this had resulted in streets clogged in a single direction, with every feeder street backing up with traffic wanting to join the glacial one-way system.

A stout policewoman in uniform was trying to direct the traffic. As well as her white blouse and black trousers, she possessed a large booty and stern expression. She was trying her best, but there was not much she could do. Whenever she ushered a driver to move forward, they gestured that they could not do so because there was nowhere for them to go. In the midst of the logjam, a gangly man in a red and green beanie hat lolloped (in that distinctly Caribbean swaggering gait) to the policewoman. As far as I could tell, he was not in a vehicle, and was merely a pedestrian.

"Alright?" he drawled.

Instead of answering him, the woman tried cajoling a massive lorry into the one-way system. It hissed its brakes and moved forward one centimetre. It was already blocking the main road and a side street. Exasperated, the policewoman shook her head. The only way the lorry would make headway in the scrum was to drive over the top of it. The man in the beanie hat watched the shenanigans with keen interest. "Miss, you need to clear de traffic dat way, ya know," he said, pointing in the direction everyone wanted to go. "When dat clear, tings will move."

The policewoman glared at him. She looked a lady not to be trifled with, especially in the hot and clammy morning. The man recognised the look. "Okay, okay, I'm just sayin', alright..."

"What are you tryin' to say?" the woman shot back.

"Notting." He bounded off, disappearing underneath the shadow of a tropically-stained long building that might have been a factory. Five minutes later, the lorry had manoeuvred into the main street, puffing out a cloud of black exhaust smoke in triumph. Everyone moved forward a few feet.

Kingstown looked typical of a Caribbean town: hectic to the point of bursting. Plenty of townsfolk were wandering the streets, lounging around in stalls or resting upon walls. The buildings looked in poor shape, often in a state of disrepair; covered with tropical grime. But they were almost all splashed in bright colours. Shops signs read: Tailor Paris, Arthur's Transport Rental Co., and the UniQue Boutique, which offered the *latest in ladies and gents clothing*. While Brian enjoyed another coughing fit, I spied a young woman wearing a clingy white T-shirt. Splashed across her chest was an obscene slogan. 'I LOVE COC–' the final letter hidden behind her ample bosom. Then she turned to cross the road and I read the T-shirt in full: I LOVE COCO.

One thing was for sure: Kingstown was not boring.

4

Getting to Fort Charlotte involved another period sitting in gridlock. It gave Brian a chance to eat a banana, a chocolate biscuit and finish his tea. The cause of the traffic was some road works. A bulldozer and a set of workmen were supposedly resurfacing half of the road, but we had caught them on a break, or they preferred leaning on their shovels. The only member of the work team doing anything was a man whose job it was to turn a handheld sign saying STOP or GO. His other job was to chat to everyone who came his way, young or old, Rasta or granny. When our side said GO, the traffic lurched forward and then stopped. The man with the sign knew a taxi driver in front and the pair decided to have a chat. Wondering what Brian would make of this new – and easily avoidable – delay, I watched for signs of annoyance. But he showed no sign of being irked at all. Instead, he applied the handbrake and told me that St Vincent didn't have any traffic lights.

"Really?"

"Yeah, man. Well, we have some, but I haven't seen any of them working. We don't need them."

I begged to differ, but said nothing.

Above us, hidden in the contours of a tall hill was Fort Charlotte. Built by the British, it was two hundred years old, named after the wife of the then King of England, George III. Unusually for a colonial Caribbean fort, the British never used it as protection from sea attack, but rather as protection against local attack. Those Caribs had been a constant source of annoyance for them.

When we eventually reached the top of the ridge, the fort came into view: an imposing fortification of dark-stained bricks and high walls. We parked in a grassy courtyard bordered by small buildings and a tall wall. A trio of goats were munching on a patch of grass. Behind us was a building that had been the officer's quarters. While Brian waited in the car to finish his breakfast, I went to investigate, entering the old quarters through a side door and finding myself in a darkened rectangular room full of paintings. A young woman, bored out of her mind, sat behind a small desk looking at a mobile phone. For the briefest of seconds, she glanced my way and then continued to stare into her phone.

"Hi," I said.

"Alright." She didn't look up.

"Is this a museum or something?"

She nodded.

"How much to see it?"

Finally she looked at me. "It's free." She looked down at her phone again.

With nothing else to say, I walked up to one piece of artwork. It showed a group of Caribs trading with some French sailors. It was the friendliest painting there because all the others depicted scenes of English mistreatment. One picture had the caption: *1763 signalled the influx of land-hungry English settlers*. It showed a horde of Caribs burning down a sugar plantation in reprisal. The next painting showed British troops leading chained and shackled Caribs towards waiting ships so they could begin their exile off the coast of Honduras.

Back in the courtyard, I climbed a stone ramp to reach the uppermost section of Fort Charlotte. At the end of a walkway was a small, pale-blue building with an antenna poking from its roof. Inside the building was a thin young man. When I popped my head in, the man smiled. "Do you work here?" I asked.

"Yeah. This is a signal station. If a ship's in trouble, they contact me." He pointed at a walkie-talkie type thing. "Then I ring the coastguard."

"Does that happen often?"

"Not too often."

I asked him whether he enjoyed working in the signal station.

"Yeah, I enjoy it. Do you want a tour of the fort? I can show you around."

"What if an emergency call comes in?"

He shrugged. "They hardly do."

I declined his offer; not wanting the deaths of some merchant seamen on my hands. Instead, I went to find Brian. It was time to visit the set of the Pirates of the Caribbean.

5

We left the last vestiges of Kingstown below in the bay. The road was covered but of bad quality. It meant furious swerving or snail-pace manoeuvring. Quant veranda-laden houses with tin roofs lay scattered on the surrounding hillsides while fruit stalls, pecking chickens and, more commonly, goats loitered in the roadside dust. Everywhere were palms and thick green vegetation. We passed a small yellow building that proudly declared itself the *Vegetable's & MEAT-MART*, its apostrophe placement and strange mixture of upper and lower case lettering making it even more appealing. It sold dasheen (a type of root vegetable) yams, paw paws, chives, pumpkins, cucumbers, tomatoes, sweet potatoes and a relish called 'home made seasons & pepper sauce'.

With conversation quiet for the moment, Brian switched on the radio. Ralph Gonsalves, Prime Minister of St Vincent and the Grenadines was a guest on a live chat show. He was telling the host that he was heading to the airport later that day so he could fly to Trinidad to attend the funeral of former Trinidadian Prime Minister, Patrick Manning, with whom he had attended university.

"I thought the funeral was not until tomorrow?" said the radio host, a deep-voiced man who sounded like Barry White.

"I'm going today so I make it in time."

The radio host laughed. It was a knowing sound of mirth.

Gonsalves laughed, too. "Tell me about it. I can't risk not getting there. If I fly there this afternoon, then I should be in Port of Spain to see Patrick Manning's body tomorrow. Fingers crossed for Liat Airlines."

“They are famous for their delays,” said the radio host. “And wasn’t there an incident at the airport last week involving you and Liat?”

“Let’s clear this up right now. I was due to fly to Guyana for a trade conference. Liat booked me onto a flight with a stop in Barbados. So I turn up at ET Joshua Airport and wait for the flight to Barbados but of course, it was late. When it eventually arrived, I mentioned to the Liat representative that I had a tight connection to make in Barbados. He told me that I might not make it but they would try their best. Anyway, I got to Barbados but, surprise, surprise, the flight to Guyana had already left. Liat tried to get another plane, and eventually they did, and that’s the flight I got on. When I boarded, I asked the pilot if he could wait for other passengers stranded in Barbados, but he said he did not have time. So we took off without them. And then, a day later, the press reported that I had chartered the plane all for myself, leaving everyone else behind. This is not true! I tried to get the pilot to wait, but I have no control over Liat Airlines. And in the end, I missed the conference anyway.”

The radio host commiserated. “That is the problem with journalism in this country. Many of the reporters have taken creative writing courses to avoid writing about the truth.”

With thoughts of Liat and delays resounding unhappily around my head, we threaded our way north.

6

We passed Protestant, Anglican, Catholic and Seventh-day Adventist churches. Religion was big business in St Vincent and the Grenadines, with eight out of ten people considering themselves of the Godly persuasion. And because of this, funerals were big business, too. The radio had switched to a programme dedicated to death announcements.

“We are sad to announce the death of Mrs Agnes Mayhew, aged 88, who died last Tuesday,” intoned a solemn man, whose voice was sounding out over a backing track of suitably sombre music. “She leaves behind six children, eighteen grandchildren, two great-great-grandchildren, one sister and plenty more relatives. Agnes’s funeral will be held at the Anglican Church on Monday. Memorial service begins at 2pm, with the burial at three.” There was a slight gap in the narrative for us listeners to pay our own private respects to Agnes, and then he announced the death of someone else. In total, five announcements were aired before making way for a well-placed advertisement for a funeral service provider.

We passed through tiny villages with names such as Rubis, Rillin Hill Layou and Barrouallie, a tiny coastal settlement that had once been the capital of St Vincent and the Grenadines. Not far from Barrouallie was a village called Wallilabou Bay that, up until 2005, no one outside St Vincent had heard of. That year, it struck gold when Hollywood filmmakers used it as part of their *Pirates of the Caribbean* outdoor film location. Since then, steady trickles of tourists have made their way to the old film set.

To get to the actual bay, Brian had to negotiate a tight hairpin bend that led down an alarmingly steep gradient. Brakes squeaked, suspension groaned but we made it to the bottom without ending up in the sea. We parked beneath a couple of palm trees. A gorgeous slice of ocean lay beyond.

“If it’s alright with you, Jason,” said Brian, ‘I might have a nap for a while. You take your time.”

What was it with Caribbean tour guides, I wondered as I left the car. They all wanted to nap on the job. But I was quite glad, actually; it would give me chance to explore at my own pace.

7

Outside, the heat and clamminess hit me. How had Johnny Depp and the rest of the crew coped with the tropical humidity when they had been in town, I wondered? Mr Depp probably had a couple of assistants with cold wet flannels on hand.

The producers of Pirates of the Caribbean picked Wallilabou Bay because of its small, isolated natural harbour that was free of modern development. To make it more pirate-like, they constructed a makeshift dock, a buccaneer-themed Port Royal building and flew in a whole load of props. I gazed at the main building, the chief draw of Wallilabou Bay. Wooden shutters and a gabled upper-storey level adorned it. A few open coffins lay along its front. From a distance, it looked authentically pirate-like, except it was all an illusion. When I inspected the exterior stonework up close, I found out it to be a veneer of thin plasterwork. The plaster covered a flimsy wooden frame. Some of it had flaked away to reveal the bare wood underneath. Beyond the front facade was nothing but a skeleton of metal scaffolding supporting a rickety roof. But so what? The producers never intended it to be a tourist site, only a background prop for exterior camerawork. And in the years since the film shoots, the set had fallen into noticeable disrepair.

Inside, someone had pasted a series of photos onto a roughly-constructed rear wall. They showed the actors and crew in various states of rehearsal or action. In another small section, some shooting schedules dating from 2005 were on display. *Shooting Day #36 - Thu, Apr 21, 2005,* one schedule read. *Scene #72: Jack and crew row towards shore.* For the scene, a few stuntmen (the only people in the shot) were needed. So was a parrot, plus a helicopter to film the scene from above. With a bead of sweat dribbling down my face, I decided to seek the fresher air outside.

I walked along a jetty that took me underneath a kitschy signpost. A plastic pirate, complete with eye patch and cutlass, was perched on one end. I gazed out to sea, noticing a white yacht anchored some distance offshore. Four months previously, a group of ten German tourists had moored their yacht near to where I now stood. While they slumbered, two men climbed aboard in order to steal their belongings. Being clumsy, one of the thieves knocked something over, waking the passengers with the resulting clatter. Instead of escaping the yacht, the pair grabbed more valuables and then shot and killed one of the passengers.

I stared at the white yacht in the distance, wondering whether the people on it knew about the terrible tragedy. Probably not, I thought. I decided go and have a drink to cool myself down.

8

Before I could reach the bar, a man in a yellow T-shirt bounded over. “Alright, man,” he said, sticking his arm out. “People call me Speedy.” His smile was broad and his face friendly. I shook Mr Speedy’s hand and introduced myself.

“So what brings you to Wallilabou?” he asked.

“To see the Pirates of the Caribbean set.” I gestured to the pretend building.

“You a pirate fan?”

“Not really, But I did enjoy the movies.”

Mr Speedy nodded. “Well, I was in the first film – an extra. Just for a few days, mind, back in 2005. If you look out by the jetty, that’s where I was, dressed up like a pirate, pretending to catch a fish. But you would not recognise me; I was in costume.”

Speedy was now a trinket peddler. He had already laid them out on a nearby wall and wanted me to look. “I can’t buy anything,” I said. “I’m travelling with Liat Airlines; hand luggage only.”

“A necklace does not weigh much and takes no room in your luggage, man.”

I could hardly argue with that and so begrudgingly looked at his wares. There were a few necklaces made up of tiny beads, a selection of wristbands patterned in Caribbean colours and some gaudy, beady earrings. “All dese tings made by Speedy’s own hands,” he told me proudly. I had my doubts about that, but in the end, I bought a small necklace for twenty East Caribbean Dollars, about five pounds.

Speedy handed it over. "Thanks man, I know you didn't really want to buy anything. So I really appreciate it. You have a great day, now."

The bar featured a few pirate waxworks, some Jolly Roger flags and masses of rigging dangling from the ceiling. Due to the recent murder and the fact that it was out of the cruise ship season, I found myself the only patron of the bar, and the owner seemed surprised to see me. He jumped up and looked flustered for a second before asking me what I wanted. I ordered a Hairoun Beer, which came in a compact little bottle that proudly declared itself St Vincent's prize-winning lager. After thanking the barman, I found a table overlooking the sea. A couple of local boys were paddling about in the water, one at either end of a surfboard. One waved. I waved back, taking a slurp of my Hairoun, happy with my lot in life. How lucky I was to be able to visit places such as St Vincent. How lucky I was to sit and savour the warm ocean breeze and the almost hypnotic flow of the waves. My fourth Caribbean nation was turning out to be my favourite so far.

9

"It was terrible. Terrible for the gentleman who got killed, but terrible for St Vincent," said Brian after I'd asked him about the yacht murder. "You gotta ask the question: why did those two boys do that? What did they think they would happen? Steal a couple hundred dollars? Take a laptop, maybe? But in the end, they killed a man." Brian sighed as we joined the main road away from Wallilabou Bay. "But let me tell you something: since the killing, tourists are not coming like they used to. The yachts are not coming – maybe only one or two a week. They go to Antigua and St Kitts, instead. Our president – that man you heard on the radio earlier – he called the people who did this a terrible stain. And he is right. I just hope they are caught soon."

Suddenly a car roared past us, and not an ordinary car: a *blingmobile*. It was sheer white with jet-black bumpers and fluorescent blue and orange wheel rims. It looked utterly ridiculous. Brian shook his head as it and a raucous cacophony of dub-reggae receded, leaving dust eddies at the side of the road. "Young folk. They like their cars. They don't realise how stupid they look."

I sniggered at his observation.

Forty minutes later, we arrived back in Kingstown so I could do a bit of exploring by myself. If anything, the traffic was worse than earlier, with street after street caught up in the absurd one-way logjam. After ploughing through it, Brian found a tight parking spot near a large Bank of St Vincent and the Grenadines building and ushered me out. As I closed the door, he shouted through the window. "I'll be back here in one hour. Make sure you're ready, because stopping is illegal. See you later."

As he drove off, I took stock. The first thing that struck me about Kingstown was its hustle and bustle. Cars, buses, mini-vans, fruit stalls, people lugging carts full of coconuts, pensioners shuffling with shopping bags, buxom-chested ladies wearing large floppy hats, people laughing uproariously: the capital was overflowing with noise and activity. After crossing the road opposite the bank, I headed downhill, negotiating a street packed with food stalls, until I came to the attractively named Bay Street, one of the main thoroughfares of the city. Hidden behind a line of shops, shacks and nondescript structures was the Caribbean Sea, and my mission was to walk far enough along the street to see it.

Along the way, I came to a building worthy of a photograph. It was a tall and wide brown structure with a fetching orange roof. Above its archway was a large black sign that read: Central Police Station. I couldn't see any policemen – possibly because they were all out directing traffic – but I could see a statue of a soldier standing upon a tall and sturdy plinth. Upon closer inspection, he belonged to yet another Caribbean war memorial.

Over fifteen thousand men from various Caribbean nations volunteered to fight in both World Wars. One of them was a young Vincentian called Ernest Hadley who arrived into a grey and mortar-blasted part of Belgium called Passchendaele. It was the summer of 1917, though it may well have been winter for Second Lieutenant Hadley: every tree was bare, the ground devoid of grass and his home was a trench of stinking mud. When his superior officers ordered him over the top on August 27th, Ernest Hadley ran for his life. He was one of half a million men who died in the Battle of Passchendaele during that dreadful summer.

10

I literally stumbled upon Kingstown Central Market, almost tripping over a fruit stall. The proprietor, a fearsome looking young woman of considerable girth, glared at me before reaching over to rearrange her melons. I limped away, surveying the tightly crammed outdoor stalls, many protected from the sun and rain (both equally likely on a hot July afternoon) by sheets of plastic tarpaulin. Bunches of bananas, slices of watermelon, shiny plums, kiwi fruit and bagged-up nuts were available from wooden shacks and plastic counters. The heat was intense, the bartering skilful, the colours vibrant.

I detected the pungent odour of fish. It was coming from Kingstown Fish Market, an indoor warehouse of fervent chopping, descaling, weighing (on ancient metal scales) and bagging up of chunks of milky flesh. Through the other side, I finally came face to face with the Caribbean Sea. It stretched before me for two and a half thousand kilometres until it swept upon the coast of Nicaragua. With my mission to see the sea complete, I decided to head into the centre of the city just as a waft of smoked marijuana drifted under my nose.

Even though a quarter of century had passed since my university days, the smell was immediately recognisable. I scanned the market for the source. It was coming from a trio of white-haired gents sitting in a shaded area behind one of the stalls. Two of them had beanie hats; the third preferred a jaunty sailor's cap. All three were smoking and chatting amicably. When they caught me looking, they invited me over. I waved their offer away, but one man stood up, wobbled a little and waved at me again. He looked stoned out of his head and so I walked over to their little pot den.

"Alright, man," the gent in the sailor's hat, the one standing up, drawled. He took a deep drag on his joint and then offered it to me. I thanked him but declined. He nodded and exhaled smoke from his nostrils like a dragon.

"Whatcha doin' in Kingstown?" one of his pals asked. Three pairs of eyes tried to focus on me.

"Just seeing the sights. Kingstown seems a nice place."

"That it is, man. That it is."

I asked, "So do you work here at the market?"

"Yeah," said the man in the white cap. "We're been toilin' all morning, you know." The other two nodded as the joint moved around. All three were sitting now, leaving me standing by some tarpaulin. "This is our little reward. You sure you don't want some?" Again, I declined, and, after a few moments of marijuana silence, I said I had to go. The trio waved me off with a billow of cannabis smoke.

Walking towards the centre of the city, I stopped to buy a coconut from a young man sitting on the back of a flatbed truck. For 30p, he hacked the top off, stuck a straw in and handed it over. It was delicious, tastier than any can of fizzy drink I could have purchased in one of the shops nearby. I walked away happy.

Still enjoying my fresh drink, I came across the most colourful shop in town. *God Bless St Vincent* it proudly declared. Below the sign, next to a painted jaguar head, the slogan added, *Mad Store.* Piled up outside the door were rolls of linoleum. Perhaps it was special linoleum because five people were inspecting the rolls. There was also a mattress hanging by the door that was attracting some attention. When I peered inside the store's murky entrance, I spied women's clothes and handbags.

"Can I help you," asked the voice of a woman, hidden in the gloom.

Briefly, I was flummoxed. "Erm … no, thanks," I managed to mutter. "I was just looking for some swimming goggles." For some reason, they were the first thing that popped into my head. To add to the ruse, I mimed doing the breaststroke.

"We don't sell them," said the voice. "Maybe try somewhere along Grenville Street."

I thanked the unseen woman and headed deeper into Kingstown, soon finding myself outside the city's barbed-wire-covered, jailhouse. Someone had painted *Her Majesty's Prison* in huge white curving letters on the side of the main building, underscored with the noble motto, *to hold, to treat, to rehabilitate.* A small sign informed prospective visitors that no leggings, armpits or shorts were allowed.

I looked at my watch. My hour was almost up and so I headed back to the bank. And dead on time, Brian pulled up and I jumped into the passenger seat like an actor from the *Dukes of Hazard.* It was time to go back to the hotel to see a prostitute.

11

The prostitute came later. First, I ate some late lunch, then decided to go for a walk around the yacht harbour I'd seen from my hotel balcony. A curved beach of powdery sand made up the edge of the harbour; I was only person on it, and, for a few moments, I stopped to admire the boats. Most of them were small white craft with tall, spindly masts. A few men were tinkering on a couple of them, inspecting engine parts and doing nautical things that I had no inkling about. One of them was cleaning a bilge pump, or maybe it was a piece of drain plug – I really had no idea – so I decided it was time to resume my afternoon stroll.

Suddenly, movement caught my eye: crabs, and hundreds of them. All of them were in a patch of sand underneath the canopy of some thick palm leaves. Before I could even focus on them, they were gone, bunkered down inside tiny sand holes. I stood still, waiting. Then one popped its eyes above the sand hole. Like a cartoon character, its eyes swivelled on stalks, searching me out. I waited for the crustacean sentinel to locate me but the crab was either not good at noticing motionless humans, or it was a poor lookout. It must have given the all clear because, suddenly, about twenty crabs (all about the size of my fist), emerged from their hideouts. Following this show of bravery, the rest of the gang bobbed their heads up and soon the forest floor was awash with red-orange crabs. When I stepped forward to take a photo of the scene, they disappeared in a flash.

I left the timid crabs and wandered further along the deserted beach. Except it wasn't deserted: a woman was sitting on an upturned boat further along. Her presence startled me – not least because she must have been watching me for some time. The woman was in her thirties, her buxom figure squeezed into a long flowery dress. She possessed a large smile. As I plodded towards the boat, she said something quite astonishing. I was sure I'd misheard her.

"Sorry?" I said.

"You want company?" the woman repeated. Her voice was so matter-of-fact that I still thought I'd misheard her. She was looking at me, waiting for my answer.

"Do I want company?" I asked.

The woman nodded coyly.

"No, thank you."

"Suit yourself."

I walked off, mentally shaking my head. I could think of no other possible reason to explain her behaviour except that she was a prostitute. This made me wonder about her business model. It seemed flawed in the most fundamental way. Surely, she would get more customers in the town, or at least on the main road. The chance of someone encountering her on the beach, let alone someone who was a willing client, was slim at best. I looked back and saw she was still sitting on the upturned boat. She looked like she was watching the yachts. Perhaps that was where her customers came from.

12

Following my encounter, I decided to leave the harbour and take the high road. It was called Windward Highway, and took me on a nice route that offered extensive sea views. Twenty minutes later, I was nearing my destination, the Paradise Beach Hotel. The receptionist at my hotel had mentioned that it had a nice bar area around the back where I could enjoy a beer or two. Before I turned down towards it, I came across a fifty-something woman sitting on a wall with some shopping bags. She looked like she was waiting for one of the minibuses that plied the route.

"You want any company?" she asked.

Again, I was stunned. "No thanks," I mumbled. She shrugged and looked back along the road. What was it with St Vincent and the Grenadines? Why were ostensibly ordinary women propositioning tourists at every turn?

Later, I found out that instead of being sex workers, the women were chancers, hoping I might say yes so they could earn a little bit of extra cash for their families. A rich white man was a bonus many couldn't refuse.

Finally, I left the highway and turned down towards The Paradise Beach. As soon as my beer came, I pressed the cold bottle to my forehead, positive I could hear the liquid evaporating. I drank an enthusiastic gulp and took in the vista beyond the tables and parasols. Opposite, about two hundred metres out at sea, was Young Island, a perfect slice of tropical niceness, bristling with palms, thick vegetation and a flawless white beach. Sun beds belonging to the Young Island Resort littered the beach. A one-night stay on Young

Island averaged $250. It was where Johnny Depp had stayed during filming of Pirates of the Caribbean.

With my body temperature still in the red, but pulling back from the edge, I raised my glass to St Vincent and his Grenadines. Although my stay on the island had been horrendously brief, I had still enjoyed myself immensely. And when I thought of the islands to come – St Lucia, Antigua, St Kitts and Dominica, my smile broadened.

Life, I decided resolutely, was indeed grand in the Caribbean.

Clockwise from top left: Me enjoying a coconut in the centre of Kingstown; A policewoman not to be trifled with; War Memorial to the thousands of Caribbean men who died in both World Wars; Blue Lagoon Marina – home to a prostitute; The signal station up on Fort Charlotte; Old film set from Pirates of the Caribbean; Kingstown's most colourful shop

Chapter 5. Liat Airlines to St Lucia

I had a whole morning to do nothing. I relished the break from constant airport runs and island hops. With nothing better to do apart from having a leisurely breakfast, I decided to wander around the yacht harbour again. The crabs were nowhere to be seen, and neither was the woman who had offered me some company. After swilling my feet in the surf for a while, I said my mental goodbyes to St Vincent and trudged back to the hotel, wondering how Liat Airlines would treat me today.

After I had packed, the hotel ordered me a taxi. I was surprised to find it was Brian again. Once more, he began the journey with a horrendous coughing fit. It lasted so long that I grew concerned. When his chest hacking ceased, I asked whether he was okay.

"Yeah, man, I'm good. Just can't shake this cough."

"Have you had it a while?"

"A few weeks. Just a chest infection, I think."

"Maybe you ought to get it checked out."

"Maybe." He started the engine. I got the impression he didn't want to talk about it any further.

The weather was sunny and warm, just like it had been every day on my trip. It looked the perfect weather for island hopping: clear skies, light wind and perfect visibility. If Liat delayed my fight to St Lucia because of the weather, then I would know they were lying.

I told Brian about the women who had propositioned me the previous day. This news made him snigger heartily, which brought about a new coughing fit. "They saw a white man and thought they would give it a go. I doubt they would ask a local man. They were thinking of the money, that's all."

Fifteen minutes later, we were parked outside the airport terminal. Brian shook my hand and said that if I ever returned to St Vincent, then I should give him a shout. "There's a lot more to see than an old movie set and a waterfall. We have nature trails, a botanical garden and, if you come in early July, Carnival. It's not as big as Trinidad's but it's still worth a visit."

I told him I would. "Mind you, maybe I'll be ringing you in a couple of hours. Liat might cancel my flight and I'll need picking up again."

Brian chortled. "But you never know; sometimes Liat are on time."

2

It was not on time. My flight was delayed by one hour, and the reason had nothing to do with the weather: it was the late departure of an earlier flight. Thus, for close to two-and-a-half hours, I sat in a stuffy one-room terminal, with no cafés or shops to keep me amused, only a single duty-free shop that I tired of after only two minutes. Instead, I found a seat and gazed at the large painting of ET Joshua, the man for whom the airport was named. The caption underneath informed me that the man's full name was Ebenezer Theodore Joshua (which was a great name, I thought), and that he was first chief minister of St Vincent and the Grenadines between 1956 and 1967.

Mr Joshua looked *stately*; presidents and important ministers usually did, especially on state-sanctioned artwork. But he also looked friendly and wise, especially since the artist had painted him with a wry sparkle in his eyes. I looked him up on Google and discovered there was very little information about the man, apart from that he was born in Kingstown and then, in his thirties, he travelled to Trinidad and Guyana where he discovered a hitherto unknown interest in politics. ET Joshua also found out something else: he could stand up in front of a crowd and speak without nervousness. Things got even better when he learned he had a talent for rallying them. Thus, upon his return to St Vincent. Mr Joshua joined a trade union party to put these skills to use. A few years later, he found himself leading the country, albeit under British colonial rule. No wonder they named an airport after him.

While I waited out the delay, it started to rain. It was the first rain I'd seen since arriving in the Caribbean. Then, ominously, the sky darkened and, after a few thick patters on the window, it let rip – a full-blown tropical storm. Outside, the palms swayed in stormy disquiet.

"Where yas from?" asked a bald man in the seat next to me. He looked about sixty years of age. He was straining to see what I was reading on my phone.

"England."

"England? Never been to England, man. I'm from St Lucia; I can't wait to go back home. St Vincent is boring, man. No nightlife, no notting. In St Lucia, you can do things all hours of the day. Not like here in Dullsville. You know what I'm saying?" I murmured in agreement, though secretly wondered what sort of nightlife a sixty-year old man was looking for. Maybe he'd been staying at my hotel.

"You going to Barbados or St Lucia?" the man asked. He was referring to the fact that after St Lucia, the flight was scheduled to fly onto Barbados. I told him St Lucia.

"Been before?"

"No, first time."

"You're gonna love it. My island is de best in the Caribbean. Best beaches, best beer, best cricket, best women, best everything, man."

"I'm looking forward to it."

With nothing more to say on the matter, the man promptly fell asleep. Either that or he'd just had a sudden heart attack. Half an hour later, the rain eased, which pleased me. The old man woke up in time to see a turboprop airliner land with a sluice of arcing water. When the plane approached the gate, I saw it belonged to Liat Airlines.

When the signal to board came, I was one of the first in line, rushing aboard like a madman so I could bag the prized space above my seat for my hand luggage., A few minutes later, the old man arrived in the aisle and checked his ticket. By a strange quirk of fate, he was sitting next to me. We nodded in recognition and then, as soon as he took his seat, he promptly fell asleep again. Within a minute, he was out for the count, head back, mouth open. Then he started snoring. At first, it was like an intermittent kettle boiling but once we had taken off, he began to trumpet like an elephant. He was causing such a commotion that people began to look for the source of the horrendous din. Because Mr Snore was slumped down in his seat, barely visible, people thought I was the culprit. When the man in front turned and glared, I shrugged and pointed. His eyes swivelled and he turned back in his own seat. The flight to St Lucia continued northwards.

3

St Lucia lies only fifty miles north of St Vincent, about the same distance as Manchester to Leeds. As we descended over its rugged, cloud-strewn southern end, it reminded me of the Isle of Man, which was appropriate approximation as both were about the same size. The old man woke up and looked confusedly about the cabin. Then, after realising where he was, he regarded the watery streaks skimming the windows.

"Still raining," he croaked, stating the obvious.

I nodded, as we descended towards St Lucia. A few minutes later, we hit the runway hard enough to bounce again. It was only for a second, but the rebound was sufficient to make someone scream. The second touchdown was better, but only marginally so. Ahead of me, sitting in a rear-facing seat next to the cockpit door, the stewardess rolled her eyes.

The old man looked outside again and grinned. "Back home."

Due to the rain, the cabin crew would not allow us to leave the plane. Instead, the St Lucia passengers and I had to line up in the aisle. While we waited, a middle-aged woman ahead of me began speaking ill of Liat Airlines.

"You know wat dey did?" she said loud enough for everyone in the cabin to hear. "They pulled me from yesterday's flight! I turned up in St Vincent airport and dey say I too late. 'So what?' I tell dem. You know what dey say back? Dey say, your seat is gone, miss; we give it to somewan else. Come back tomorrow."

The man standing near the woman shook his head at the callousness of Liat Airlines. Then he asked why they had done such a heinous thing. Everyone strained to hear the answer, including the cabin crew.

"Cos I was five minutes late! *Five minutes.* I told Liat it was cos of de traffic, but dey did not care. Told me to come back in the morning for this flight. I had to call my nephew to come and pick me back up from de airport. He'd only just dropped me off! Dey should be ashamed of demselves, Liat Airlines."

The cabin crew rolled their eyes again: water off a duck's back.

"And if dey lose my bag," the woman added, "I will take 'em to court. Dey shouldn't be allowed to mess people around like dat."

Finally, the rain eased enough for the cabin crew to give us the go ahead to leave. With only a handful of passengers passing through immigration, I was stamped through and sitting inside a taxi ten minutes later. Country number five of my adventure was now in front of the swishing windscreen wipers.

4

My taxi driver, a young man in his twenties, turned out to be a Good Samaritan. As we drove through the outskirts of Castries, St Lucia's diminutive capital, he spied a damsel in distress. The soaked woman's car would not start and she didn't know what to do. After a protracted manoeuvre to allow traffic to slip past our two-car blockage, the driver stopped his engine. "You don't mind me helping her, do you?"

I scowled. "Yes I do. I need to get to the hotel so I can have some rum punch."

Except, of course, I said no such thing.

I smiled and told him to go ahead. He nodded, climbed out and produced some jump leads from the boot of the car that he proceeded to attach to the woman's failed battery. A minute later, with rain almost drenching both of them, he restarted our engine and gunned the accelerator. Her stricken engine hiccupped into life and then ran smoothly. The woman looked eternally grateful, like she wanted to kiss the taxi driver. Like a Knight of Olde, he nodded, grabbed his jump leads and turned chivalrously on his heels.

"That was nice of you," I remarked when we set off again.

"Everyone on the island looks out for each other. It's a friendly place; that's why I stay here. How long you here for?"

I told him.

"Two nights! You come to St Lucia for two nights?" he gestured outside with one hand. "I hope the weather clears up for you, then."

"Do you think this is the start of a tropical storm?" The thought had crossed my mind a couple of times already.

"Nah, man. Just a bit of water."

Five minutes later, we were sloshing our way through an area of St Lucia called Gros Islet, the location of my hotel. Renowned for its bars, restaurants and late night parties (which was a world away from its humble origins as a fishing village), I hoped my hotel would not be full of drunken louts. Luckily, it wasn't, because it was located at the furthest reaches of frivolity in a place called Rodney Bay.

As soon as I got to my room, I did something long overdue: clothes washing. Travelling with hand luggage meant washdays were a frequent necessity. While I waited for my smalls to ferment in the sink, I availed myself of the facilities to empty my bladder. Afterwards, I discovered that the flimsy flushing device failed upon the first yank of the 'chain'.

Mentally swearing, I lifted the lid of the cistern. After staying in countless hotels, I had developed a basic knowledge of toilet plumbing and after peering into the ceramic gloom, I saw the perpetrator immediately. I prodded the strange plastic device attached to a short metal chain and heard the gush of water starting. As the cistern began to fill, I nodded in appreciation at my skills. A minute later, the flush flushed and I was happy again.

To celebrate my skill at fixing hotel toilets, I decided to have a shower. Before getting in, I elected to test out the fixtures, wanting to check that they were not as flimsy as the toilet. The shower, I noted, featured a handheld hose, and so I stepped into the booth, fully clothed, and picked it up, directing its angle towards my outstretched hand, well away from my body. I turned the water supply on, and screamed like a girl. A hidden overhead sprinkler system was now drenching my head and body. I sidestepped its cruel onslaught, but still ended up dripping wet. And then the hotel's fire alarm went off. Cursing St Lucia, I draped myself in a towel and headed for the door just as the wailing cacophony ceased. I waited, unsure of what to do. Then I stepped back into the room to attend to my washing in the sink.

And people think travelling is glamorous.

5

The next morning it was still pouring down. Mist shrouded everything beyond a couple of palm trees on the other side of my window. Rain splattered the ground and waterfalls gushed from the roof. I opened the balcony door and gingerly stuck my hand out to assess the strength of the downpour. An instant drenching was my reward. Just then, my phone rang. I grabbed it and listened to the voice. It was my guide for the day, a man called Kenny. Unsurprisingly, he told me that the 9am tour was off. "You won't see a thing," he told me. "Maybe this afternoon will be okay."

I put the phone down and felt wholly disappointed. After all, I only had one full day in St Lucia. But what could I do? Cancel the weather? Go rolling in the mud? No, I had to hope it cleared by the afternoon. So, for an hour, I sat and caught up with emails, keeping one eye on the rain. Thirty minutes later, it slackened off. When my restlessness became too much, I donned my hat and headed downstairs. As I stepped outside, I was pleased the deluge had turned into drizzle.

I hopped over a puddle and wandered along a line of all-inclusive beach hotels, passing bars and restaurants (one agreeably called the Razzmatazz Tandoori Restaurant) until I came to the Rodney Bay Police Station. Either the police officers were still asleep or they were having their breakfast, because all was quiet. Not like a few years ago when three or four masked gunmen staged an audacious robbery in broad daylight in St Lucia. A group of 55 cruise ship passengers had been enjoying a delightful walk around some botanical gardens when the robbers brazenly stepped in front of them, pointing their guns and demanding that everyone hand over their valuables. Job done, the quartet fled and has never been caught.

Incidents such as this are rare, but they do cause jitters in St Lucia's tourist industry. If the cruise ships stopped coming – because their owners deem things too dangerous – then the island would face a severe crisis. Therefore, a few years ago, when an independent report surfaced that claimed the St Lucian police kept something called a 'death list', people took note. According to the report, *Operation Restore Confidence* allowed the police to bypass the lengthy judicial process of arrest, questioning and then, perhaps, giving evidence at a trial, so they could simply shoot the bad guys dead, a claim they vehemently deny, of course.

I carried on past the police station, waving to a Western man jogging on the other side of the road; he looked at me as if I was a lunatic. I found a small path that led to the beach. Apart from a couple walking hand-in-hand at the edge of the waves, and a hawker trying to sell me a carved coconut in the shape of a shark, I had it to myself. Had the sun been shining and droplets of rain not been falling on my head, the sea, palms and the white sand might have been just about perfect.

6

Back at the hotel, Kenny rang me back. "The weather is clearing. I'll pick you up in ten minutes." I put the phone down, grabbed my camera and then ran around in circles for a minute, stopping to apply mosquito spray to my head, feet and arms. During the night, tiny winged beasts had assaulted me in six different places, the worst of which was on my forehead. The red patch made me look like a Cyclops.

Kenny pulled up in an expensive Toyota 4x4, which suggested his tour company was doing well for itself. I climbed into the passenger seat and shook his hand. He was a stocky 49-year-old gent with a warm smile and, best of all, a high-pitched Caribbean laugh. Within two minutes, I decided I liked Kenny a lot.

"First time in St Lucia?" he asked.

I told him it was.

"I love this island. I really do. It's the best of the Caribbean islands. Better than Barbados, better than Antigua, better than Trinidad, better than Grena—"

"Have you been to many others, then?" I asked, cutting him off from his list.

"Most of them. The difference is the beauty of this island. You will see this for yourself. The only thing that is wrong with St Lucia is the economy. We rely on tourism, right? You already know that; well, we also rely on bananas. But South America has bananas, and they can sell them cheaper than us. If the banana crop fails in St Lucia, like when a hurricane hits, then that's it: the country will be in trouble. We would only have tourism to fall back on. This is the only thing that worries me about St Lucia. We need to diversify before it's too late."

We were driving away from Gros Islet and Rodney Bay, back towards the capital, Castries. As we rolled past terraced hills and velvet-coated highlands, quaint houses came into view, where chickens pecked in the dust and men in reggae-themed beanie hats toiled at building work.

"Have you been to the States?" I asked.

"Many, many times. For one thing, my son lives there, He's a marine in California. He's lived there since he was twelve. I visit Florida mostly, though. I stay on Miami Beach and enjoy myself. I'm not married anymore, so Miami is a lot of fun for me. I've been there fifty-five times. Mind you, with the way things are going up there, I might not be going back anytime soon. "

"You've been fifty five times?" It seemed an extraordinary number.

Kenny laughed. "I know what you're thinking. How can a simple taxi driver from St Lucia afford to fly to Florida fifty five times? Well, it's because my sister works for American Airlines. She works in the offices but she gets me cheap standby flights. I once flew first class for $120 US."

"So I take it you prefer Florida to St Lucia?" In the distance, Castries was starting to take shape. It wasn't a big city by any stretch, but compared to Gros Islet, it was a metropolis.

"No, man. St Lucia would win every time. America is fun; St Lucia is home. Besides, I know everyone here, and it's a much … much simpler life here. If I want to drink a beer on the beach, then no one will stop me. If I want to drive without a seatbelt, which I sometimes do, then no one will stop me. Well, the police might. In fact, I have about thirty tickets from the police but I've not paid a single one. That's because one of my best friends is in the police!" He guffawed at this and, because his laughter was so infectious, I did too.

Then we arrived in Castries.

7

The French founded Castries in the mid-seventeenth century. They liked it because its large harbour offered fair protection for their ships. The problem was the British also liked the harbour. They liked it so much that when a hurricane, followed by a terrible fire demolished most of the fledgling settlement, they stormed in, all guns blazing. Not that the French offered much resistance: they had grown tired of the heat and had wanted out for a while. But as interesting as all this is, the most curious European to land in St Lucia was not a settler, but a privateer.

Francois Le Clerc was a noble name for a pirate. The Spanish called him something less pleasant: Jambe de Bois, *Peg Leg*, due to his missing appendage. According to popular history, Le Clerc was the first recorded pirate to ever have a wooden leg. Anyway, Peg Leg set sail for St Lucia around 1550, after he and his men had successfully looted Cuba, escaping with 80,000 pesos, a phenomenal amount of money in those days. Once his band of cutlass-wielding buccaneers made landfall, Le Clerc set up a camp close to Rodney Bay and attacked passing Spanish ships. After a while, they grew bored of this hit and miss approach, and so they all sailed to Panama, and then the Azores, where Le Clerc hobbled around for a bit and took to wearing a large black pirate hat. In the Azores, Le Clerc was killed while trying to attack a passing Spanish treasure ship.

Today, Castries is home to governmental buildings and offices. None of them is particularly high-rise, and the overall look of the St Lucian capital is one of functionality rather than beauty. Instead of a pretty waterfront, Castries has a line of shipping containers, a spindly blue crane and the head office of the Inland Revenue.

Kenny dropped me off outside a large, orange-and-white building called Prio's Country Palace, which may have been a music hall, a market place or something else entirely. Kenny was a little sketchy on the details and could not offer any insight other than concerts might have been held there at one point. Whatever it was, it was closed for the day and so I sauntered along the street, enjoying the sea breeze, when I chanced upon a large notice painted in red capital letters

DO NOT PISS HERE by order of CCC (Castries City Council) the sign read. I blinked and read the sign again. It was daubed across a bright orange wall tucked away from the main road. I was smiling about it when I climbed into Kenny's car a few minutes later.

"Every tourist sees that sign," he said, chuckling. "It should be in a guide book, because the number of tourists who take pictures of it is amazing."

We stopped again a few minutes later. There were hardly any people about. I mentioned this to Kenny. "That's because it's Sunday. You should see it on a weekday."

I climbed out to explore by myself. I walked past a little grey-brick Roman Catholic Church with a small archway called the Arch of Mercy. I stepped inside, finding a service taking place. The flock was scant, taking up only the front pews, but the pastor, a bald-headed gent in glasses, bellowed through a microphone like he was in front of thousands. When he regarded me quizzically, I raised my hands in apology and retreated outside.

Opposite the church was the Court House, a colonial-looking building with white wooden shutters set against red brick and red plasterwork. It would have made a nice hotel, I thought, especially with its sweeping second-storey veranda and sloping, wooden red roof. Four white-shirted police officers (two men and two women) were standing on one corner of the court house, merrily chatting away. Whether they were awaiting the arrival of a miscreant or simply having a break, I had no way of knowing. One of the officers, a man in his fifties sporting aviator shades, had two pens in his shirt pocket. A real stickler for paperwork, I assumed.

A rotund woman carrying a bag of shopping swayed past me and then turned a corner. From around the bend, I could hear some carnival-type music. I followed the woman, and found that she was cutting through an area of parkland called Derek Walcott Square. Unusually for someone with a part of a city named after them, Derek Walcott was still alive and kicking, though at 86, he presumably was not kicking as much as he used to. In 1992, Mr Walcott, a son of

Castries, won a Nobel Prize for Literature; as soon as the city planners heard of this momentous event they renamed the park. Derek Walcott Square has a bandstand, a bronze bust of the great man himself, a copse of trees and, on the day I visited, a set of schoolchildren dressed up in bright and vivid costume. Some were dressed as birds, others as butterflies and a few as pieces of fruit. Most, though, were just decked out in bright orange dresses with elaborate headwear. Each had something in common: their mother fussing over them. Kenny later told me that the children were taking part in a mini-Carnival parade to be held later that day.

8

Unsurprisingly, Castries looked much better from above. Kenny parked at an elevated spot where a few enterprising and patient hawkers awaited. As soon as they saw me climb out from the car, they were upon me: bangles, folds of cloth, magnets, sunglasses and a plethora of postcards were flashed my way. I said no to all, which did not seem to surprise any of the sellers, and they quickly retreated, keeping a keen eye out on the road for any new and potentially more agreeable tourists.

I gazed down upon the St Lucian capital, a city with a population of just 20,000, which in England would make it a large village. Castries was nestled between a lush border of green hills on one side, and a swirling arc of blue ocean on the other – exactly the same as all the other capitals I'd visited. The sea would have looked better if they sky hadn't been so grey and overcast, and I might have seen Martinique, the coast of which was only about thirty miles distant, but as it was, there was nothing to see except a dismal haze. I looked down at a thin peninsular on the far side of the harbour. It was home to a sliver of concrete that formed the jetty for arriving cruise ships. The first thing the 600,000 or so passengers who arrived every year in St Lucia would see was a large, purpose-built complex of duty free shops and street entertainers. After negotiating them, they would hit the well-oiled machinery of shore excursion tour guides, who would whisk them off on historical tours or deposit the less adventurous ones on a hotel beach somewhere.

"The water looks good for swimming," I said to Kenny.

"Yeah, it is. Nice temperature. But I never go in – well, maybe up to my knees if I'm feeling brave. I'm scared of water and have never learned to swim."

"Scared of water? What about rain? Are you scared of that?"

"Rain? No, man! I'm only scared of deep water, like in the sea or lakes and things like that. Rain doesn't bother me, which is good, because when the storms come, there's lots of it. The last bad one we got, Hurricane Tomas, was about six years ago. It closed the airport. There were floods everywhere. People had to be airlifted by helicopter. I spent the night in a layby, waiting things out in my car because a mudslide had blocked the road in both directions."

I asked whether any warnings had been given.

"Oh, we always get warnings. Usually two days before they hit. But I didn't think Tomas would be that bad; that's why I was out driving. Now I know better. Whenever I hear the warning, I bunker down with my supplies. Anyway, let's get back on the road. Time to see some bananas."

9

Like most roads on Caribbean islands, St Lucia's were thin, winding and bounded by thick vegetation and pastel-coloured houses. Heading into the centre of the island, things took a turn even more tropical. Gone were the villages: the interior was a profusion of palm trees, leathery leaves and seas of luxurious green grass. Behind all this, the hills were the colour of asparagus. I could not recall a time when I had seen so many shades of green.

Twenty minutes later, we were driving along some lower ground. On our left was a massive banana plantation – a huge area of land that farmers had reclaimed from the jungle. Each individual banana tree wasn't particularly tall, but as a collection, the plantation commanded respect. Kenny pulled over so I could see them up close.

Many of the banana bunches were covered in thin, blue plastic. It was to protect the fruit from insects, Kenny told me. "And banana trees only produce one crop of fruit in their life. Then they die. But before they go, they send a little shoot down to the ground so a new banana tree can grow. It takes about nine months for a new tree to grow and produce fruit again."

I walked along a muddy avenue of banana trees. The bananas carried on as far as the eye could see, spreading out on my left and right in all directions. I walked over to a huge bunch dangling from one tree. There were well over a hundred green – almost ripe – bananas in the stem, and I asked Kenny how much the bunch would be worth.

"These are Cavendish Bananas – the type you see in your supermarkets in England. I'm pretty sure most of these bananas will end up there. For this stem, maybe the farmer will make five US dollars."

"Five dollars? For all these?" I did a quick mental calculation. "That's about three to four cents per banana."

"That's the price. Bananas are cheap nowadays and other countries are selling them even cheaper. And then your supermarkets in Europe want to buy them cheaper than that. They will only pay the lowest price for these bananas. And here's something else you should know." Kenny studied the bunch closely. "Not all these bananas will be acceptable for British supermarkets. They have got to be *just* right." He pointed at one sad little banana at the bottom of the bunch. "This one's too small." He pointed to another one. "This is not the right shape – it's too bent out of shape. But at least this farmer will make some money. If a hurricane hit, he would have nothing."

Back on the road, we did a small detour to a little village called Canaries, pronounced Kan-arr-ees, as opposed to the yellow birds. One upon a time, Canaries had been a thriving settlement servicing a huge sugar plantation, with a large enough population to support two schools and a church. Then, in the 1950s, when the price of sugar dropped, the plantation owners closed their production line, leaving the town to wallow. Most people jumped ship – quite literally – and moved to England. The few that remained turned their hand to fishing (the men) or street vending (the women). Today, fewer than two thousand people remain in Canaries.

The school was still there, or least the primary school was – a long green building surrounded by a tall red wall. And even though it was a Sunday, it was busy with the chaotic sound of children's chatter and laughter. Kenny and I both looked over a wall to see what the kids were up to, finding a whole troop of them dressed up in fine orange gowns and yellow mortar-board hats. A large notice board told us that they were preparing for their graduation ceremony.

We wandered to a small beach to find a whole row of brightly painted pirogues lined up waiting for the next morning when the men folk would take them out to sea to catch fish. Further along, three women were washing clothes in a narrow inlet, chatting contentedly as they did so. Out in the surf, a group of children frolicked in giddy frivolity. Two men, mending fishing nets, were smiling, too. Perhaps that was the answer, I thought. Get rid of material goods and concentrate on the necessities. Make life simple again and enjoy the moment rather than worrying about the future.

10

We stopped on a hairpin bend, pulling into a layby at the summit of a tall hill. We climbed out to take in the panorama; before I did, I watched a barefoot man walk past with a net. The net was attached to one end of a stupidly long wooden pole. The only reason for having such a lengthy net, as far as I could discern, was to catch butterflies. While we watched, the man stopped by a tree and deftly lifted his pole and swung it at a mango. In one swift motion, he managed to dislodge the fruit. If it had landed inside the net rather than plopping onto the ground, I would have clapped. Undeterred, the man retrieved his prize and stuffed it in his pocket.

Kenny and I walked to a concreted area that looked out over the hills. Now that the weather was clearing up, I could see a nice horizon of blue in the distance. It was a good view, I had to admit, and the people who lived in the houses perched on the nearby hillside would see it every day. Kenny pointed down at one of the homes, a large aquamarine bungalow on stilts. "My friend built that house in his spare time. It took him years. He and his lady friend moved in a few years ago. She's the one who paid for it."

Kenny told me that the woman had lived in England for many years, working as a nurse before she had met his friend. "That's how she made her money. She has a son over there. He lives in London now: a solicitor. Anyway, my friend and this woman lived in that house until she died."

"Died?"

"In a car accident. She was driving down the hill we just came up when her brakes failed. And this is the bit I don't understand. You've probably seen the gulleys at the edges of St Lucian roads, right? I just don't get why she didn't drive into them. Yes, her car would've been a write-off, but at least she would be alive. But she decided to drive up a side track leading around a steep bend. Maybe she thought it would slow the car down. But she lost control and flew off the side. When it landed, the car set on fire. Horrible, just horrible."

I didn't know what to say.

Kenny breathed out heavily. "My friend was devastated. But then it got worse. The woman hadn't left a will; everything she owned went to her son: the house, the money, everything. So this house now belongs to a solicitor in England and he wants to sell it. My friend has got nothing because he wasn't married and the son doesn't like him. He's got nothing to show for all the effort he put into building his retirement home, nothing. All the son thinks about is the money he will make."

I shook my head at the unfairness of it all. To lose him companion, then his home, all in a short period of time did not bear thinking about it. "So what is he going to do?"

Kenny shrugged. "I don't know. Maybe he'll live with a relative."

I gazed down at the delightful house with a perfect view. It seemed tainted now.

11

St Lucia's most famous landmarks are two jagged volcanic spires known at The Pitons. They are so famous that the local beer is named after them and they adorn the island's flag. En route to Soufriere, St Lucia's second town, we stopped at a viewing platform so I could admire them. And admire them I did, for they looked fabulous. Like a gigantic pair of green shark's teeth jutting upwards from a mouth of tropical greenery, the majestic volcanic plugs rose to over 2500 feet, towering over the vivid buildings of Soufriere, occasionally spewing sulphurous air towards it, thereby explaining why the French called the town Soufriere, *Sulphur in the Air*.

I asked Kenny whether it was possible to climb The Pitons, to which he nodded. "Is that what you want to do?" He looked worried.

I shook my head. "No, just wondering."

"Good, because it takes about three hours to reach the top. I've never done it, but I've been told it's hard work – lots of trudging through jungle, then climbing over rocks and dealing with the heat, humidity and flies."

"Sounds like hell."

Just then, a minibus pulled up and from it spilled a platoon of Chinese tourists. Unmindful of me, they swarmed the viewing platform, taking photos from every conceivable angle and generally making a racket while they did so. When I was nudged for the third time, I took this as my cue to leave. I wanted to see Soufriere up close.

In the thick of town, I felt underwhelmed. From above, Soufriere had looked gorgeous: vivid splashes of blue, yellow and red edged against the sea. Up close, it was just another chaotic Caribbean town of crumbling wooden buildings, cracked plasterwork, peeling paint and corrugated metal roofs. But then things improved when we turned a corner. The street was clean and bright, the wooden verandas and wooden panels freshly painted and bright. If they could get the rest of the town looking like this, then Soufriere would be stunning.

We arrived on the sea road where crowds of people had gathered to enjoy the weekend. Many were dancing in a tight jumble along a stone pier. Others were sitting in the shade offered by a large petrol station. Music was blasting out from speakers, and everyone looked like they were having a great old time, including some scrawny chickens ruffling their feathers like they were in a hen parade.

Kenny left me to my own devices to explore Soufriere; while he chatted to someone he knew, I walked at right angles away from the sea, passing a blue-and-yellow building that proudly declared it sold Piton Beer, and then a dilapidated blue hut that claimed it peddled Prime Time Videos. Soon I found myself standing beside a church that looked like it had been lifted straight out of an English country village. It had a gorgeous stone steeple, a series of carefully-constructed stained glass windows and freshly-painted white arches. If church bells had sounded, and a blushing bride appeared, I might have believed I was in the Cotswolds. It was infinitely better than the building opposite – a garish monolith that looked abandoned due its charred and blackened upper level.

"You want me to show you 'round?" said a withered old man wearing a baggy pink shirt unbuttoned halfway down his chest. Through the gap, I could see his clavicle, sternum and ribs. In contrast, his grey beard was scraggly and thick. With his bare feet, he looked the epitome of an aged drug user.

I ignored him and walked back towards the busy pier.

"Okay, how 'bout I show you where the stores are? You want a beer, some cigarettes? Maybe a Coke?"

I considered this. I *was* thirsty, and a Coke sounded like a good idea. I turned to face the old man, noticing just ill he looked. He had probably not eaten anything substantial for a while. "A Coke would be good."

He flashed me a decayed smile. "Follow me, man." He bounded though a crowd of dancers, checking that I was keeping up and then stopped outside a dingy little shop. I thanked him and passed him a handful of change, which he accepted gratefully. Then he was off, bounding back to where we had come from. I bought my drink and was just enjoying it when I heard a commotion. Over the din of music and raucous laughter, I could hear shouting. I headed over to a large crowd, and then through a gap saw two men. One was middle aged and muscular; the other younger, perhaps in his late teens. The older man was wrestling the younger man to the ground, and as we all watched, both fell with an audible thwack. The crowd gasped.

"I'll teach you a lesson, boy," screeched the older man, who now had his victim in a headlock. "You hear me? You hear me, boy?"

The younger man looked petrified but was not in a position to speak, not with his larynx being half-crushed. Wondering whether I was witnessing a serious assault or, worse, an actual murder, I was glad when a few men rushed over and manhandled the older man away. But he was not done. Mr Muscle grabbed the young man again and then punched him in the face. The young man looked stunned, wobbled for a second and then fell back towards a wall. At this point Kenny came over and joined me. I asked him what was going on.

"The young man is a thief. He has stolen someone's phone. The other man is trying to get it but it looks like it's already been passed on. Come on, we better leave." The older man was standing over the thief, telling him to get up. The young man wisely decided to remain slumped.

We got back into the car. Just along from us was a small police station. Kenny pulled up outside and lowered his window. Through the open door of the police station, a couple of officers were lounging around, unmindful of the noise just down the street. "You boys might wanna see what's going on along there," said Kenny, pointing towards the altercation. "Some fighting going on." The officers nodded but remained seated. Kenny shrugged and we moved forward.

As we headed uphill away from the madness of downtown Soufriere, I asked Kenny whether the young man would be okay."

"Oh, yeah, man. They'll just rough him up for a while. But, hopefully, he'll learn his lesson and not steal from his neighbours again."

12

Our final stop was, according to Kenny, the Caribbean's only drive-in volcano. The Sulfur Springs turned out to be a prime tourist attraction of St Lucia and, as such, was home to a proliferation of tourist tat shops (mostly selling special 'volcanic' soap). As soon as I stepped outside, the smell of rotten eggs invaded my nostrils, a not altogether unpleasant smell, but not one I was keen on either. The smell was the sulphur, or more accurately, the hydrogen sulphide gas escaping from the bowels of the earth all around me. Kenny handed me over to a Sulfur Springs guide, a young lady in an official Sulfur Springs T-shirt, who smiled thinly, then admitted she was scared to death.

"Why? Is the volcano about to blow?"

The young woman's eyes widened. "No nothing like that. It's my first day. I'm a nervous wreck."

She led me up a rocky incline, describing the rocks around us, the age of the rocks and the type of rock it was. I listened patiently, nodding in all the correct places. With a break in her monologue, I asked whether she'd had to memorise what she'd just said.

"Was it that obvious?"

I told her she was doing really well, which finally brought a real smile.

"I've been up most of the night learning my notes," she admitted. "My family is sick of hearing about volcanoes and hot springs. I don't blame them: I've been going on about them for weeks."

By now the smell of rotten eggs was receding as my nose grew accustomed to the smell. The guide and I were standing by a fence that overlooked a landscape of hissing, bubbling, steaming and generally volcanic-looking terrain. "The area past the fence used to be accessible to the public," intoned the guide, reciting her memorised notes. "But that was until an unfortunate accident. A guide called Gabriel was showing some tourists around when the ground beneath him cracked and he fell into a boiling pit of mud. He did not die but he suffered severe burns to the lower part of his body. If you look over there, you can see the pit. It's called Gabriel's Hole."

I looked and saw a gaping crack in the grey surface. Steam was billowing out as if an old locomotive had somehow been buried under the surface. "So are you sure the volcano isn't going to erupt today?" I asked in jest, but with a serious undertone.

"Do you think I would be here if it was about to erupt?" The guide was laughing heartily now. She was going to make a great guide, I felt. "No. They check the seismic activity all the time. Any chance of volcanic movement and this place would be deserted."

On the way back to the car, the guide and I stopped to peer over the side of a small bridge. Below us were a few groups of mud-covered tourists. The mud was hot and supposedly full of medicinal properties, including the ability to cure sunburn, asthma, sinus problems and a whole range of allergies.

"You want to try it?" the guide suggested.

I smirked, shaking my head. The last thing I wanted to do was cavort around with a bunch of strangers while smearing hot mud across my beer belly. "I think I'll give it a miss."

"Well, in that case, the tour is finished. I hope you enjoyed it." She looked at me hopefully.

"I did. You were great. You have nothing to worry about. You'll get lots of tips." I shook her hand and handed her a generous tip. It was time to head back to the hotel.

13

That evening, while enjoying a scrumptious fish meal cooked in the tastiest blend of spices I'd had in a long time, I received a jolt from the netherworld. It came from Liat Airlines. The subject of the message was enough to make my heart leap. It stated: *Flight Delays & Distruptions.* Even the awkward misspelling didn't take away my trepidation. I opened the email with mounting horror.

'LIAT has issued a travel advisory for Monday 11th July 2016. Due to unplanned industrial action, a number of LIAT flights originating or connecting from or through Antigua are experiencing delays. LIAT wishes to apologies to its passengers for any inconvenience caused.'

I re-read the email, trying to make sense of it. But of course, it made perfect sense. The airport I was flying into the next morning was experiencing delays, delays so bad that Liat Airlines, an airline famous for its delays, felt they ought to give passengers the heads up. I closed the email and regarded my fish. My appetite had gone and so had my sense of adventure. I was halfway through my Caribbean island hopping and there was now the real possibility of industrial action derailing it.

I decided to hedge my bets and did a quick search for alternative flights to Antigua. The only one that came up was with British Airways. When I saw the price, I almost collapsed from my seat: they wanted over two thousand quid for a one-way hop across the Caribbean Sea! Were they insane? Then I realised the reason for the ridiculous price was that it went via Gatwick Airport. So that was it, then – I had to throw in my lot with Liat Airlines, unless I wanted to charter a yacht. So with little else to do, I picked at my food, drank my bottle of Piton and then retired to my room to pack.

Clockwise from top left: Possibly the best sign in the world; a whole load of bananas, probably bound for a British supermarket; The Pitons towering over the town of Soufriere; Pleasant wooden buildings of downtown Soufriere; Small fishing boats at Canaries; Looking down over Castries

Chapter 6. Little England in Antigua

The shrill, upsetting electronic wail of my alarm roused me from my uneasy slumber at 4.30am. Despite my valiant efforts at ridding the room of mosquitoes, one had evaded my diligence and had bitten me thrice. I saw the blood-ingesting felon hanging on the high ceiling: a female, as all biters are. Its spindly, angular legs and wings were now motionless, the insect's body sated from its midnight meal. I couldn't face climbing on a chair to punish it, so left it alone, my own weary eyes dragging with gravity. I just hoped the insect had not been carrying anything nasty like Zika, Malaria, Dengue or the horrible sounding Chikungunya Virus, a disease that begins with a fever before kicking in with some muscular and joint stiffness. A nasty rash follows this and then a worrying symptom called flaccid paralysis, where a person's muscles become limp, which is especially worrying if the muscles in question are helping respiratory movement. As it stood, I absently scratched my new set of bites and prepared myself for Liat-induced angst.

The taxi picked me up at 5.30am; I was still barely awake. The driver took one look at me and asked whether I'd had a hard night of partying.

"Only a hard night of hardly sleeping. In fact, I reckon I should've stayed in bed and not bothered with the airport."

The man looked at me quizzically. "Why is that?"

"I'm flying Liat." I explained about the email.

The driver laughed. "Liat, man. They run their airline like the government runs this country! They do whatever they want and the people cannot do a thing. They cancel a flight, so what? They lose your bag, so what? They have no competition and so don't care."

"I take it you've flown with them?"

"Many times. But I think you will be okay today. The weather is good and they do not like to cancel flights when it is busy. If they do, they get lots of hassle. Even this industrial action in Antigua will not affect you, I think."

And, by God, he was correct. When I checked in at the airport (another open-air check-in counter as opposed to an air-conditioned interior one) and asked about any cancellations, the man told me everything was good.

"So no delays?"

"Oh, yes, we have a delay. But it's only about twenty minutes. Notting to worry about, man."

To celebrate, I retired to a café and sat down with some much-needed caffeine.

2

Despite the good news from the check-in agent, I did not totally relax until I was sitting inside the Liat Airlines ATR-72 Turboprop. Even then, I fretted, thinking that one of the pilots might take ill, air traffic controllers might go on strike or we would run out of aviation gasoline. Only when we left the runway did I smile. The flight to Antigua was on!

For the next fifty minutes, I tried not to fall asleep, fearing my snoring would be far worse than the gentleman I'd been sitting alongside on the way into St Lucia. There was a young woman sitting beside me near the window, and I had no wish to upset her with my dinosnore. Thankfully, every time I was in danger of entering the Land of Nod, my head would flop forwards, resulting in a constriction of my airways that would jolt me back to reality. The third time this happened, I chanced a glance at the woman. She offered me a withering look. I looked at my watch and discovered I'd been asleep for fifteen minutes. I wiped the dribble away.

VC Bird International Airport, named after Sir Vere Cornwall Bird Senior, the first Prime Minister of Antigua and Barbuda, was the largest airport I had been to in a while. Instead of a small terminal servicing Liat aircraft, VC Bird was a sprawling complex of gates and airbridges. Large jets belonging to American Airlines, JetBlue and British Airways littered the apron. So much for the industrial action, I mused – it was all systems go and I was through security in a flash, dragging my hand luggage behind me like the veteran passenger I was. As I did so, I passed the best flag in the Caribbean.

Antigua's flag has a striking design quite unlike any other I'd seen. It features two red right-angled triangles at each end that form an inverted triangle in the middle. A squeak of blue and white forms a stark line between the red, all finished with a spiky yellow sun (on a black background) that rises from the centre. I snapped a quick photo and then, before I knew it, I was sitting in the back of a taxi, traversing some gorgeous beaches lapped by clear blue water. The view, the sun and the calypso music blaring out from the radio buoyed my mood. I was in Antigua, for God's sake; what was there not to be happy about?

3

My hotel room had a large balcony overlooking a portion of Antiguan delight. The Caribbean Sea was a gorgeous mixture of blues, all of them delightfully tropical and a world away from any water surrounding the United Kingdom. The slivers of sand looked perfect, too. No wonder Antigua was the destination of choice for the discerning beach lover, people such as Eric Clapton, Paul McCartney and Oprah Winfrey.

All the same, I was weary and fatigued and so, after doing some washing in the hotel sink, I decided to lie down for five minutes. Within a minute, I was asleep and did not awake until midday. When I discovered the time, I was cross with myself for wasting a few hours of my only day in Antigua. I rushed down for a sandwich and asked the hotel to order me a taxi for the afternoon.

"Where do you want to go?" asked the hotel receptionist, a woman who had been awarded Employee of the Month according to a large sign on the wall.

"I'm not sure. Just the usual places."

“The usual?”

“Yes, the normal things that tourists like to see.” The woman was annoying me a little bit. I wondered how small the workforce of the hotel reception staff had to be for this obtuse lady to win Employee of the Month. “Can you suggest anything?”

“Are you interested in cricket?”

“Not really?”

“Okay…what about an abandoned sugar factory?”

I nodded. “That sounds okay, I suppose.”

“I’ll tell you what. I’ll order a taxi for say, four hours, and you and the driver can decide where to go between you. He’ll know places to visit. How does that sound, Mr Smart?”

“That sounds great. Thank you.” Maybe she did deserve the award after all.

4

Clive turned up in a taxi mini-van. He was about sixty, lithe, with a stubbly grey beard that curled around his chin before petering out along his cheeks. One of the first things he asked me when I jumped into the passenger seat was whether I was a fan of cricket. When I told him I used to watch it at university, Clive nodded excitedly. “You’ve come to the right place, then. Antigua is the home of cricket!”

We reversed out of the hotel car park. “You’ve heard of Richie Richardson? Curtly Ambrose? Viv Richards?”

I nodded.

“Well they’re all from Antigua and played for the West Indies. In a minute we’re gonna pass Viv Richard’s house. We can stop so you can take a photo.”

To be honest, I wasn’t that bothered about cricket or Viv Richards’ house but, because Clive seemed so enthusiastic, I kept quiet. We were heading downhill along a thin country road that followed a line of telephone wires. Every now and again, the wires would split off towards individual homes. One of them belonged to Sir Isaac Vivian Richards. We stopped just outside his house but, as far as I could tell, the great cricketer was not at home or, if he was, he was not a curtain twitcher, for all was still at his windows.

"Take a photo," Clive urged. "Viv won't mind."

The home of Viv Richards was a modest, burgundy bungalow with a corner veranda and white windows. I took a photo. "Have you ever seen him?" I asked Clive.

"Yeah, yeah, yeah. I see Viv all the time. He's a nice man. I went to school with him. He wasn't in my class; he was in the year above."

"Does he still play cricket?"

"Not much now; he's sixty-four. He works on the radio and TV. He does commentating and things like that."

We pressed on, and then pulled over a short while later. This time it wasn't a cricketer's house Clive wanted to show me, but a view. Below us, sprawling towards the distant sea was St John's, Antigua's tiny capital. St John's was home to a few shopping malls, a sprinkling of designer stores and a heady collection of investment banking offices, not to mention a couple of churches, a museum and a botanical garden. Absently, I wondered what Christopher Columbus would make of it if he were still alive.

Five hundred years previously, the first European ships arrived upon the windswept shore near St John's. At the helm of one galleon was Christopher Columbus, who regarded the island, pondered for a moment, and then decided to call it Antigua, after a church he'd once seen in Seville. That done, he moored his ships long enough to mark his landfall and then set sail for St Kitts and Nevis.

A century and a half passed before anything else of note happened on Antigua, and this time it involved the British. They established a settlement so they could plant some sugar. The sweet stuff had become such a valuable commodity that even the richest London merchant could only afford a single spoonful a year – and that was if he was lucky. Sugar was, quite literally, worth its weight in gold. And so the British dug up the Antiguan soil, planted the sugar cane and forced the native population to toil the fields. When the local slaves began dying (due to a mixture of European-introduced disease and severe malnutrition), the British had a rethink and began importing slaves from West Africa. These new slaves were far hardier and, because the British allowed them to have relationships and therefore children, their numbers increased dramatically. By the beginning of the eighteenth century, there were twelve slaves for every white person on Antigua.

Despite being allowed to have families, the slave workers of Antigua were treated badly. For instance, if a white person killed a slave in anger, then the courts classed it as a misdemeanour. No judge in his right mind would send a white man to prison for administering a well-deserved beating. And so some slaves rebelled. One such slave was a man called Hercules.

Hercules (a nickname coined due to his size and strength) was a slave carpenter by trade. As well as being skilful with tools, he was clever, quick-witted and charismatic. One day, when he talked of how brutal the British slave overlords were, and how other slaves on different islands were not suffering in the same way, people took note. When they saw the British meting out draconian punishments such as whipping and hanging on slaves for trivial crimes such as spilling their masters' wine, they listened even more, especially when Hercules hatched a secret plan.

One can only imagine the hushed shock in the barn as Hercules' co-conspirators took in his plan. Not only would they attack a few slave owners, they would kill every white person – man, woman and child – on the island. Everyone would die! After making everyone swear to secrecy until the time was right, Hercules told them all to go back to work as normal while he ran through the finer details of the plot in his mind. Unfortunately, while he did this, some of his conspirators grew nervous and informed the British. Soldiers quickly arrested Hercules and took him to the centre of town where he was punished by being hanged, drawn and quartered.

Understandably, this put off other burgeoning slave rebellions but, a few years later, a slave with the improbable name of Prince Klaas began to rouse the spirits of his fellow workers. Like Hercules, Klass wanted to massacre the entire white population of Antigua, and plotted to do so with a few trusted pals. Once again, though, someone spilled the beans and Klaas ran for it. He didn't get far and was arrested. When the British paraded him around the centre of St John's, Prince Klaas probably thought he was facing the hangman's noose. He was wrong. Waiting for him in the centre of a small square was Britain's latest execution method – *Breaking on the Wheel*.

Instead of being an unusual TV game show, Breaking on the Wheel was a fiendish way for a person to die. First, the victim was laid down, spread-eagled, and tied onto a large, horizontal wooden wagon wheel. As someone slowly rotated the wheel, a man with a hefty hammer bludgeoned the criminal's fingers and toes. Round and round the victim went, with the hammering moving further down the arms and legs, then onto the shoulders, hips and ribcage, until virtually every bone was mashed and pulverised. As a final insult to Prince Klass, his bloodied and crushed body was left to hang in the town's square for weeks so that everyone could gawp at.

Clive was about to show me the place where Prince Klass had endured his Breaking on the Wheel.

5

The traffic was light. Unlike in Kingston a few days earlier, St John's thin streets were a breeze to negotiate. As we made our way into the centre, Clive asked me where my wife was. He'd noticed the wedding ring on my finger.

"She's back in England making a shed."

Clive did a double take. "Your wife is building you a shed while you are on holiday? Respect, man." He gave me a high five.

Clive told me he was married with two grown-up children. His son worked in China. "He lives in Shanghai with his Ugandan girlfriend, if you can believe that. My daughter lives in New York with her husband and their five-year-old girl. I speak to my granddaughter most days on Skype. The little one is usually on her iPad. When she talks, her voice sounds American to me. I suppose that's to be expected."

There was a little park on my right and a small primary school on my left. Some kids were playing on a small patch of weatherworn grass. Ahead of us, passing the park and clinging to the edge of the road, a man was wobbling on a bicycle. He looked as if he might fall off at any moment. As we overtook him, Clive tutted.

"I don't like bicycles," he said by way of explanation. "When I was a young boy, I used to ride a donkey or, if I was lucky, a horse. My grandfather owned a few. That's why I have no time for bicycles and that kind of thing. They're not natural, are they?"

Before I could answer, pointing out that a car was even less natural than a pushbike, Clive said, "When my son was young, he always wanted a bike. 'Pleeeassse, Mum!' he wailed. 'Pleeeassse, Dad!' In the end, his mother bought him one. And do you know what? He lost it within a week! Nowadays, when he flies over from China, he always wants to drive my car. So I have to clean it up, polish it, you know. One time I said to him, 'Why can't you walk?' He looked at me like I was from the moon! 'Every time you turn that key', I tell him, 'you cost me money, boy.' But he is not bothered. Kids his age don't care about money – as long as it's not theirs."

We pulled up outside some tall gates in the centre of the capital. At first, I thought we were at a cricket ground, but Clive told me it was the Antiguan Recreation Ground. If I had been here 280 years previously, I might have seen Prince Klass being strapped to a wagon wheel. There was nothing, not even a commemoration plaque, to suggest that this had even happened.

Clive and I stood outside the gates looking in. "The grounds are used for football matches and Carnival celebrations," Clive told me.

"But it used to be a cricket ground. I must have watched a hundred games from those stands. From up there, I watched Viv Richards step to the crease and score the fastest test century in history – this was back in 1985. He knocked six after six. One hit a bottle of rum in the grandstand. It took him fifty-six minutes. His record stood until just last year. None of us could believe the skill of the man." Clive smiled at the memory. "Now, cricket is played at another stadium a bit further out of St John's. I'll take you there if you like."

I shrugged noncommittally, but then thought, why not? Clive was clearly a major fan of the game and, besides, he sweetened the deal by saying it was on the way to our next stop anyway.

6

We passed the city's prison. I couldn't see much because of its sturdy white wall topped with ugly coils of barbed wire. Clive told me that crime was low in Antigua. "All the bad guys are locked up in there."

They may have been locked up, but some of the prisoners were still having fun. A couple of years previously, some footage emerged showing a group of inmates enjoying a prison party. The short clip, filmed on a mobile phone, showed dancing, boozing and hookers. It looked like a nightclub and not a place of punishment.

More shenanigans from the prison came to light in February 2016. It involved a prisoner called Kaniel Martin, who had filmed himself singing a rap song. He thought it was so good that he posted it on YouTube, soon enjoying the exposure it was receiving. Nothing wrong with that, you might suppose, except when you consider what Mr Martin had done to warrant his incarceration.

Eight years previously, aged twenty, Mr Martin and an accomplice had burst into a hotel chalet and ordered the frightened British newlyweds to kneel against their bed. Then they shot them dead. The murdered couple, Ben and Catherine Mullany, were from South Wales, celebrating the last night of their honeymoon, paid for by their family and friends. And while they bled to death, the gunmen fled with a mobile phone, a camera and some cash. Two lives for a few hundred pounds. But at least one of them got a YouTube video out of it.

Clive turned off a roundabout and then trundled past an aisle of palm trees that ended at a giant white stadium. The Sir Vivian Richards Stadium looked modern, sleek and expensive. On a plinth by the entrance stood a statue of the great man, his cricket bat brandished like a weapon, a warrior about to go into battle.

"You want to look inside?" asked Clive. I nodded, more for him, really. Just then, an open-topped jeep pulled up beside us. The passengers were two couples, part of an island tour according to the sign on the side of the jeep. The men, obviously cricket fans, bounded out and rushed up the stairs leading to the entrance of the stadium, leaving the women sitting in the back. Clive and I climbed out into the heat.

I followed the men up the steps and found myself on terrace full of new plastic chairs. Behind the seats was a café in the process of being refurbished. Pots of paint lay on large plastic sheets on the floor. Beyond the chairs was a huge oval of green and, further back, some massive spectator stands, their chairs coloured to represent the Antiguan flag. Every seat was empty.

The two jeep men were marvelling at the sight, taking photos and talking animatedly. I was less enamoured and keen to move on, but Clive wanted to point things out – the Curtly Ambrose stand, the huge vertical floodlights that flanked them. He then showed me the oval and the ticket counter. I nodded and murmured in the appropriate places.

"The Chinese paid for all this," Clive told me. "They also built the new airport and most of the street lighting in Antigua." He laughed. "One day soon, this island will be called the Chinese Republic of Antigua."

Like half of the world, then.

7

In the centre of the island, we passed through a little village called All Saints. This rural community is notable for two reasons: one, it is actually Antigua's second-largest town, with a mighty population of three and a half thousand, and two, it has a single set of traffic lights – the only ones found outside the capital. They were on green when we passed through.

Our destination was the far south of the island, a place called the English Harbour. From my scant research, I knew the harbour was an old Royal Navy base and that Horatio Nelson had once visited. I was hoping for some prime Antiguan history to pore over when we got there.

"Did you see that video of the man getting shot by the policeman in America?" Clive asked unexpectedly. Ahead of us, a sliver of deep blue, dotted with yachts, was nestled between vividly green headlands.

I nodded.

"There's something wrong with America. Too many guns. That's what happens when people can buy weapons from supermarkets, and children can get a gun from their father's arsenal and shoot their teacher because they got a detention. It's all gone very bad over there and I feel sorry for my granddaughter growing up in such a place."

I asked whether Antigua had a gun problem.

Clive considered this. "We have them. But they are mainly with the gangbanger kids. They don't go for tourists; you are safe, don't worry."

The pretty bay turned out to be Falmouth Harbour, a marina for visiting yachts. We didn't stop, and I only saw it fleetingly, but what I did see was *wealth*. The yachts were not the little, paint-flecked vessels seen in English seaside villages – no, these were the super yachts of the very rich. Falmouth Harbour was a millionaire's playground.

The English Harbour (sometimes called Nelson's Dock) wasn't far from Falmouth; when we got there, I was disappointed. To attract tourist, the owners had turned the original eighteenth century buildings into plush restaurants, cafés and bars. The Admiral's Inn and the Porter's Lodge (which tried, but failed, to conjure images of the harbour's naval past) stood next to Linley's Bar & Restaurant, the Picture Frame Shop and Dream Yacht Charter LTD. The latter, Clive had told me, could hire me a yacht for the princely sum of $15,000 per week.

Clive decided to stay in his vehicle, leaving me to wander alone. I visited an outdoor bar called Pillars, finding a scattering of wealthy-looking Europeans enjoying sneaky afternoon Pimms and rums as they took in the fresh sea breeze. I considered getting a drink myself but carried on and exited the bar at its far end, finding myself in gentrified Middle England. I regarded the British red phone box standing on the corner of the Copper & Lumber Hotel. I could have been in Exeter, except for the palm trees. Shaking my head, I rounded a corner and came to the harbour itself. It was even worse.

Instead of evoking feelings of old naval ships, shifty buccaneers or swashbuckling heroes, the harbour was home to more million-dollar yachts. Sleek white craft lay out in the bay while their owners wandered about in white shorts and blue pullovers draped across their shoulders. A few families were picnicking on the lawn overlooking the water and I caught snippets of conversation about stocks and shares, their children's horses and about a fabulous restaurant in Guadeloupe one of them had tried.

"Casper," said an American voice belonging to one woman, "go and tell your father we need some more drinks."

I smirked despite myself. Who in their right mind would call their child Casper? Only the uber-rich, that's who.

I found an information sign. It told me that Admiral Nelson, in his late twenties by this point, had resided in the dockyard between the years 1784 and 1787. Nelson was not particularly fond of Antigua. In his diary, he claimed the island, and the dockyard specifically, was an 'infernal hole' and were it not for the good company of a certain Mrs Moutray (an attractive young lady married to the commissioner of Antigua) he would almost certainly have hanged himself. Apart from dwelling on how horrid his life was in Antigua, Nelson's main duties were to oversee building work and, occasionally, preside over court-martials. One notable case involved a sailor called William Clarke.

8

Clarke's crime was being young. As soon as his ship arrived in Antigua, the young man went on a mammoth bender of drinking, whoring and debauched partying. When he eventually returned to his ship, drunk and incapable, his commanding officer hauled him before the court under the charge of dereliction of duty. With Nelson at the helm, young Clarke was duly sentenced to hang, except, at the last minute, for reasons unknown, Nelson took pity on the erring seadog and spared him. Following this brush with death, Clarke decided to toe the line, turning himself into an able seaman, quite unlike the following gentleman, whose story begins with a sundial.

Hidden behind a circular metal railing at the edge of the English Harbour is a small sundial. The timepiece itself is interesting, but nowhere near as interesting as the story behind its location. The sundial marked the spot where, in 1798, a 23-year-old gentleman called Lord Camelford (a man so posh that William Pitt the Younger was his cousin) killed a man in a duel. The problem arose due to the hot-headedness of Camelford, a newly promoted lieutenant in the British navy.

A few years prior to his arrival in Antigua, Camelford was stationed on the island of Tahiti. While in dock, he tried to curry sexual favours with the local women by unbuttoning his tunic and offering ship contraband in return for their willingness. None fell for his advances and eventually his commanding officer found out about his antics and had him flogged.

Later, when his ship arrived in India, Camelford began illegally trading with the locals. Again, his commanding officer found out about these deals and punished him with his trusty whip. On another occasion, Camelford was found snoring away on his watch. For this, the young man was placed in irons, and the grudge he had formed against his commanding officer grew exponentially. Things culminated in England a few months later. By a horrible coincidence, Camelford found himself walking along the same street in London as his commanding officer. Without pause, the young seaman beat him so severely that the officer ended up hospitalised. Yet because of Camelford's family connections, no charges were ever pressed.

Despite these antics, the navy promoted Camelford to lieutenant and posted him to Antigua. Once in the Caribbean, he made a new enemy – a fellow lieutenant called Charles Peterson. After quarrelling about who was the better officer, Lieutenant Camelford did what any cad would do and challenged Lieutenant Peterson to a duel. The poor man, feeling unable to refuse the request, accepted the challenge; so the pair met at dawn, more or less on the spot the sundial now stood. After standing back to back for a few seconds, the men began to step away from one another. When they turned, Camelford fired first, shooting his rival dead.

A few months later, back in Blighty, Camelford and his best friend had a falling out. After accusing one another of uncomplimentary remarks, the pair met in a meadow with pistols at the ready. After walking an appropriate distance, the men turned and fired. Unfortunately, Camelford's shot went wide, while his friend's hit home, striking the 29-year-old in the chest, paralysing him instantly. Camelford died three days later, ending his colourful and violent life.

To finish my time at the English Harbour, I found a small shop and bought myself a can of Diet Coke. When the shop assistant rang the till, I realised that piracy was still an issue in the harbour. The price was quadruple what I would pay in the UK. With a bitter taste in my mouth, I headed back to find Clive.

9

As we made our way back to St John's, I spied a delicious scene of palms, sea and boats. I asked Clive to stop so I could take a photo. He duly obliged and remained in the car while I walked along a sandy track leading to the beach. Ahead of me, under the shade of some palms sat two women. Both watched my approach. I smiled and said hello, but neither woman returned any sort of greeting. In fact, one looked decidedly unfriendly. Shrugging, I carried on past them and began to take a few photos of the vista: the rolling surf, the sand and the palms – its remoteness making it even more appealing.

One of the women shouted something. I didn't hear what she had shouted but I turned to see her in a hostile posture, hands on hips, furious expression on her face. "Go away, white man!" she yelled.

I was utterly taken aback. I lowered my camera and could only stare at the woman.

"Go away," she repeated. "We don't want any white man here." Her friend glared too.

"I'm only taking a photo," I blurted but took the hint and started to leave the beach. Passing the women, neither said anything, but I could feel their eyes upon me with every step. Back in the sanctuary of Clive's car, I felt angry more than anything else. I told him what had just happened.

He nodded knowingly. "They think you are an American. White men from America are not popular in Antigua right now."

We rode in silence for a few minutes. In my mind, I found it remarkable that the actions of a white police officer in Minnesota could affect my visit to an island four and a half thousand kilometres away. Little did I realise that this ripple effect would meet me again before the end of my trip to the Caribbean.

"So are they going to be angry with every white person who comes their way?"

"For a while, yes. But they will soon forget. By the time the cruise ships start coming, they will be fine, laughing and joking with the tourists as they sell them mangos and bananas."

As we hit the outskirts of St John's, my mood improved. Clive was telling me about Antigua during cruise ship season. "It's *so* busy. Sometimes we have four, five, maybe six ships in port, and everyone in Antigua is working their asses off. Unemployed people get jobs as drivers and guides; housewives sell trinkets by the side of the road. Money pours in. I work every single day of the winter. The money I save sees me through the rest of the year."

I asked Clive what the cruise ship passengers usually did on their day in Antigua.

"I would say half go straight to the beaches. They can get some lunch, buy some bits and pieces and then sunbathe for a few hours. The rest might do buggy adventure trips or catamaran tours. A few do a tour like yours – seeing the history and some of the island. Most passengers don't even leave the ship." Clive shook his head. "I can't understand that, though. Why come all the way and not see anything except their balcony?"

I concurred wholeheartedly

We drove through the remnants of St John's daily outdoor market. Colourful parasols and stretched fabric covered stalls with fruit, vegetables and iceboxes full of cold drinks. In the centre of the capital, we came to a small statue of VC Bird, the first prime minister of Antigua. His representation was unusual because it was full colour, and almost cartoonish in its design. I climbed out of the car to take a photo, noticing that the street beyond the statue was dirty and chaotic. There was a shop selling mops, another peddling pizza and a few more that seemed to be convenience stores. Near doorways, men lounged around on plastic seats while stray dogs ran freely along the road. Music blared out from somewhere. I watched the citizens of St John's wandering hither and thither, armed with shopping bags or broken expressions as they emerged from the Paradise Casino, and decided it was time to go.

10

On the way back to my hotel, we pulled up at some traffic lights. Ahead of us was an open backed white truck. Three men were sitting in the back: two looking utterly bored and a third, sporting a black beanie hat, staring at me.

His eyes were the same as the woman's earlier: hostile. I hadn't done anything to deserve this scrutiny except being born white. The man saw I was watching him and raised one hand and formed a gun shape. He mimed shooting me. Clive tutted. "I'm sorry for this. It's that shooting in America." Thankfully, the lights turned green and the truck turned left. As we pulled past the vehicle, the man was still staring at me. It was unnerving.

"You know what I think?" Clive said, "If more young people got into cricket, then the anger might go away. When I was a teenager, all I thought about was cricket – same with my friends. And none of us were angry about anything. Not like now. I see a lot of anger in our youth."

And on that sad note, Clive and I arrived at the hotel. After thanking him for his time, I retired to my room. As I closed the door, I realised I was ridiculously tired and a little bit perturbed by what had happened today. I collected my washing from the balcony and packed it into my luggage, hoping that my next port of call, St Kitts, would offer something more relaxing and welcoming. Antigua had left me with a strange taste in my mouth.

Clockwise from top left: Antigua has the best flag in the Americas, I reckon; The view from my hotel balcony; Wadadli Beer – Antigua's tipple of choice; Aerial view of St John's; An English country village otherwise known as the English Harbour/Nelson's Dockyard; Downtown St. Johns.

Chapter 7. St Kitts and the Cruise Ships

The next morning I was back at VC Bird International Airport. Once again, nobody checked my hand luggage and so, in a quiet area of the airport, I repacked everything from my pockets and socks into the main bag. That done, I shuffled through security before buying myself a soothing latte, watching the information screens with familiar jitters. The screens claimed that the Liat flight to Saint Kitts was on time, a claim I did not believe. But it turned out to be true. For the first time, Liat Airlines was dead on time!

Taking off was mesmerising. The aircraft hugged the north-eastern coastline of Antigua, where coves such as Dutchman Bay and Jabberwock Beach played second fiddle to the stunning ocean colours: a palette of turquoises, cyans and azures, all gently swirling over shallow reefs and white sand. And then we were out over open ocean, skimming above the waves at five thousand feet.

Fifteen minutes later, we were flying over Nevis, St Kitts' smaller sister island, a round mountain dome that the Four Seasons chain had more or less hijacked with one of their prized resorts. And then we hit some turbulence.

And I mean turbulence.

In all my years of flying, with close to five hundred commercial flights under my belt, it was the worst turbulence I have ever experienced. One second we were flying smoothly over Nevis and the next, I was weightless, my body and feet suspended in the air, my passport floating around my face, my seatbelt the only thing stopping me from crashing my head onto the overhead panel. In the next second, gravity thrust me back into my seat, and it was only then that I became aware of the screams. They continued as we careened on the Rollercoaster from Hell. Up and down. Side to side. Then a terrible jolt that sent a sickening lurch through my innards. It felt like we were about to crash and I genuinely felt afraid. As I wondered whether to compose a final text message to my wife (at the same thinking that my phone would never work once it tasted the salty depths of the Caribbean Sea), things righted themselves. It was as if someone had flicked a switch on the airborne rodeo, stopping its insane bucking and twisting.

After I'd retrieved my passport from the floor, the young man next to me, a member of the Antigua and Barbuda Football Association, according to his T-shirt, turned to stare at some of his teammates further back in the cabin. He looked as shocked as everyone else but tried to take a selfie of himself, no doubt to appear on Twitter with a caption saying: I cheated death with Liat Airlines. For the next few minutes, the cabin was deathly silent. Even the cabin crew looked shocked. Then we landed at Robert L Bradshaw International (another airport keeping with the tradition of naming their establishment after famous statesmen) and people began talking again. A minute later, the incident was forgotten as we climbed out into the sunshine of my seventh Caribbean nation.

2

"You're only in St Kitts for one night?" asked the incredulous immigration officer.

I nodded, as he looked for an empty space in my passport. With pages at a premium, I had blue tacked some blank ones together to avoid the unfortunate event of someone stamping the centre of an empty page. These pages, of which I had only six remaining, were vital for any future visa stickers I might need. By blue tacking them, with the most miserly but adequately sticky spots of blue, I hoped to keep them safe and free of ink. So far, they had escaped the scrutiny of every Caribbean immigration official. This man didn't notice them either, despite flicking through every page. He looked up and noticed my wedding ring. "Where's your wife?"

"Back in England."

"Well, you need to come back with her for a week at least." He resumed his flicking, searching for a space to place his stamp but after eight or nine full places, he closed my passport. “For one day, I don’t think I’ll bother. Welcome to St Kitts.”

As the first person outside the terminal, I had to face the mad crush of waiting taxi drivers alone. All four of them looked at one another, then at me and waited for me to make my move. I picked one man, the oldest of the bunch, and gestured that he was the chosen one.

“Which flight did you come in on?” he asked. His pals looked at me, too.

“Liat from Antigua.”

“But it only landed ten minutes ago, man.”

“I’m a quick mover.”

“You must be.”

And then, after jumping in his airport taxi, I was delighted to find that the hotel was only nine minutes away. To celebrate Liat Airlines’ excellent time keeping, I decided to have some lunch before setting out to see the island.

3

St Kitts and Nevis is the smallest country in the Americas. Its population is about the same as Guernsey’s. The largest island, St Kitts (also known as Saint Christopher’s Island) is shaped like a fat tadpole (or maybe a chicken drumstick), with its spindly tail reaching towards Nevis, a roughly circular blob. At their closest point, only three kilometres separate the islands. If a bridge was in place (and there is talk of one being built), it would take someone on a bicycle about six minutes to cross between them. As it is, people sometimes swim across; the record is 58 minutes.

The first Europeans to sight the islands were the Spanish. When Christopher Columbus spied the main island’s three distinctive volcanic peaks through his binoculars, he marked them on his nautical charts and then, just as he had done in Antigua, set sail again.

A century later, a fluffy-bearded English explorer, John Smith, sighted the islands. Even though he was on his way to Virginia, USA, he decided to lay down his anchor for a while, setting up what turned out to be the first European settlement. His stay was brief but productive, because, as well as fishing, sampling new types of fruit and generally relaxing among the palms, Smith and his cohorts discovered that the island of Nevis contained soothing hot springs. Even so, Smith and his crew, growing bored of island life and the harassment they were receiving from the locals, resumed their journey northwards.

Another group of Englishmen arrived. Instead of fighting with the local chieftain, they made friends, bribing him with spices, beads and trinkets. Then they established St Kitts as the first permanent British colony in the Caribbean. Soon more Brits arrived, and then some Frenchmen. Each set up their own settlements on different sides of the island.

The chieftain of St Kitts was starting to get annoyed with all the white people traipsing around his island: first the British and then the French. When more of them started arriving, he gathered his elders and shook his fists at them. "We will stop these white men," he possibly snarled. "And we will do it in the dead of night. We will kill these Europeans with our knives, with our axes, with our hands." Everyone nodded. It was a good plan. The only thing standing in the way of it was a woman called Barbe.

Instead of being a blonde plastic bombshell, Barbe was an aggrieved slave woman, stolen from her own island, brought to St Kitts and forced to marry a man against her will. She despised her new husband and caused him no end of trouble. At the same time, she began to fall in love with a married British officer called Thomas Warner. With her beauty and guile, she soon had Warner trapped in her charms and, during a tryst, she furtively whispered the plot to him.

Understandably, Warner was shocked. Flinging Barbe aside, he gathered as many troops and weapons as he could and stomped off to the Chieftain's stronghold. The locals didn't stand a chance. By the time the British (and a few French) soldiers were done, two thousand tribesmen were dead and their bodies dumped into the nearest river. When dawn broke, the river was still running red. The only locals the British spared, allegedly, were a handful of beautiful women, whom they took as sex slaves.

In the decades that followed, no more rebellions befell the British, and St Kitts went on to become the sugar production capital of the British colonies. Then, like other islands before it, the plummeting price of sugar in the mid-nineteenth century meant the glory days were over. When the final sugar factory closed its doors for business in 2005, St Kitts and Nevis was forced to change its way of generating income. Nowadays, offshore banking and high-end tourism are what fill the government's coffers.

4

After unpacking a few things from my luggage, I spied a ring binder. As well as thanking me for staying in their hotel, and telling me about what time the restaurants opened, it had a section dedicated to hurricane awareness. I found out that the difference between a tropical depression and a tropical storm was to do with wind speed. The former blustered along with wind speeds up to 38 mph while the latter tore across ocean and land with speeds up to 74mph. One mile per hour beyond that and it was a fully-fledged hurricane. The information outlined what I should do should a hurricane be approaching.

Phase A was simply a *Hurricane Alert*. When a Phase A warning was given, it meant that a hurricane was in the vicinity, though it could be hundreds of miles away. People might look out of their hotel window and see some ominous clouds but go about their daily business as usual.

Phase B notched things up a little. *Hurricane Watch* meant that a hurricane was probably approaching, but it was still a day and a half away. Guests of the hotel might want to leave the island. If anyone had not yet arrived, then they should probably not come at all. Gallantly, in the case of a Phase B hurricane warning, the hotel would waive any cancellation fees.

Phase C: *Hurricane Warning* was the scariest. This meant that the hurricane was almost certainly going to make landfall within 24 hours. A full page of notes was set aside for what would happen should a Phase C Hurricane Warning be given. It read as follows:

1. Secure passports and important documents inside the hotel safe.
2. Pay any outstanding amount owed to the hotel.
3. Pack a small bag of essential items.
4. Pack everything else inside a suitcase, and put the suitcase inside a plastic bin liner (provided by the hotel staff) and secure by masking tape. Guests should leave the suitcase in their room.
5. Then, when the imminent arrival of hurricane signal is given (it didn't say what this signal would be, but I imagined it to be a hotel employee hollering through a klaxon, 'People: get your shit together and run for it'), Guests should make their way to the nearest hurricane shelter. (My shelter, should this situation arise during my stay in St Kitts, was in one of the lower hotel rooms.)
6. Guests should run like hell and take photos of palm trees being uprooted and goats disappearing over cliffs.

I looked outside and regarded the blue sky; I deduced Saint Kitts and Nevis was in Phase Snooze.

5

My balcony offered a view of the St Kittian (the correct term, believe it or not) capital, Basseterre. It looked small and dainty, with little in the way of tall buildings. Towering over it like a white monster, though, was a gigantic cruise ship, the first one I'd seen on my trip. It was almost as long as the town was wide.

After watching it for a while, I decided to see some of the island while the weather was good. As I'd done in previous hotels, I asked the receptionist to order me a taxi driver for a few hours. When she told me the earliest that one could arrive was an hour, I nodded and got her to book it. Then I decided to go for a walk.

Across the street was something called the Historic Fort Thomas Hotel. By swishing some bushes aside, I could see an old cannon standing by a broken white fence. I approached the fence, deciding that it looked exactly the type of barrier seen in *Scooby Doo* cartoons. A faded sign on it read OUT OF BOUNDS. I ignored the warning and sneaked into the grounds, finding myself on an expanse of cracked concrete edged by a few old (and bare) flagpoles. A line of overgrown shrubs and the shell of a once-grand hotel that resembled a prison lay further off. There was nothing remotely attractive about the Fort Thomas Hotel.

I walked to the rear of the building and found an area of windswept grass leading to a cliff. At the edge of the drop were a few abandoned fortifications. The sorry collection dated from when the British were stationed in St Kitts. As well as the battlements, the British had constructed a military hospital, which was now the abandoned hotel.

I left the grounds of the hotel and passed a series of well-to-do houses with thick walls and high fences. One such dwelling had a sign saying BAD DOGS: a good name for a rap band if ever there was one. I rounded a corner and came across a tall stone obelisk. After scattering a few basking lizards, I circumvented the small monument, reading the names of the 26 St Kittian soldiers who had died in both world wars. One was a 23-year-old airman called Sydney Sapenne. His crew had taken off on an overcast day in October 1944 on a mission to drop supplies to Italian partisans. Unfortunately, as they flew towards their target, the weather took a turn for the worse and the plane crashed and burned, killing everyone aboard.

I left the memorial and crossed to other side of the street, where a path led along the sea front. Basseterre lay in the far distance: a riot of multihued buildings that littered the harbour front, most of which looked purpose-built for cruise ship passengers. Beyond the harbour was a less pleasing jumble of shapes and styles: squares and rectangles, even cylindrical water towers, which in turn led up to some lush green hills dotted with expensive looking domiciles.

Along my route, I only saw two people. One was an old man sitting on a portion of seawall eating fruit from a Tupperware box. Lying beside him was a stout fishing rod. He nodded as I passed, tucking into his healthy lunch, seemingly without a care in the world. The other was a younger man. He was standing in a small boat out in the water. A couple of pelicans were bobbing around in the water next to him, with a couple more flying above. Apart from them, I had the whole sea promenade to myself.

My goal was to locate a shop from which to purchase some provisions. I found one about half way to Basseterre called the Daily Food Chinese Supermarket. I entered its welcome air-conditioned interior and found exactly what I was looking for: a bottle of water and a bottle of beer, hidden among the noodles, sauces and myriad other Asian-themed items. Back outside, I guzzled the water like a drunkard, thinking about how odd it was to have a Chinese supermarket in the middle of St Kitts. But perhaps it wasn't so unusual.

In 2014, the government of St Kitts, in an attempt to attract foreign investment, set up a scheme whereby anyone with a spare US$400,000 could buy themselves a St Kittian passport. Why would anyone want to do this? Well, with St Kittian citizenship, a person could travel to over one hundred countries visa free. For a Chinese businessman, this is a desirable outcome since his own passport will get him to only around twenty countries. Anyone with a St Kittian passport could also live in St Kitts, enjoying a tax-free income. So, for anyone with a spare lump sum, the proposition may sound attractive. It seemed unlikely, though, that a Chinese family would pay almost half a million dollars so they could open a grocery shop in the Caribbean.

Thinking about this, I set off back to the hotel to meet my taxi driver.

6

Chris was a thirty-something, bald-headed man who had a distinct American twang with his Caribbean brogue. In his spare time, he installed satellite dishes. "The dishes are my fall-back," he said as we set off along a thin road that would take us along the south-western coast of St Kitts. "In the off season I need something to pay the bills."

We headed away from Basseterre and passed through a small village. "This place is called Challengers," Chris told me. "It was the first village on the island to be freed from the plantation owners. A man called John Challenger – he was a British customs officer – sold the land to the newly-freed men and women. I know Challengers doesn't seem much to look at, but as part of our history, it is vital. I just hope someone decides to fix things up."

I looked at the houses – they were jauntily painted but in need of attention. Wonky fences, broken doors and rickety verandas seemed to bind the village together. Not far from the village was a tiny trickle of water known locally as Bloody River, the same place where the British massacred the local indigenous population thanks to information from a slave woman called Barbe. Known later as the Kalinago Genocide of 1626, the only thing to suggest such a terrible thing had occurred was a small signpost. It told me that in the year 2000, a ceremony was held at the river to release the spirits of those massacred.

I scrambled across a few loose rocks until I came to the river. It was as dry as a bone, with a little bridge spanning it. Underneath the bridge, a goat was munching on some leaves; from behind some high walls, I could hear children playing. The scene was almost fairytale-like (if I ignored the abandoned, rusting shell of car) and I trip trapped onto the concrete span and stood in the middle looking down at the goat. After a few quiet moments of reflection, I crossed to the other side and returned to Chris. When we set off, I asked him about his experiences with Liat Airlines.

"Why do you ask?" he said guardedly.

"Because tomorrow I'm flying to Dominica with them, via Antigua."

Chris whistled. "Let me tell you this. Last year, I was due to fly to St Martin for a family get-together – my sister lives over there with her husband and two children. So I arrived three hours early for my 10am flight and guess what? They told me there was a delay. So I sat and waited, and waited, and then waited some more. Ten hours later, Liat finally cancelled the flight. So I went up to the desk and asked what I should do. They told me I was booked on the next morning's flight. I said this was no good because I had already missed my family get-together. I said I wanted my money back. You know what they told me?"

I shook my head.

"They said I could have a voucher. *A voucher!* They said they never refund money. I was mad as a dog. But do you know what? There was nothing I could do and they knew it. I've never used that voucher – I never want to fly with Liat ever again. So does this answer your question about what I think about Liat Airlines?"

I told him it did.

7

On the way to the marvellously named Brimstone Fortress, we drove along a stretch of road that had the sea on one side and some high ground on the other. Chris told me that if the wind were of sufficient strength and the temperature of sufficient heat, then the smell of sulphur would cascade down the hills and flow upon the road we were now travelling. I wound down the window but could only smell the sea.

I gazed up at the hills. Somewhere in the distance was a volcano – the source of the sulphurous odour. Clouds were obscuring its jagged, ominous point, but I already knew that Mount Liamuiga's last eruption was over one hundred and fifty years ago. Therefore, I felt perfectly safe, quite unlike some Caribs in 1626. Prior to St Kitts' independence in 1983, the volcano was called Mount Misery due to an unpleasant side effect of the Kalinago Massacre. In an attempt to escape the British onslaught, some Caribs fled their camp and rushed up the side of the volcano hoping to find somewhere to hide. When they realised there was nowhere, and that the British were coming up after them, they committed suicide by jumping into its deep volcanic crater.

The name, Brimstone Hill Fortress, conjures images of hellfire and damnation. However, the reason behind the name is more mundane. When British engineers first designed the fortification and tried to think of a suitable name, one of their group just happened to smell some brimstone from the nearby volcano and thus the name was born. As we turned onto a track towards it, Chris gave me two options: walk or drive to the top.

Walking would be tortuous, he told me. The trail, abundant with insects, snakes and possibly monkeys, led upwards through dense forest. Driving would take about five minutes. I rubbed my chin and pretended to consider things, then told him to drive on. "So St Kitts has monkeys, too?" I asked.

"Plenty of them. But we eat them here," Chris told me matter-of-factly. "But before you ask, I've never tried any monkey meat. In fact, I think mainly its kids who eat monkeys now." Chris began to do an impression of a teenager. "Hey man, we're totally drunk; let's cook a monkey." While I digested this morsel of island life, Chris explained some history behind the Brimstone Hill Fortress.

"The British designed it in 1690, but they didn't build it – they made African slaves do all the heavy work. They called it the Gibraltar of the Caribbean because of how high it was. They thought no one would ever breach its walls. They were wrong, because the French took it."

I asked Chris how he knew so much about everything. He was like a tour guide.

He laughed. "It's because I drive taxis for a living. In the tourist season, all I do is drive people around. They all want to know the same things and so, about five years ago, I decided to find out all the answers. Now I just tell people what they will ask anyway." Suddenly, he frowned. "I'm not boring you, am I?"

"No, not at all!" We were passing through a relatively flat piece of terrain punctuated by large trees filled with delightful red posies. I wondered how many times Chris had seen them, and the fortress, and so asked him.

Chris calculated the answer. "Hundreds of times. I couldn't really guess. But it's rare I come in the off-season like this. It's so much easier right now. From January to April, when four or five ships come in a day, this track is gridlocked with buses, minivans and taxis: all trying to come up at the same time. You should hear the beeping and swearing! It's madness. Mind you, if we had been here an hour ago, the fort would have been swarming with passengers from the cruise ship. But have you noticed something about the track?"

I looked at the thin road leading upwards. It looked like a regular country road in the Caribbean, like scores I'd already travelled upon. I shook my head.

"It is only wide enough for one lane of traffic. When a bus comes down, everyone has to move over and stop. It can take up to an hour to reach the fort. If I were in charge, I would build a second road: one for traffic going up; the other for traffic going down. But the people in charge either have not thought of this or they like to watch us suffer."

8

Brimstone Hill Fortress was the best fort I saw in the Caribbean. It was massive (its grounds covered an area larger than eighteen football pitches) and was astonishingly well kept. Everywhere I cared to look, sea walls, bastions, cannons, ramparts, stone steps and old military buildings filled my view. Film crews seeking an authentic fort setting would not have to look anywhere else.

Leaving Chris to chat with another taxi driver, I huffed my way up a large stone ramp to the core of the complex – the citadel. In the middle of its huge courtyard was an elderly white couple with their guide. The old couple looked at me briefly but I was already bounding up more steps to reach the uppermost level.

Once there, I paraded past a line of cannons, then gingerly made my way towards the central section where a sheer drop into the courtyard awaited unsuspecting visitors. Unprotected by any sort of fence or safety barrier, there was a small sign saying *Caution, stay clear*. I did so and then wandered to the furthest end of the bastion where a flag of St Kitts flapped in the breeze.

The wind soothed my perspiring brow as I gazed down at the northern coastline of St Kitts. It tapered away to reveal an expanse of prime blue Caribbean Sea. In the hazy distance was an almost perfect conical-shaped island called Sint Eustatius, part of the Caribbean Netherlands. After lingering for a few moments, imagining I was a British soldier on the lookout for enemy ships, I climbed down to courtyard level.

At the bottom, I discovered a series of rooms that formed the fortress museum. One showed how the sleeping quarters might have looked during colonial times: basically, six hammocks in close proximity. Next to the hammocks stood two plastic life-size soldiers decked out in period red-and-white costumes.

In another room, a series of wall displays described the punishment meted out to errant troops. If a soldier lost an item of military clothing or didn't sufficiently tidy up after himself, his pay was docked. If a soldier was caught mildly inebriated, or had been fighting, then he would was flogged. The accompanying illustration showed a man with a freakishly large bald head whipping a man tied to a post.

If a soldier was caught stealing he might be put in prison. If he killed a slave in anger, he could look forward to a ride in the *whirligig*: the prisoner was housed inside a cage that was placed on top of a horizontal wheel, his head covered by a fabric mask (to aid disorientation) and the whirligig was spun violently around. The result was always the same: profuse vomiting and possible concussion.

Moving up the ladder of crimes was refusing the order of a superior. For this, a man would get to ride the *wooden horse*. Unlike a child's favourite plaything, this wooden horse was a block of pure torment. According to the illustration, the only similarity with an actual horse was its colour (brown) and its legs (four). Essentially, it was a triangular sledge of wood on stumps with the sharp edge of the triangle at the top. After the prisoner's hands were tied behind his back, he was placed on the edge, straddling it, legs dangling over the sides and weighed down with heavy logs. Testicles were mashed and mauled as men in red coats shouted giddy up.

At the top of the Brimstone Hill Fort's punishment hit parade was the simple and effective execution by firing squad. Four categories of crime warranted this final solution. One was murdering a fellow white man. Second was assaulting a senior officer. Third was being caught having homosexual relations. Number four was the most bizarre – having sex with livestock. And on that note, I left the citadel and went to find Chris.

9

Chris and I turned inland from the coast and began a leisurely upwards drive through lively little villages. Children played giddily in small gardens while old men lounged on verandas. Chickens scattered as our wheels encroached upon their dust. Every now and again, we would pass empty wooden shacks that, come the tourist season, would be selling curios and knickknacks.

We were on our way to an old sugar mill called the Wingfield Estate. It dated from 1625, when the first European settlers arrived on the island. A man called Samuel Jefferson ended up owning the estate and, as well as overseeing his plantation, he managed to sire a clutch of children who went on to have their own children and so forth, until one of them grew up and became Thomas Jefferson, the third president of the United States. As well as being a breeding ground for future presidential stock, the Wingfield Estate grew sugar, tobacco and produced its own rum. The current owners have turned the old plantation buildings into a tourist attraction.

I had a wander around them all, occasionally stopping to gaze up at a massive stone chimney towering above the whole estate. In the days when sugar cane was refined into raw sugar, the chimney formed an escape route for the massive amount of steam produced. "How many slaves worked here?" I asked Chris. We were peering through a dark recess called a firing tunnel. It was where sugar cane stems not used for sugar were burned to heat the boiling vats.

"I think there were about a hundred of them."

"Were they treated well?"

Chris harrumphed. "What do you think, Jason?" He smiled at me, and I realised the absurdity of my question. "Of course, they were treated harshly, but I think there were different levels of harshness. I believe the slaves who worked at this plantation were treated better than most. The strongest slaves worked in the fields – manuring, cutting and planting. Older slaves, or ill ones, worked in the factory. Even children did jobs – like scaring birds away and picking weeds. They all worked long hours. But one thing you have to remember, Jason, is that each of these slaves was the plantation owner's property. That's why the white men whipped them so much. To them, they were just one step above dogs."

I didn't know how to respond to that and so said nothing, peering towards a line of thick forest that bordered the far side of the old plantation. Thankfully, Chris's phone started ringing and he excused himself. It gave me time to wander towards the trees.

Stepping through a clearing, I found myself enveloped by screeches, squawks and the raucous call of a million insects. And then I saw a lizard. It was the biggest one I had seen in my life (outside of nature documentaries). Its head alone was so large that for a moment it thought it might be a caiman or an alligator, except St Kitts didn't have any. Maybe it was a monitor lizard, I thought, and crept forward, trying to keep my footsteps as soft as possible so as not to disturb the reptilian beast.

After a few metres, I stopped to regard the lizard again. It was sunning itself on the forest floor, its head turned upwards as if attempting to catch the scant sunlight coming through the canopy. I tried to take a picture, zooming in the lens as far as it went. Afterwards, I checked the image. The thing was massive, the size of a Komodo dragon and I suddenly realised the folly of my ways. As far as Chris was concerned, I was looking at the old sugar-making equipment, yet here I was, in close vicinity to a creature that looked large enough to eat me. Maybe an alligator had escaped from a zoo, I suddenly thought. I gingerly sidestepped under the shade of a mango tree and took stock. This also gave me chance to take another photo. When I zoomed in, I discovered that it wasn't a lizard, after all: it was a tree stump. That was it, I decided, I turned tail and fled with a cacophony of insects accompanying my elephant-like crashes through the undergrowth.

10

Heading back towards the capital, Basseterre, I asked Chris about crime in St Kitts. My question was loaded because I'd read that the small island nation had one of the highest murder rates in the world. Chris did not dodge the question.

"We have a tiny population: about 55,000 people. And we don't have much violent crime, but when we do, it skews the figures. Look, if there was a murder in England, the statistical chance of you being murdered the next day is still very low. You agree?"

I nodded.

"But if someone is murdered in St Kitts, then probability wise, you are suddenly much more likely to be killed. But it means nothing. Do you see what I'm saying?"

I nodded again, though with less conviction.

"I think there were about twenty five murders last year. Jamaica had about 1200! When I read that we had a higher murder rate than them, I laughed my socks off. Jamaica is a country I would not feel safe in. But I feel totally safe in St Kitts. The only murders we have are young kids in gangs: sixteen-, seventeen-, eighteen-year-olds with guns and chips on their shoulders. But – and this is a very big but – these gangs would never shoot or rob a tourist. Even if a cruise ship passenger was lost and wandered into a gang territory, the gangbangers would not touch them. You want to know why? Because they know that if they murder just *one* tourist in St Kitts, then the cruise ships would stop coming and that would be the end of St Kitts. We would die an immediate but painful death. The cruise ships are our only source of income. We don't have sugar, we don't have bananas: all we have is cruise ships."

"What about Cuba?" I interjected. "Cuba's opening up to tourism now. Are you worried that they will take away some of your potential customers?"

Chris nodded vigorously. "Jason, you are exactly right. We are very worried about Cuba. We are worried about Cuba becoming a new cruise ship stop. Most cruise ships we get here are part of a five-port journey. Five ports are what most tourists seem to want and so, if Cuba opens up as a new hot spot, that's one port gone. Someone will lose out – Antigua, Dominican Republic, Puerto Rico, us? Whichever island is chopped from the itinerary, that's their economy up in smoke."

Chris seemed to know a lot about cruise ship economics. I asked him to give me some figures about how much money a country makes from them.

"Whenever a cruise ship comes into port, our government makes ten dollars per passenger. The cruise ship company pays this. They pay whether the passenger stays on the ship or comes ashore. And if, say, seventy percent of these passengers take part in a shore excursion, then that's a whole load more cash floating around our economy. Last year, 1.2 million passengers arrived in St Kitts. You do the math and tell me how much that is, because I already know. Imagine us losing that kind of money." Chris fell silent for a moment, as if considering such a calamity. "It doesn't bear thinking about."

We rode in silence for a while. There was nothing much to say about that.

11

Basseterre does not loom over the horizon like, say, London, or even Manchester, does. Rather, it gradually reveals itself, like a lustrous stone hidden behind veils of green hills and curling grey roads. Except the gem is tarnished. Grime, decay and, worst of all, the rampant flavour of commercialism marks the city.

The St Kittian capital is a town built solely, at least as far as I could tell, to service the needs of foreign visitors who arrive on the island for their half-day of island fun. As soon as they disembark, they walk along a narrow quay before entering a world of duty-free stores, jewellery outlets, casinos and restaurants collectively known as Point Zante, a hideously showy conglomeration of false colonial-looking architecture meant to wow tourists into shopping heaven.

With Chris waiting in the centre of town, I walked past stores with names such as Tropical Word, Sharky's Souvenirs and Kay's Fine Jewellery, ignoring the touts with ease. Some cruise ship passengers were returning to the ship in preparation for their 5pm departure. Most were ambling past the stores with shopping bags full of bountiful duty-free. Beyond the shops was a huge triple-arched yellow edifice that served at the filtering point for passengers and locals. Large signs said *Restricted Area: Passengers Only*. Behind the arch, but towering above it, was the great ship itself, a white behemoth called the Carnival Valor. This $500 million cruise ship could house three thousand passengers across its thirteen decks. And it was only a medium-sized one! When the larger ships called into port, some of them could entertain double that number.

I left Port Zante and found a route that took me into the heart of Basseterre. More or less in the middle of the town was a small roundabout full of small shops. The redeeming feature was a green, ornately decorated clock in the centre. Built in Glasgow and then shipped to St Kitts in 1883, the clock honoured Thomas Berkeley, a former president of the St Kitts legislative council. Unfortunately, Mr Berkeley never saw the clock, as he died two years prior to its placement.

Nor far from the Berkeley Memorial was Independence Square, a rough patch of parkland frequented by people taking shortcuts and old ladies sitting on benches. A few people looked my way but most turned around when I glanced back. It was as if they were afraid of upsetting me in any way. I sauntered through the park, from west to east, stopping to admire a little fountain along the way. A few sombre-looking, bare-chested women stood rigid above the slight cascade of water, their stony gazes fixed and unreadable. Hanging onto their sarongs were children. The square in which they stood was a former slave market; the statue was a symbol of this.

If an African slave survived the dreadful voyage across the Atlantic, they could expect the following upon arrival in Basseterre. First, their captors would hose them down and put them in chains, naked. Then they were locked up in dungeons for twenty-four hours so they could recuperate. The next day, some of the more muscular (or beautiful) slaves were oiled up in preparation for their appearance at the market. While various plantation owners waited with their purses, the slaves were paraded in the centre of the square, while spectators eyed them up as if they were cattle.

Strong, younger male slaves usually fetched the best price, for they were the ones who could toil under the most difficult conditions. A young female slave, though, would also get a high price. She might bear children one day (who under the rules of slavery, would be the property of the plantation owner), thereby giving two slaves for the price of one.

An elderly slave often went for the lowest price, or even a negative price, unless they had skills such as carpentry or cooking. But sometimes plantation owners bid for elderly slaves in order to keep their younger slaves happy. It was basic economics: they knew that a young male slave would work more efficiently if he knew his mother was working in the plantation building behind him. It was a different ball game, however, if a slave arrived into Basseterre's market diseased or disabled. If that was the case, then they came with a 60% discount. After enduring six to eight weeks on the Atlantic, on a diet of biscuits, starch and beans (with the occasional slurp of limejuice to ward off scurvy), many slaves arrived ridden with measles, smallpox, dysentery, rickets and blindness; some of them even arrived insane. Some unlucky souls deemed too weak were shackled on the dockside and left to die. Sometimes, a diseased slave was simply thrown in the harbour to drown. With only this statue to remind me about St Kitts' grisly and grim past, I left the park.

Aimlessly wandering Basseterre's backstreets, I uncovered some beautiful examples of old colonialism: wooden, two and three-storey structures punctuated by elegant balconies, handsome doorways and fancy frilled decoration. Some looked like they belonged in a Wild Western saloon town, and, because of them, I re-evaluated my thoughts about the St Kittian capital. It was certainly not a diamond or an emerald, but it was a shiny stone worthy of inspection beneath its veneer of sharp commercialism. I rounded a corner and found myself back at the car. It was time to head back to the hotel.

12

In my room, I retired to the balcony. The cruise ship had departed, its berth readied and prepared for an almost identical vessel to arrive by the time I arose the next morning. But for now, I perched my feet on top of the wooden balustrade and looked out over Basseterre. The sun was receding but the pelicans were still out, flouncing around on the warm air currents. Beneath them, the waves washed against the shore.

I opened a beer and ruminated on my trip thus far: seven countries in little over a week, and most of them with Liat Airlines. The following morning I was flying back to Antigua, and then onto Dominica. But for now, with a gorgeous sea breeze caressing my brow, and a cold bottle in my hand, I could only look forward to whatever fate threw at me from across a darkening Caribbean Sea.

Clockwise from top left: Brimstone Hill Fortress – don't touch the livestock; Port Zante (note the huge cruise ship behind the arch); A rather charming clock tower in the centre of Basseterre; Looking towards the St Kittian capital, Basseterre; Wingfield Estate: a former sugar plantation; War memorial of St Kitts

Chapter 8. Dominica is not the Dominican Republic

I threw back the curtains to bathe in the glorious sunshine of a new morning in the Caribbean. I blinked the last remnants of slumber from my brain, made myself a coffee and retired to the balcony to look at the new cruise ship in port. It was even larger than the Carnival Valor and, after typing its name into Google, I discovered that the *Ocean of the Seas* was one of the largest cruise ships in the world, capable of housing a staggering 6000 passengers, which was about half the population of Basseterre. As I sipped my Nescafé, lines of passengers, like an army of ants, were traipsing along a walkway towards the duty-free shops of Port Zante.

I checked Google for something else, too: weather conditions for my flight. As far as the weather bots were concerned, today's forecast was fine: glorious, in fact. When the march of the cruise ship passengers slowed to a trickle, I went to pack. It took five minutes.

At the airport, I looked at the board and saw that my first Liat flight to Antigua was showing an on-time status. Nodding to myself, I entered security where, for some unfathomable reason, my hand luggage came under scrutiny as it passed through the scanner. The woman in charge asked whether I had any liquids and when I told her I had, she nodded knowingly and called over a colleague. He came over with a sniffing hound by his side. The woman pointed at my bag and then me. "This man has suspect liquids."

The man nodded, handed the dog over to the woman, and donned some gloves. Simultaneously, I felt some suspect liquids stirring inside my bowels. After unzipping my bag, the man rummaged until he found my little bag of liquids, sprays and gels. First, he studied my tiny travel bottle of shampoo, then pored over a miniature tube of toothpaste, which he turned around in his fingers as if he fully expected to find wires attached somewhere. When he didn't, he picked up a bottle of mosquito repellent I'd bought in Barbados. It contained 90ml of liquid, ten less than the forbidden 100ml. He looked at the front of the bottle and then at the rear. With sweat bubbling on my face, and a hound sniffing around my gels, the man nodded. He held the repellent up to the woman.

She studied the label. "I knew it," she said.

The man showed the rear of the spray to me. There was a tiny graphic of a fire, almost invisible to the naked eye. "Flammable material," he whispered. "You can't take it with you."

I pulled a face. "Really? I've taken it everywhere else."

"It's against civil aviation rules."

There was nothing I could do. As I escaped security, I found solace in the fact that my hand luggage would have less of a bulge from now on.

2

I took my seat in the departure lounge and waited. When the time to board came and went, I was not surprised. When the time to take off came and went, I began to fret. While I paced about, occasionally casting worried glances at the sky, a horde of American passengers arrived and filled the tiny departure gate. Most of them were elderly and quiet as they waited to board their American Airlines flight to Miami. One voice was loud, though, and it belonged to a sixty-something gent standing near the small snack bar. Ignoring all the people waiting to buy beer, crisps and sandwiches, he bellowed in the direction of the woman behind the counter, "Hey, miss, can you tell me where the restaurant is?"

To her credit, she ignored the rude man.

"Miss," he shouted, his leathery lips flapping in disquiet, "where can I find the airport restaurant?"

A fellow countryman, nursing a final Caribbean beer, answered for him. "This is it."

The cantankerous old git shook his head in disgust and hobbled away.

Just then, an airport announcement crackled through the speakers. "For all passengers waiting for Liat flight 315 to Antigua, please be advised there is a fifty-minute delay."

My stomach flipped. Fifty minutes? What the hell for? A quick Google search revealed that Liat 315 was composed of three different flights. The first sector originated in Beef Island (a great name, I thought), which flew to Saint Martin with a flight time of just thirty minutes. The next sector was Saint Martin to St Kitts, a journey of only twenty minutes. So how come they were already fifty minutes late? My two-hour transfer window through Antigua had now been cut in half. I found a seat and fitfully watched the sky.

3

The aircraft arrived and, once we had all boarded, I looked at my watch. I still had time to make my connecting flight, but it was going to be tight. I flicked through Liat Airline's flight magazine, the zanily titled *Zing*. One page was dedicated to Liat's male cabin crewmembers. According to the article, only five men worked as Liat cabin crew, and the piece featured photos of each one. I studied the pictures because a male crewmember was aboard my flight. Except none matched the man at the front of the cabin.

Was he an imposter? A fake cabin purser? No, he was probably new to the airline and Liat had not had chance to update their magazine.

I replaced the magazine in the pouch as we rolled for take-off. Twenty minutes later, we landed at VC Bird. Once off the plane, I rushed through to the transit area and saw that my flight to Dominica was just about to start boarding. It left me with barely enough time to grab a cup of coffee, but I didn't care; I had thrown the Liat dice and had played a double six. I was going to Dominica and no one could stop me now.

As I took off into the clear blue sky again, the lady in the next seat regarded me. She was a kindly pensioner with a mop of frizzy grey hair. The woman introduced herself as Elizabeth and told me she lived in Roseau, Dominica's capital. She had just visited Antigua to see her sister. "I don't like going there too often, though: too much crime now," she told me. "Drugs, you know. Not too many drugs in Dominica – no one can afford them!" She chuckled at her own joke, and then asked me whether I was a food connoisseur. I had no idea what warranted this question, except that maybe my stomach was rumbling as much as the engines. I'd not eaten anything except a simple sandwich for breakfast.

"Not really," I said, "I like a good curry, though"

She nodded. "I like spicy food, too. But tell me, have you heard of the mountain chicken?"

I admitted I hadn't.

"Well, when I was a little girl, mountain chicken was a popular meal."

"Is that the bird in the middle of the Dominican Flag?"

The pensioner guffawed. She found it so funny that she turned around and told the people behind us. They laughed, too. "You are a funny man!" Elizabeth said, turning back to me. "No, the mountain chicken is not the bird in the middle of the Dominican flag. That bird is a parrot. No one eats parrots. The mountain chicken is food. My mother uses to give me it when I was a little girl. I loved it until I found out what it really was."

My ears perked up.

"Mountain chicken is frog – big frogs from the jungle. They are bigger than chickens. They have powerful legs that help them jump ten feet, but people still catch them all the same. But as soon as I found out my favourite chicken was frog, I have never eaten it. Not once."

"So what did it taste like?"

"Like chicken!" The old bird chortled. "My mum served it in a bowl and it looked like chicken, too – you know, on the drumstick 'cos of the frogs' big back legs. And it wasn't green; it looked like regular chicken. I tell you, if you had a plate of forest chicken and vegetables, and no one told you it was frog, you would never know. It was our national dish!"

I asked whether people still ate mountain chicken in Dominica.

"Not really. Some of the frogs caught a disease or something. As soon as people found out, they stopped hunting them. No one wanted to catch a disease from forest chicken. So the frogs are still there, if that's what you're asking."

"So could I go into a restaurant in Dominica and ask for some mountain chicken and fries?"

For some reason, this thought really tickled her. She guffawed like a lunatic. "No, you could not order mountain chicken in a restaurant. They would be closed down."

I noticed a gorgeous island below the wing. It was Guadeloupe, a large circular mound of green. Then we were back over the ocean, descending toward Dominica. It was an island also dominated by a thick coating of luxuriant green. And then, we were on the runway. Ten minutes later, I said goodbye to Elizabeth and was stamped into my eighth Caribbean nation.

4

Because I'd read that taxis were scant in Dominica's only international airport, I had organised my own transportation. Imagine my surprise, then, to see two men holding pieces of paper with my name written on them. One man was old, the other young, both standing side by side. My eyes swivelled between them in confusion. Both men looked at me.

I quickly decided that the chance of two Jason Smarts being aboard the flight was nil, and so, like characters from a Spaghetti Western, I watched the men's eyes narrow as they waited to see who would make the first move. I surprised them by doing it myself, heading towards a barrier at the far end. Both men followed my movement, almost barging one another as they fought for supremacy. “Mr Smart! Mr Smart!” the young guy yelped. He vigorously pointed to the piece of paper with my name written on it.

Jason Smart!” the older man shouted. “I’m your driver, not him.”

I reached the end of the barriers and stopped, looking from man to man, from name to name. Then I had an idea and got my phone out. “Okay, who is Green Tour Taxis?” I said, looking up.

The young man smiled. “That’s me.”

The old man grimaced and said nothing.

I addressed this second driver. “So who are you? And how did you get my name?” The old gent told me his boss had sent him to pick up a Jason Smart and deliver him to the Fort Young hotel in Roseau. “Is that where you’re staying?”

I nodded.

The young man cut in. “Same as me. Airport transfer to Fort Young Hotel. And I’m from Green Tour Taxis.”

Both men looked at me, awaiting my verdict.

“Sorry,” I said to the old man.

He shrugged and walked away. As for me, I followed the man from Green Tour Taxis, who turned out to be called Zack. As we walked to his minivan, he told me that sometimes hotels booked taxis for arriving guests. “Maybe that’s what happened here.”

I nodded. That made some sort of sense. I climbed into the back of the van and only then did I notice the young woman sitting in the front passenger seat.

5

The woman’s name was Lycelle and she was Zack’s girlfriend. She told me that collectively, they owned the Green Tour Taxi service. “We started the company two years ago and, at the moment, we do tours and taxi services in our down time. I work as a graphic artist and Zach is a presidential policeman.”

Zach murmured assent and then said something in such a quiet voice that I couldn't hear what. Instead, I asked him whether the president was a good person to work for.

"Sometimes," he muttered.

We began a sunset journey of tight road turns guarded by thick jungle. Nature Island – Dominica's nickname – was about right; nature was brushing against the wing mirrors and fluttering around the vivid red flowers. That said, compared to Antigua and Saint Kitts, Dominica seemed almost third world. Pot-holed road, tiny tin-roofed shacks, fume-belching trucks and women carrying bundles of sticks on their heads were common. I could have been in West Africa.

As darkness engulfed us, the only light was from our car's headlamps. They illuminated the foliage-laden forests for the briefest of turns before coating the road in stark white. As we drove along, I asked Lycelle about the hurricane that had hit Dominica the previous August.

"It was really bad," she told me. "But it wasn't a hurricane. By the time it reached Dominica, Erica was a tropical storm. And, instead of wind, she was rain. And lots of it. It hit Dominica at about 2am and the rain did not stop for 24 hours. And when I say rain, I mean rain. It was torrential, unrelenting. It was like a waterfall. Isn't that right, Zach?"

Zach nodded, and Lycelle continued. "Dominica is very mountainous and has many rivers, but none could cope with the amount of rain, and so torrents began rushing along river beds. There were floods and mudslides and ... well, let me give you an example. Zach's father owned a shop in Roseau. It sold pots of paint, paintbrushes and things like that. When he found out about the storm, he and Zach rushed to the shop so they could save as much stock as they could. By this point, it was windy but not raining. They put a lot of stock into the back of a van and drove somewhere safe. When they returned to the shop a few days later, it was gone.

Everything had been washed away – the walls, the doors, the windows: everything."

I whistled at the thought of this. "The rain was that powerful?"

"It was unbelievable. Whole roads were washed away as if they were cardboard. Bridges stood no chance and this meant that villages were cut off for days. Helicopters and ships had to come from Antigua and Barbados to save people. It was a disaster. The church I went to as a little girl was gone. My grandmother's home: gone into the ocean. When Erica moved on, and I looked at things, all I saw was devastation. I have never seen anything like it. It was like a disaster movie. Tomorrow, when we drive you to the north of the island, you will see some of the damage caused by Erica with your own eyes."

6

We reached Roseau after an hour's drive. With night firmly settled over the capital, it was hard to make out anything beyond a few dimly-lit stores. Lycelle tried her best to point things out, but with a noticeable absence of street lighting, it was like pointing to a star constellation in the night sky and telling me it was the Night Dancer.

We passed the prison, though I would never have known. Lycelle told me it housed about three hundred prisoners, of whom nine were female. "Plus three Chinese tourists," she added juicily.

"Chinese tourists?"

"Yes. No one really knows why the Chinese men have been locked up, but I have heard rumours that they stole a lot of money from a bank. They did it electronically, I think, not with guns. I'm surprised at this, though; Chinese people are important here, and they have lots of money. They have been rebuilding the roads and buildings that Erica destroyed."

"So the men in prison came to Dominica to work?"

"I don't know for sure, but probably."

Outside the Fort Young Hotel, I said goodbye to Lycelle and Zach for the time being. Just before they drove off, Lycelle offered some words of advice "If you walk around Roseau tomorrow before we pick you up, please be careful. Some people see foreigners and try to rob them."

In a rare display of disagreement, Zach cut in. "Don't listen to her. You'll be fine. Just act as if you know where you're going and don't flash your cash: common sense, man." He then spoke privately to Lycelle, probably chastising her for worrying me needlessly. He turned to face me. "Roseau has a lot of vagrants. They might ask you for money, but just wave them away and they won't give you any bother. They know better than to hassle a tourist. In fact, if you came on a cruise ship, you wouldn't see them at all. We keep them hidden in vagrant compounds. But at this time of year, they're out and about, looking for trouble."

I thanked them for their assistance and entered the Fort Young Hotel, a former eighteenth-century fort that overlooked the sea. As I checked in, I could hear a bar band playing a hip-swaying tune in the courtyard. After I'd collected my key, I went to watch them for a while, tuning into a great bass player grooving along behind a leggy female singer. After I deposited my things in my room, I went to watch them again, savouring a gratis rum punch provided by the hotel management. It was a welcoming start to Dominica.

7

Many people confuse Dominica with the Dominican Republic. Even post offices sometimes confuse the nations. Letters sent to Dominica often end up in the Dominican Republic, and vice versa. Getting them mixed up was never a problem for Christopher Columbus, though; he knew exactly which one was which because he discovered both, naming them after the Latin word for Sunday.

When Columbus sailed away from Dominica, the French and later the British settled there and, like the other islands of the

Caribbean, Dominica became a hotbed of plantations. By 1978, Dominica was ready to go it alone. It could not have chosen a worse time. A spate of devastating hurricanes swept over the island more or less as soon as the government signed their independence papers, obliterating its only export – bananas. While the fledgling nation scrabbled about trying to make ends meet, a group of white supremacists from the United States and Canada planned an invasion. Thankfully, they failed, due to a mixture of utter incompetence and members pulling out at the last minute. But their attempt to take over Dominica proved just how tenuous a hold the government had onto its sovereignty.

By the end of the 1980s, just as the government were finally getting things together, the worldwide price of bananas plummeted, sending the island's finances into meltdown. Today, Dominica remains one of the poorest of all the Caribbean nations with a GDP per capita around half that of the citizens of Antigua and St Kitts, and a third of Trinidad and Tobago's. And because of its relatively poor tourist infrastructure, Dominica is one of the least visited Caribbean nations.

But despite these setbacks, Dominica has something in its favour. For some unfathomable reason (scientists are trying to work out why), the people of Dominica live unusually long lives. The number of them who have reached the grand old age of one hundred years is three times the world average. Perhaps it is to do with their easy lifestyle, the food they eat, or perhaps something more complex like their genes or their penchant for forest chicken. Thinking on this perplexing conundrum, where some of the poorest people on Earth live the longest lives, I bought myself a beer and watched the band finish their set.

8

For some reason I arose at 6am and was completely awake. Maybe it was because I had not completely closed the curtains and therefore allowed the room to bathe in Dominican sunshine. But waking up early was good; I could see the city without the full roar of the sun's heat and without shysters trailing my movements.

Half an hour later, I was outside, pleased to find the capital still asleep. Even the vagrants, of whom there were many, were slumbering in closed doorways or benches. The only part of Roseau open was the Farmer's Market, which was a clustered and chaotic area of stalls overlooking the Roseau River, a rubble-strewn inlet of the Caribbean Sea. I passed a woman setting out an array of exotic fruit as reggae music played out behind her. Another woman was carrying a huge bunch of bananas on her head. Pineapples, coconuts, mangos and endless bunches of bananas were in the process of being arranged across individual tables. I stopped at one such stall, doing a double take at the huge bananas for sale. Each of them was far bigger (about twice the size, by my reckoning) and wider than the puny ones sold in British supermarkets. They were like yellow clubs and I decided to buy one as breakfast. After handing over one East Caribbean dollar, about 30p, I walked away, marvelling at the size of the thing, scoffing it until I came to a bridge. I gazed out over the ugly Roseau River, pondering whether to cross it, when something distracted me.

"Hey!" a man shouted. Inwardly, I sighed. Long ago, I had learned to ignore these calls. Most people who shouted at me in foreign lands were taxi drivers, hawkers or vagrants, and so, when this man shouted, I simply pretended I hadn't heard him and continued eating my mammoth banana. After a few bites, I decided to head back into the main part of the city, towards a street lined with old wooden buildings. If the makers of Pirates of the Caribbean decided to make another movie and wanted an authentic smuggler's port, then Roseau might fit the bill. They would have to clear the crazy telephone wires first, but apart from them, it was ripe for buccaneers.

The man shouted again and he sounded closer. I turned to see he was following me. This left me with two options: carry on and ignore him or turn around and confront him. Thinking it wise not to have my back turned against a potential troublemaker, I chose the latter. He looked about fifty but was probably much younger. Half naked, with bare feet and a scraggly beard, the man stopped about five feet from me. "You got any money for me, sir?"

I shook my head. "No money, sorry. I don't carry money when I'm walking the street."

"Except when you buy a banana..."

He had me there. The evidence was still in my hand. He'd obviously seen me buying the damned thing.

"Sorry," I shrugged and walked away, wondering whether he would shuffle after me. When I stole a glance thirty seconds later, I was thankful to see he had gone.

I turned along another street, finding a few more people were awake now. A man was brushing a shop's doorstep, and a couple of old ladies were plodding towards a corner further along. In an alcove, another homeless man was sitting upright, staring about as if he had just woken up, which he probably had. I walked past him and stopped at one of the fine wooden structures. It advertised itself as a laboratory.

The large sign outside said: Dr Erica Joseph's Diagnostic Lab. According to the information, the good doctor offered treatments such as *Therapy for Slow Learners, Word Therapy for Cancer Victims* and something called *Blank State Disorders*, which included ADHD, Dyslexia and Broca's Aphasia, the latter being an affliction affecting speech. As well as these treatments, Doctor Erica's lab offered motivational courses, of which the most popular seemed to be *Become a Self-Discipline Master as a Cruise Ship Employee.*

Getting a cruise ships job was a sought-after position among Dominica's unemployed. Once they received their sea passage, they would get to see some of the world, receive free board and lodgings and have money in their pockets. No wonder people such as Doctor Erica were cashing in on this.

Unemployment is a big issue in Dominica, with a quarter of its young people out of work. The island's unemployment rate is the third highest in the Caribbean, with only St Lucia and Grenada topping it on the list. When young Dominicans leave school and find themselves with no job, they grow disenfranchised. And so what do they do? Some lucky ones return to school, a few might persuade rich relatives to pay for cruise ship courses and others turn to begging or petty crime. There are simply no other options.

Roseau had woken up. The shops were open and the small trucks servicing them were clogging the narrow streets. Mini-van taxis exacerbated the problem, stopping to pick up passengers or ushering people out into the street. A bakery was doing a roaring trade, selling rolls, rotis and cakes to passers-by. Most of the vagrants were awake too, wandering around, searching through bins and or poking around in street rubbish. Whenever one noticed me, he (they were exclusively men) asked for money. I passed a bus stop where two cute children were waiting: a boy and a girl aged about six. They waved, so I waved back. Seeing this, they rushed over. "You have dollar for us?"

I shook my head.

"Only one dollar. We're hungry."

Before I could falter and hand them some change, a woman rushed out of a shop, sending the children fleeing for cover like a couple of scared rabbits. "Scat!" she shouted after them. "Don't you be bothering people now."

I was about to thank her but she was already returning to her store.

9

Just along from a little roundabout, well away from the hustle and bustle of downtown Roseau, was a tiny patch of green called Pebble's Park. Who Pebble was, I had no idea, but I stepped into his park, nonetheless, aiming towards a white octagonal bandstand in the centre. As I approached, I noticed a couple of vagrants slouched inside. Though groggy eyed and horizontal, the grizzle-chinned gents spotted me in an instant and were up before I could make my escape.

"Got any spare dollars, man?" one asked, the thinner of the two.

"Or anything?" added his pal. "Just something to help us out, you know."

I held up my hands. "Sorry, I don't have anything."

They looked annoyed but accepted my response, returning to the bandstand and their bags of belongings. I left the park and found a lonesome statue standing on a tiny, grass-covered traffic island. I stopped to look. A man in broken shackles was blowing into a conch shell: a symbol of slave freedom. A placard told me it was the Neg Mawan Emancipation Monument, the strange words translating to 'brown man'. Slaves arriving in Dominica were sold in Roseau Slave Market. I decided to pay a visit.

I found the cobblestoned market behind the Dominica Museum. A group of women were in charge of the stalls selling woven baskets, trinkets and T-shirts. All were chatting, laughing or regarding me. As the only patron, I was attracting a lot of attention.

"You want a hanging basket?" jeered one woman in my direction, who possessed an infectious laugh that all the other women found hilarious.

"Or some scented candles?" another woman added. More laughs, but good-natured ones. These women were used to the cruise ship passengers, and today, with no boat in town, they had time on their hands to toy with me.

I smiled, looked around and didn't know what to say. I certainly had no interest in any of the displayed wares, but the women already knew this. "If you're looking for where the slaves were sold," said the woman in charge of the basket stall, "then look over der." She was pointing towards a red structure with arches on all sides. It was about the correct height to accommodate a single slave in chains.

I thanked her and began to take a photo. Another woman rushed over and stopped me. At first I thought it was because taking photos was forbidden, but it was because she wanted to remove the T-shirts she had draped over the base. “Now you can take a picture.”

I did so, thanking her, too.

“So why you in Dominica?” asked a third lady, this one holding court at a stall selling hats and brightly coloured dresses.

I lowered my camera. “Just visiting. Seeing what’s what, you know. Enjoying island life.”

She considered this. “What you think so far?”

I answered truthfully. “It’s a beautiful island. And everyone’s so friendly, especially all of you.”

The women seemed to like this. “Well you can come back anytime. We’ll give you a special discount.”

After leaving the vendors, I entered the Dominica Museum. A teenage girl guarded the entrance. Like all teenagers, working in a museum was clearly a major chore for her and she could barely be bothered to issue me a ticket. When I inquired about whether the museum was any good, she shrugged and looked at her phone.

Undeterred, I had a wander around the small rooms, pausing briefly at some old pottery and tools, and then at some photos of Dominica’s past rulers. None particularly interested me, and, when I gazed at some old clothes, I yawned. Not even a glass cabinet intriguingly called Grinders and Graters could keep me interested. Instead of torture implements, a collection of pebbles and sharpened rocks lay inside. A pair of black and white photos caught my attention for longer. They showed Roseau market, the place where I had just been, from the 1920s. Easy to make out was the red arched podium where the slaves were paraded. The podium and the rest of the market place looked the same as it did now, except for one thing: the square was brimming with well-do-do black folk wearing fine black hats and Sunday best, or carrying large sun parasols, all of the people frozen in a scene of jolliness.

In a quiet corner of the museum (though all of it was quiet, since I was the only visitor) was a section dedicated to a woman names Jean Rhys. I had never heard of her, but the display told me that she was a novelist prior to her death in 1979. I studied one of the accompanying photos. It showed Rhys in her younger days. With her coy expression and delicate features, she looked like a 1930s starlet. Her story turned out to be interesting.

Born in Roseau in 1890, Jean Rhys was the daughter of a Welsh doctor and Creole mother. After spending a pleasant childhood in Dominica, her parents packed her off to England so could live with her aunt. What sixteen-year-old Rhys thought of the cold and drizzle of Cambridge after living on a tropical island is anyone's guess. But with no choice in the matter, she tried to make the best of things, but found that, due to her mixed heritage, she was an outsider.

Her island upbringing didn't help. With her strange twang of speaking and her lack of finery, Rhys found it hard to fit in. She longed to return to Dominica, but with no way of making this happen, she decided to become a rebel. By the time she was twenty, she had embraced the hedonistic lifestyle fully, dallying with alcohol, drugs, nude modelling and even becoming a mistress to a series of wealthy men. It wasn't all fun and games, though; at one point, she spent some time in Holloway Prison for assault, which, apparently, gave her time to take stock. When she was released, instead of cavorting in the dance halls of East Anglia, she began to flesh ideas out for what was to become her first novel. When *Voyage in the Dark* was published in 1934 – a dark tale of a mistreated woman who harked from the Caribbean – it sold enough copies to warrant Rhys writing another book, and then another. She eventually died in Devon, aged 88, where her name fell into relative obscurity.

I looked in a glass cabinet. It contained some of Jean Rhys' books, most of them in tatty condition. With one last look at the photo of such a colourful woman, I left the museum in search of sights anew.

10

Before I left the museum, I stopped by a striking painting on the wall. At first glance, its subject was a seated woman cupping her face in her hand. Except it was no such thing: the painting was one of those glorious illusions where the painter had depicted a collection of objects which, when looked at from afar, or with squinting eyes, looked like something else entirely. Her legs were the curved supports of a wooden table. Her waist was a basket. Appropriately, her bosom was a pair of ripe melons. A cheerfully placed bunch of bananas was the woman's left hand. Cleverly, the artist had painted her right hand as a vase holding a flower, the leaves forming a hand cupping a face. When I studied the woman's face, I discovered the lips to be an orchid, the nose a tall-masked yacht, and the eyes some canoes. Her eyebrows were a pair of distant islands. It was amazing.

Outside, I began to wander aimlessly, keeping to shaded spots as best I could. Then I realised I had no water and so found a grocery store. As well as a bottle of water, I could not resist picking up the local newspaper, delightfully titled *The Sun: Dominica's Hottest Newspaper.* As I traipsed along a quiet street, I read the headline. *Man Vanished*, it read. Intrigued, I stopped in an alcove to read more. According to the tabloid, the whereabouts of a British-Dominican man who had disappeared more than a month ago was still a mystery. Where could he be, the newspaper hypothesised? Who had seen him last? Was he murdered? Had he fallen off a cliff? No one knew. Compounding matters was that Marsley Williams, the gent in question, was a 77-year-old, quietly spoken man who had never gone missing before, and, as the newspaper took pains to point out, had no reason to disappear. The story was front-page news, not because Williams had gone missing, but because some of his extended family had flown over from the UK to help in a 'fruitless search' as they complained about the 'indifference' of the Dominican authorities to finding their absent relative.

I closed the newspaper, folded it and stuffed it into my trouser leg pocket. At the end of the road, I came to the Dominica Botanical Gardens. Once upon a time, the gardens had been one of the finest thoroughfares of tropical greenery in the Caribbean, until a devastating hurricane struck in 1979. At that time, I was eight years old, blissfully unaware of anything happening beyond the borders of England, let alone thousands of miles away. And even if news of the hurricane had filtered into the Smart household (which, as far as I can recall, it hadn't), it would not have caused a flicker in my young mind. But maybe it should have done, because the hurricane that bore down upon the island of Dominica on the morning of 29 August 1978 was one of the worst the world has ever seen.

11

Hurricane David was a Category Five hurricane, the highest there is. As it spun and gained supremacy over the Atlantic, meteorologist believed that Barbados would take the brunt. Thus, when it altered its terrible course at the last moment, making a beeline for southern Dominica, the island was wholly unprepared. Winds of up to 150 mph tore over the island for six hours, lashing 250 millimetres of rain down in the process, which equated to three months' worth of rain in England. When the hurricane departed, it left Dominica in devastation. Aerial photos showed Roseau after what looked like a bomb attack. Eighty percent of the town's homes were gone, leaving thousands homeless. Miraculously, only 56 people lost their lives, far lower than the death toll in the Dominican Republic, where two thousand died a day later.

Roseau's botanical gardens took its fair share of hurricane damage. Trees were uprooted; others simply vanished, never to be seen again. One tree, an enormous African baobab tree, fell and landed on an empty yellow school bus that had been parked in the gardens for safekeeping. The baobab crushed it like a hammer compressing a tin can. The bus is still there.

I stared at the crushed yellow bus. Only the front driver's portion looked recognisable, as behind it, the bus was completely caved in like an accordion. The enormous tree trunk still lay on top of it. If you wanted a stark image of the power of nature, this was it. I could not stop looking at the cracked windows, the flattened tyres and the mashed-in seats. It was one of the most bizarre things I'd seen in the Caribbean.

Managing to tear my eyes away, I wandered along a well-groomed pathway, which cars, pedestrians and cyclists were using as a shortcut. Some people slowed down to look at me, but most were not interested. I turned off the path and headed over some grass instead. And that was when someone took more of an interest in me. The man was wearing overalls that said he was a botanical garden worker. He was collecting fallen palm fronds and stuffing them in a large sack. He stopped and watched my passage. When I noticed him studying me, I waved. He didn't wave back. Instead, he walked over to me and asked where I was going.

"I'm looking for Jack's Walk." Jack's Walk was a hillside climb that supposedly offered commanding views across Roseau. It was supposed to be in the gardens somewhere. "Is it around here?"

The man shook his head. "Never heard of it."

"Its nickname is the Thirty-Five Steps."

"Oh yeah. The steps are over there behind the trees." He pointed towards a thick copse of foliage. He then picked up another palm and stuffed it into his sack. "Watch out for snakes."

I moved in the direction the man had pointed, now keeping a wary eye out for snakes in the grass. I found the steps hidden behind some breadfruit trees, their fruit dangling menacingly above my head. Near the steps was a sign warning me that catching giant ditch frogs (mountain chickens) was illegal. There was a picture of one of the brutes, too. The amphibian looked like it could crush a man's neck with its muscular back legs. Good luck to anyone who wanted to catch one of those buggers, I felt. And so, wary of giant frogs now, I began my climb.

At first, it was great: a hillside trail full of pretty flowers and swift, darting lizards. Then, when the steps became less step-like and more like precarious mounds of mud, I enjoyed it less. More so, when I realised that the name, 'thirty-five steps', was an outrageous lie. More like three hundred and thirty-five steps. And if one of them should be a false step, most likely caused by an upturned tree root, I could tumble, head over heels, to the bottom of the forest where I would lie dead for many days, my flesh picked clean by the centipedes, worms and mammal scavengers. Additionally, should a sudden downpour occur, the path would turn into a mudslide. Not only would the bugs pick me clean, but also I would be brown and slimy before it happened. Grimly, I clambered upwards, every pore in my body oozing sweat until I reached the summit.

But it was worth it. Not since Trinidad had I observed a hummingbird in the wild. A dazzling green-plumaged bird darted over some bushes and blossom that overlooked Roseau. I perched myself on a rickety wall and angled for a shot of the tiny bird, aware that if I reached too far, I might topple to my demise, but I did not care. And, even though almost every one of my photos turned out to be ridiculously blurred, I was a happy man, at one with the wildlife of Dominica.

12

After lunch at the hotel, Zach and Lycelle picked me up. Their dual mission for the afternoon was to show me a fort in the north and then deliver me to a hotel on the other side of the island. Though the Fort Young Hotel was a fine place to stay, with an early flight to catch the next morning, I felt a hotel closer to the airport might be more prudent, if only to give me an hour's extra sleep.

As we drove north from Roseau, we passed a large signpost in red and white. It said, ALERT: DIVERSION. At first I didn't think anything of it, not even when our car began to bump and shudder over the rough terrain of the diversion track, but by the third such sign, I asked Zach and Lycelle about them.

Lycelle answered. "The signs warn drivers that the road no longer exists. Erica washed it away. In the village where my grandmother lives, all of the roads were washed away. Or if the road survived, then mud covered it. The people in her village could not do anything: they were trapped. No one could go anywhere or do anything. In the end, they had to zip line food in. Can you believe that?"

I told her I could not.

"It was a scary time for me, and for everyone. There was a house in her village that I used to love. It was big and sturdy, and it was built on pillars so that floodwater could go underneath. After the hurricane, there was no house left. Everything had been washed away, apart from some stumps."

Zach was still silent, occasionally tooting his horn when we approached one of the many hairpin bends. At one point, we passed a rusting shell of a Mr Whippy ice cream van, then a couple of JCBs. Lycelle couldn't explain the ice cream van, but she could explain the JCBs. "The Chinese brought them over after Erica, but they didn't take them back. We think it's because it's cheaper to leave them than pay for them to go back to China."

We came to another diversion. As we negotiated our way through a rutted sidetrack that took us away from the ocean, I could see why the Dominican authorities had closed the road off. The road ended as a jagged cliff. After a metre or so, standing as an island of its own, a section of broken road stood, one end coated in mud so thick that vegetation now grew in thick sprouts. Wrecked chunks of tarmac and twisted safety barriers made it a scene from a disaster movie, and I couldn't believe that this road – one of the major routes north from the capital – had been left in such a state. Why hadn't the government fixed it? Why hadn't the Chinese done something? Lycelle told me it was all down to money, or lack of it.

Later, as we took yet another diversion, Lycelle said a most unusual thing. "This used to be a porn farm before the storm." She gestured outside at the fields of grass, marked by occasional trees. "And even though the owner lost all his buildings and equipment, he still allowed the government to build this diversion track on his land."

"Porn farm?" I asked, incredulous that such a thing could exist in Dominica.

Lycelle nodded.

I stared at the overgrown weeds that showed nothing to indicate it used to be a place of prime debauchery. And to call it a farm! Were the actors bred on site, I wondered? Or did the filmmakers churn out such a prolific amount of adult entertainment that the only way to describe it was to call it a porn farm?

"They were all washed away, every last one of them."

"The actors?"

Lycelle shot me a glance. "No, the prawns."

To change the subject away from floods, I asked Zach and Lycelle about life in Dominica in general: what was good and bad. Uncharacteristically, Zach chipped in first. "The pace of life is sometimes too slow. If you want something doing, it can take a long time." He emphasised the word 'long'. "I also get annoyed when people get Dominica mixed up with the Dominican Republic. I have a sister in London who sends me birthday cards and things like that. When they don't arrive, and I look into it, the post office tells me the cards were sent to the Dominican Republic. It's happened about five times now."

Lycelle jumped in. "Zach also thinks he does not earn enough money." She gave her boyfriend a sideways glance. Zach shrugged in acknowledgement. "But I say this to him: yes, you do not earn as much as a policeman in, say, Antigua, but here you are respected."

Zach nodded.

"And here you will not be shot."

Zach nodded again, adding, "I've sometimes thought about moving to Antigua and getting the big bucks as a police officer. I have family there, so it would be no problem. But Lycelle is right. I could be shot over there. Antigua has a big crime problem. Here, I am safe and well respected."

The journey continued northward.

13

We passed through the town of Picard. It was essentially a service settlement for young Americans and Canadians studying at Ross University School of Medicine. I could see a few young Westerners wandering along, piled-up books expertly hugged against their chests. The existence of the medical school in Picard is a simple one. Overseas students with poor grades, not high enough to secure places at well-established medical schools back home, can train to be doctors in Dominica. In the US, potential medical students must obtain a score of at least 31 on something called the MCAT. In Dominica, the acceptance score can be as low as 17. That said, since the course's began in the late 1970s over 11,000 former students of Ross University are practising doctors.

According to Lycelle, around one thousand medical students lived in Picard. I could see a few sitting at a Subway fast food join. Their medical training facilities looked modern and glass-fronted, a world away from the flimsy buildings that dotted most of the island. Not far from Picard was Portsmouth, Dominica's second largest town. With a population of about three thousand, it was compact but beautiful, with picturesque bays nestled between gorgeous headlands. One building was covered from ground to roof in conch shells. It looked like something from a Disney film. I looked past it to the ocean. Sloshing around in the glistening water was a flotilla of fishing boats that vied for my attention almost as much as the hand-gesturing men playing outdoor backgammon in the centre of town.

But we did not stop in Portsmouth, for we had a fort to see: one named Shirley.

14

Fort Shirley stands tall upon a rocky peninsular on the far north-western coast of Dominica. In its heyday, the complex housed six hundred British troops, plus all their assorted slaves, support staff and hangers-on. As we traipsed towards a trail that led up to it, Lycelle pointed out a nondescript-looking tree. It had cute little leaves and green fruit dangling from its branches. They looked a little like apples. In every way, it was a normal tree.

Except it wasn't.

The tree, a *manchineel*, was the most dangerous tree on the planet. It had the power to kill, and the Spanish were first the first Europeans to discover this. When they first arrived on Dominica, weary after their arduous Atlantic crossing, they noticed the delectable-looking fruit and climbed some trees to grab some. After turning the small apple-like things over in their hands, a few mariners decided to eat some. These brave souls commented on the pleasant sweet flavour that quickly gave way to unusual peppery aftertaste. Then they began to clutch at their throats, gasping and spluttering. Some fell to their knees, screaming. Onlookers could only watch in horror.

What was actually happening was that the fruit was causing oropharyngeal burning, a condition that needed immediate medical attention. But, of course, none of the Spaniards knew this at the time, and so the only course of action they could take was to stretcher the poor men away, hoping they would recover. Some did, but most, following a horrendous period of intestinal agony and profuse vomiting, died. It is not surprising, therefore, that the Spanish named the fruit *manzanilla de la muerte* (little apple of death).

The tree could harm a person in other ways too. The Spaniards realised that if a soldier took cover underneath a manchineel tree, perhaps during a rainstorm, then they were at risk of harm. The tree produced milky toxins that, during rainstorms, would splash and fall on anyone or anything underneath. If any of this substance made contact with a person's skin, it formed agonising thick welts of pure burning. Speaking of which, in retaliation at the terrible tree, some Spaniards tried to burn a few down. The resulting toxic smoke emitted from the manchineel trees made some of them go blind. After this, the Spanish, and everyone else who came after them, left the trees well alone. In fact, it was only the locals who found a use for manchineel. For years, they had been dipping their hunting arrows into its sap, making very effective weapons.

I looked up at the tree with renewed respect. Its branches were teeming with death apples. One had fallen on the ground between my shoes. I moved away a few inches, not wanting any of its murderous juice to spill onto my foot.

At the top of the trail, Fort Shirley was quiet. Only the distant sound of the sea sounded below the walls. I had a quick walk around, but to be honest, I was bored of forts. This was my sixth fort of the trip, and they were all merging into one. But then something interesting happened. Lycelle spotted a snake.

The long thin black serpent was splotched with white. It was slithering tight against a wall in an attempt to escape our attention. Lycelle was already screaming, simultaneously jumping back in alarm. "Oh God, a snake! I hate them."

Zach laughed. "It's a harmless grove snake, Lycelle. It's more scared of you."

Lycelle looked unconvinced, moving well away from the wall, scanning the ground where the snake had once been. It was long gone, hidden inside the cracks underneath the wall. Then she looked contrite. "I'm sorry, Jason. But I do not like snakes. I think it started when I found one in my bedroom when I was a little girl. I screamed the house down and I would not sleep in that room for two weeks. In the end, my mother had to sleep in the room with me."

"She always finds snakes wherever we are," Zach cut in, finding the whole thing mildly amusing. "Every day we see a snake somewhere."

Lycelle nodded. "That's why I never wear sandals. And I'm always watching the ground."

With the excitement over for the time being, Zach and I wandered around the old officers' quarters and then stopped by a set of cannons. Lycelle was following close behind, scanning the ground for reptile foes. As I knelt down to study a heap of cannon balls on the grass, she screamed again.

"Snake!" she yelped, jumping back like a gazelle.

She was right. Another black and white snake, about two feet long, but as thin as a pencil, was slithering quickly away in the grass. Lycelle decided enough was enough and returned to the well-trodden pathway. As we walked towards her, Zach told me that someone had tried to steal a couple of cannonballs from the fort a few years ago. "I think he was a tourist from one of the cruise ships. A security guard saw him carrying them and stopped him."

"Why was he trying to steal cannon balls?" It seemed an absurd thing to steal. For a start, they were bloody heavy. "And what would he have done with them?"

"I'm not sure. Maybe he wanted a memento of Dominica?"

"What's wrong with a fridge magnet or a T-shirt?"

Lycelle took time out from her snake spotting to look at her watch. "It will be dark in an hour. We really should get moving." What she really wanted to say was, hurry up you oafs, stop talking about cannon balls; there are snakes waiting to kill me.

15

Sunset was fading as we arrived at my place of stay for the night. After thanking Zach and Lycelle for their services, I found myself at the bottom of some steep steps. With a wave and quick beep of their horn, Zach and Lycelle were off, heading back to Roseau.

I dragged the luggage up the steps, pausing to catch my breath near a tiny swimming pool at the halfway level. The hotel was still above me and, as far as I could tell in the fading light, it consisted of a main building and two or three separate structures. I looked at the pool. It looked distinctly unloved; a few leaves floated upon its greasy surface. Picking up my luggage again, I clambered the final few steps and found a check-in desk that also served as a bar. There was no one there apart from a man watching TV. He checked my name on his list and then nodded, producing a huge key. "Lodge number two," he said, pointing to my right.

When I reached my room, I realised it was a major downgrade from the Fort Young Hotel and, even though it was only twenty minutes away from the airport, I was beginning to regret my decision. For a start, I was in the middle of nowhere, with only a couple of buildings further along the road, and, secondly, the room had no air conditioning. To allow some air to circulate, I flung open the veranda shutters and took in the spectacular view – a vista of Dominican nature in all its glory: vast, wide swathes of rainforest palms; hills covered in thick vegetation and the silhouette of a distant peak shrouded in sunset mist. When a couple of mosquitoes flew in, I closed the shutters and the view was gone.

Later, after night had fallen, I retired to the hotel's tiny restaurant, not surprised to find I was the only person there. As I ate some bizarre, Caribbean-tinged spaghetti bolognaise, washed down with a cool Kubuli beer, I tried to make the best of things. After all, I'd survived eight Caribbean island nations and, the next day, I would be heading to South America, to Guyana, no less. Guyana was one of the tiny countries along the northerly coast of South America. Going there would mark my final jaunt with Liat Airlines. Would they come up trumps or would they let me down at the final hurdle?

Back in my room, with the constant screech of tropical crickets resounding from the pitch-black jungle outside, I prepared my luggage again, looking forward to my penultimate country. Little did

I know, that in less than 48-hours' time, my enjoyment would come crashing to a dramatic and painful halt.

Clockwise from top left: Caribbean-themed doorway in downtown Roseau; Is it a woman or a basket of fruit on a table?; Crushed school bus caused by the 1978 hurricane; It's not hard to work out why Dominica is known as the nature island; One of the many diversion signs dotting the island; The old slave market; Me, enjoying the scenery of Dominica; The Neg Mawan Emancipation Monument

Chapter 9. Broken and bruised in Georgetown, Guyana

It was the most horrendous night ever. Cooking in my own juices, battling with an invasion of disease-ridden mosquitoes – I was a broken man. The deadlock was finally halted by my alarm at the ungodly time of 4.30am. I felt like weeping.

I hadn't slept a wink. The previous night, more or less as soon as I'd turned off the light, I had heard the first shrill buzz of a mosquito. I knew instantly it was going to be a bad night, and I was correct. Without my insect repellent, I was fair game to the colony of six-legged beasts that called my room their feeding ground. When the itching started, I knew I was heading towards never-ending torment.

The heat had been another factor in my night of misery. The large ceiling fan had been dormant all night, because, as far as I could tell, its operation depended on the light. Switch off the light, the fan stopped turning. Turn the light back on, the fan moved. So, either I could sleep with a blazing light bulb or I could sleep without the fan. I chose the latter. But without any form of cooling apart from draping a wet towel over my chest (which I did over twenty times), I was grateful for the alarm giving me an excuse to get up and douse myself in the perpetually-cold shower. That done, I regarded myself in the cracked mirror. I was not a pretty sight: my eyes were redder than I'd ever seen them before. I looked like a demon. I would have had a cup of coffee, but the provisions in the room were non-existent. I packed my stuff and left the room, locking it behind me.

It was pitch black outside; I had to use the torch on my phone to find my way to the reception/bar area. After leaving the key on the table (as instructed the previous evening), I wearily made my way down the stone steps and almost fell into the dank hotel pool. In the dark, it had looked like a slab of concrete. That would have finished me, I realised. With my pockets full to bursting, I'd have sunk into its grimy depths.

Huffing and puffing, I made it to the bottom to street level. The previous evening, I'd asked the barman to order me a taxi. He told me he had a friend who was a taxi driver. "He'll be there at five thirty. He's always a few minutes early, so you won't have to worry about getting to the airport."

The taxi wasn't anywhere to be seen. It was 5.31am.

My Liat Airlines flight was due to leave at 7am, but I had to check in by six, otherwise there would be a chance the airline would bump me from the flight. I had twenty-nine minutes to get to the airport.

As I stood wondering what to do, a cockerel crowed, and then another joined it: a portent of doom, I felt. Across the horizon, the first stirrings of dawn were appearing. The burgeoning sun was casting a faint orange glow across the distant peak. Then I spied the silhouette of a man approaching. He was jabbering disconcertingly to himself, pointing at shadows, and so I grabbed my luggage and climbed back up the steps, panting with the exertion of it all, especially since my new mosquito bites were itching like hell. I considered jumping into the pool for the fun of it, but instead climbed to the top of the steps where I shouted hello in the direction of the dark hotel building. I expected no answer. I was right. Silence. I called out again just to make sure and almost jumped out of my skin when a voice sounded. "What do you want?" said the hidden voice: a man in the shadows.

My mouth opened and then closed again. Who the hell was he? "Who are you?" I croaked.

"Night manager. You woke me up."

I looked at my watch. It was 5.40am, meaning the taxi was fifteen minutes late. Fifteen minutes I could not afford to lose. I explained to the invisible man my plight. I heard him yawn. "The taxi will come."

"What if it doesn't?

"It will."

I asked him to ring the driver, just to be on the safe side, but he claimed he did not know the number.

With nothing else to do apart from throw myself down the steps, I absently scratched at a bite on my wrist and then made my way down the steps again. When I arrived at the bottom, I saw the strange silhouetted man standing in the middle of the road about two hundred metres away. He looked like he was dancing and jabbering to demons. Then, at precisely 5.50am, with the sun coming up firmly above the horizon, a taxi rounded the corner and stopped beside me.

2

"Sorry about dat, man," said the driver, an affable fellow with a sprinkling of salt and pepper stubble. "I thought I was picking you up at quarter to seven. My wife noticed the right time. Otherwise no one would have come for you." He chuckled at this thought while I plotted his murder. We set off and he put his foot down. Then, at five past six, we stopped outside the airport terminal. "Dere you go, man," said Mr Stubble. "Plenty of time."

After checking in for my flight, I sat in the departure lounge, surprised to see my Liat aircraft already at the gate. Before I even finished my cup of coffee, the call to board came. Within one minute of the posted departure time, we took off into a gorgeous blue Caribbean sky.

Fifty minutes later, I was in Barbados with four hours to kill before my next Liat flight to Guyana. I made my way to a café and bought a Jamaican Jerk Chicken sandwich for breakfast, washed down with a caffeine-heavy Diet Coke. I then found some Wi-Fi to read up on Guyana. What I discovered sounded chilling.

Crime levels are high, stated the British Foreign Office website. *Police capacity is low. There are regular armed and violent robberies. Muggings have taken place in broad daylight. Avoid walking alone around Georgetown, even in the main areas and don't walk anywhere at night*. It also went on to warn visitors about the ride to and from the airport. Some taxi drivers were part of gangs, picking up unsuspecting tourists in order to drive them to secluded spots where accomplices waited to rob and harm them.

I delved further into Guyana's crime levels. Just eight months previously, Bernard Hughes, an eighteen-year-old British man, arrived at Georgetown's main international airport. The immigration officer who stamped him into the country was the last person to see him alive, apart from the five men who abducted and bludgeoned Mr Hughes to death. He had been in Guyana just a few hours. Thankfully, all were captured and later charged.

I closed my laptop and frowned. This certainly put a dampener on things. The day's fraught beginnings looked even worse now. But I had been to plenty of so-called edgy countries before. When I had visited Iraq a couple of years back, people thought I was mad. The same people scoffed when I told them I had stayed in one of the roughest neighbourhoods of Johannesburg. Still, the warnings about Guyana did make me pause for thought. Maybe it would be best to keep a low profile in Georgetown.

3

As chance would have it, my final Liat flight of the trip left the gate dead on time, too. And to think that up to this point, I'd been worried about Liat Airlines cancelling one of my flights. Well, they had done themselves proud. Nine separate flights and not one of them cancelled. As we took off from Barbados, the last island I would be seeing until I landed in the United Kingdom, I hailed all things Liat.

Instead of flying into Guyana's main airport, we were heading to Ogle Airport, which, as well as being closer to the capital, had the greatest airport name ever. Sex pests could go about their sordid business with impunity. About forty minutes into the flight, a woman's voice came over the intercom. "Good morning from the flight deck, this is your captain speaking. Due to a build-up of thunderstorms on the approach to Georgetown, we'll be moving around quite a bit. I'm putting the fasten seatbelt signs on early because we might encounter some turbulence."

I looked outside at the carpet of white beneath the wing. In the distance, a scattering of cumulonimbus clouds had broken free of the main layer, towering like misshapen white mushrooms. They were the thunderclouds of which the pilot had spoken. Inside these cells, vast amounts of energy were waiting to be unleashed, and if our small Liat aircraft got caught up in any of it, the results could be catastrophic. When the sky turned an ominous grey, I caught my first flash of lightning. Other passengers had seen it, too, for there was a collective gasp in the cabin. Almost immediately, the aircraft began shaking and going up and down. In 2009, a packed Air France Airbus A340 had crashed into the Atlantic Ocean after taking off from Rio de Janeiro due to flying near a tropical thunderstorm. All 228 people on board died. Knowing this fact did not help my current mood.

The lady sitting next to me by the window looked like death was already on the way. She was a forty-something woman in a Salvation Army uniform. She had a large rosette pinned to her chest. Gripping the armrests, she breathed heavily as we shuddered our way downwards to the northern coast of South America. I smiled in her direction but she was incapable of returning the gesture. A woman on the opposite side screamed when we hit another batch of bad turbulence. When a second and then a third burst of lightning lit the cabin like a horror film, a man screamed. I was surprised it was not me.

To be honest, the shakes, ducks, dives and belly fops were bad, but not the worst I'd experienced – that accolade went to the flight to Dominica a couple of days previously. But even so, this Liat flight was up there with the best of them, and I grimly hung on. Two minutes later, things calmed down. We cleared the turbulent air and emerged underneath the cloud layer. There was a collective wave of euphoria about the cabin, brought about first by a few nervous laughs, and then quiet conversation.

“Dat was scary, wasn’t it?” said the Salvation Army lady.

I nodded. “Bad turbulence.”

“Turbulence? More like bein’ in a blender. I thought the Lord was callin’ me.”

We were still flying over the ocean but I could finally see the coast of South America. It looked *big* and it looked green. The mighty Essequibo River, a meandering, thousand-kilometre snake that served as the lifeblood of inner Guyana, was visible, as was the sprawl of Georgetown. A minute later, the aircraft banked to the right and headed straight for the city. When we made landfall, I saw that Georgetown was a blend of low-level buildings interspersed with wiry electricity pylons. And then, before I even had time to take a photograph, we touched down on a small runway flanked on both sides by dense jungle. It looked the sort of airstrip drug smugglers might choose when flying in narcotics.

4

My method of dealing with airport taxi drivers was well honed. Instead of responding to catcalls and shouts, I waved them away, eyes firmly fixed forward until the pack was behind me. The problem with Ogle, though, was the airport was so small and I had nowhere to hide. Instead, I switched to option two. Retrieving my phone from my pocket, I mimed making a call and then speaking to someone. The taxi drivers could hear snippets of my pretend conversation.

Yeah, just arrived, Mike . . . , flight was good, no delays . . . No, I think I’ll just get a taxi . . . Yeah; see you in about half an hour.

My pretend phone call suggested I knew people in Guyana and that my disappearance would cause questions. With the ruse over for the time being, I pocketed my phone wandered over to the pack; all of whom were watching me.

“How much to Georgetown?” I asked.

“Where in Georgetown?” one man asked, a wiry man with East Indian features and a small ponytail. “It is a big city.” His companions sniggered.

“I know,” I lied. “I’ve been here before. I need to get to the Guyana Forestry Commission.”

This brought looks of astonishment from the assembled drivers. The Forestry Commission was opposite the Marriott Hotel, my place of stay. I’d already looked it up; I didn’t want the taxi drivers to know where I staying because, at the very least, they would double the price.

The pony-tailed man pulled a face. “You’re going to the Forestry Commission with a suitcase?”

I mentally berated myself. It did look a stupid thing to do. My brain kicked into overdrive. “I’m meeting my contact there; he’s driving me to the hotel later.” The story sounded flimsy and the driver looked at me as if I was a nincompoop. Nevertheless, he led me to his taxi, quoting a reasonable price for the ten-minute journey. As I followed him, I tried to gauge whether he was carrying a concealed weapon, and then gave up. Who did I think I was – James Bond?

As we set off, I mimed another phone call, this one more crucial.

“Yeah, in a taxi right now … What? Oh yeah . . . his ID number is 5647.” I also gave the name of the driver. If the taxi driver decided to kidnap me, I’d just made it very awkward for him.

To calm myself down, I took in Georgetown from my passenger seat window, noticing the well-kept townhouses peppered with the odd palm tree. Then I surreptitiously glanced at the man next to me. He was definitely Indian looking and not Afro-Caribbean. Later I learned that about half of Guyana’s population was of Indian heritage, almost all of them descendants of Indian servants brought over by the British in the 1830s. After slavery was abolished, the British plantation owners shipped in Indian indentured servants to fill the void, promising them a better life in the Americas in return for four to seven years of hard labour. Most of them did their time, and did well for themselves in Guyana.

We stopped at some traffic lights. All four lanes of traffic were at a standstill, and the reason soon became apparent. A few seconds later, a convoy of black limousines, topped and tailed by police cars flashing their lights, was coming through.

"The president?" I guessed.

The driver nodded. "Going home. For him, all the traffic stops."

"Good president?"

The driver shrugged. "Depends on who you ask."

Eventually, we moved on and, as we followed a long coastal road bordered by a sturdy sea wall, I spotted the Marriott Hotel. The Guyana Forestry Commission was near it somewhere, though I couldn't see it yet. Two minutes later, when we pulled up outside a nondescript cream building with a long green roof that said Forestry Commission on the front, I paid the driver ten US dollars and waited for him to leave before turning tail and walking across the road to the Marriott. It was a quarter to three in the afternoon and, as I was checking in, the Liat Airlines crew that had flown me into Ogle turned up. I smiled to myself: I had been so quick off the mark that I had beaten the pilots to the hotel.

5

From my window, I looked at the empty pool and beach beyond. It was nothing like the other Caribbean beaches I'd seen because it was a long line of dirty beige sand edged by a sediment-heavy brown ocean. South America might be green, but Georgetown was definitely brown. My eyelids fluttered and then I realised how weary I was. My night of mosquito-hell was paying me back big time. I decided to lie down.

When I awoke, I looked at my watch. It was almost five in the afternoon. Spreading out a map of Georgetown, I looked for anything of interest. There was something called the African

Liberation Monument close by. That might be worth a visit, I felt, but did I dare risk venturing outside alone? Georgetown was the most dangerous place I'd been on my trip and, with the way things were going in America, I wondered how safe a white man would be wandering around by himself.

I sat and deliberated. If I didn't go out exploring, then what would I do to fill up time? I could have something to eat, maybe a few drinks, but then what? Carry on boozing until lights out? Actually, that sounded like a tempting plan; it wasn't as if I *had* to see the city tonight – I had a tour organised the next afternoon. But it was also a cowardly recourse, I felt. That was it, I decided: I would throw caution to the wind and walk into the city. After plotting a rectangular course past the liberation monument, I locked all my belongings in the safe and headed outside.

Even though it was past five in the evening, it was still hot and sweaty. Taking the thin road that led directly south of the Marriott, I passed the Forestry Commission again then walked towards a tall lighthouse patterned in vertical red-and-white stripes. It was some distance away, and I took purposeful strides towards it, keeping a sharp eye on my surroundings, especially since I was in the middle of some sort of industrial area. I wasn't alone, I noticed: a few security guards were sitting behind tall spiky fences, but none paid me any attention. A man wearing a yellow high-visibility vest, riding a pushbike, trundled past. He glanced my way but said nothing. Then a young man turned a corner and waltzed towards me, looking at me as we approached one another. I nodded but he didn't nod back. When he passed, I quickened my pace, hating the feeling that every young Guyanese man might be an assailant wishing me harm.

I came to the lighthouse. It was a tall stick of seaside rock that looked absurdly out of place in the middle of the industrial area. My hotel was to blame. When the Marriott constructed their huge ocean-view edifice, they rendered the lighthouse obsolete. But in the end, the city decided not to pull the beacon down because they thought it might make a good tourist attraction. Well, there were no tourists that I could see, apart from me. Besides, it was closed.

I carried on walking. Coming towards me were a couple of lanky teenagers. Both wore backpacks that probably contained packed lunch tubs and textbooks. To me they hid hammers and knives. They passed without a flicker and I shook my head at the absurdity of the situation. The warnings I read were really preying on my mind and I needed to get a grip.

6

Unlike much of the Americas, the first Europeans to arrive on Guyana's rugged coastline were the Dutch. At first, they contented themselves by trading with the locals, but, when they saw what the Spanish, British, French and even the Portuguese explorers were doing, they got in on the act, grabbing land and turning it to plantations. They did so well that they invited a few British farmers over to see how well they were running things. The British were impressed, so a few more came and some stayed until eventually, when Brits outnumbered the clog-wearing folk, they decided to seize Guyana. When they stuck the Union Jack everywhere, and called their new acquisition British Guiana, the Dutch moved next door to Suriname. And that was how the state of play remained until 1966 when Guyana declared its independence. And since then, crime has slowly increased.

I pressed on, turning left by a warehouse that declared itself the Toucan Food Importer. A car passed me slowly, its young male occupants eyeing me. I ignored them and passed a few government ministries; the car continued to trail me. Wondering whether I was in an episode of *The Wire*, I was relieved when it sped off at the junction of a busy road. Main Street was a gaudy whirl of shops and businesses. Evidently, schools had just finished because uniformed children were everywhere: big-bloused teenage girls in billowing skirts, gawky boys loitering as they chatted and joked, cooler kids in mixed groups as they sized one another up. Seeing the kids cheered me – if they were not in a hurry to get to the safety of their homes, then perhaps Georgetown wasn't as bad as made out in the media. In fact, the most dangerous aspect of walking the street was found in the gaping rectangular holes at choice sections of pavement. Falling down one would certainly result in a painful injury. They were flood drains, allowing water to run into underground channels.

With a newfound bound to my steps, I carried on along Main Street. I watched some women pushing a pram, a man lighting a cigarette, a couple of schoolchildren holding hands as they sauntered along. No one was giving me suspicious or hostile looks. No one cared. Perhaps the car hadn't been trailing me. Maybe the driver was just being cautious around the potholes. And so what if a few people stared at me – they were probably wondering whether I was lost. And while I thought about all of this, I came to a quite remarkable-looking building – my destination of the afternoon: a large, conical thatched structure that called itself the African Liberation Monument.

It looked like an oversized traditional West African hut, but I was wrong. It was a traditional Amerindian hut. In 1972, sixty Wai-Wai Amerindians constructed it after the Guyanese government decided they needed a traditional building for their conference centre. It had stood proud for almost forty years before burning down in 2010. The building I was staring at was a reproduction built only a couple of years ago.

While I wondered why it was called the African Liberation Monument, a man approached. Aged about fifty and in possession of a white beard, he emerged from the side of the hut and looked like an employee of the monument.

"If you want to visit," he told me, "I'm afraid it's closed. You can come back on Monday when we open again."

I told him I could be in Suriname by then.

"So you're Dutch?"

"No, English. Can I ask you something? Why is this hut called the African Liberation Monument?"

The man nodded. "Lots of people ask that question. The hut is not the liberation monument. That is the monument there." He pointed in the direction of five sturdy logs sticking out from a huge stone boulder. They looked a bit lacklustre compared to the massive hut.

"So what is the hut?"

"It's called Umana Yana, which means Meeting Place of the People. It's used as an exhibition centre." The man changed the subject, asking me where I was going. When I told him I was on my way back to the hotel, but had a tour organised for the next day, he nodded approvingly. "It's good that you are seeing some of the city. Many people are too scared to do that. It's a shame because Georgetown is not as bad as people say. Yes, there are robberies in the city, but they involve mainly businesses and shops. Stabroek Market sees a lot of crime, too – if you go there, watch your pockets – but, as a tourist, you will be fine."

I thanked him and walked back towards the hotel before the first stirrings of dusk began to fall over the city, a time when criminals might emerge from their hiding places, seeking devilment.

7

The worst case of devilment to affect Guyana occurred in 1978. It was so bad that for a number of weeks, Guyana found itself the number one news story across the globe. It all began with an American man called James Jones.

Growing up in 1930s Indiana, neighbours described young James Jones as a little bit odd. Some claimed they saw the boy presiding over mock funerals for cats, some of which they suspected he had killed himself. Despite these rather odd beginnings, James Jones managed to grow up, earn a degree and get married.

But beneath the surface he was as mad a mongoose. Aged 24, he founded the Peoples Temple of the Disciples of Christ, a mouthful to say and a mouthful to accept. After securing himself a place of worship, he immediately began preaching his strange mixture of rampant religion and socialism. And people listened. When his congregation began to swell, he bought himself some dark shades, a white suit and got the local hairdresser to fashion his hair into a thick black quiff. He was the Elvis of Christian cults.

At first, his more unusual left-wing leanings were tempered by a noble crusade to fight for black rights. Even though his father was reportedly a member of the Ku Klux Klan, James Jones (now calling himself Jim) and his wife, Marceline, became the first white couple to adopt a black child in the state of Indiana. More people joined his flock after learning of this.

By the time the 1960s rolled around, America was a hotbed of communist war mongering. Cuba, North Korea and the Soviet Union were real and present dangers. Beneath this backdrop, Jim Jones moved his church to California and played on this fear by telling his – by now, considerable – flock that Armageddon was around the corner. The only way they could avoid it, he told them, was to move to the Caribbean where they could live in sanctuary.

What most of them did not realise was that Jones had been preparing the move for quite some time. In downtimes from his sermons, he and a few trustworthy cronies had secretly flown to Guyana to lease a large plot of land located about 150 miles west of Georgetown. The soil was poor and the nearest source of fresh water seven miles distant but, for Jim Jones, it was ideal. It was isolated from the world and so, perfect for brainwashing. After leaving his trusted temple members in the Guyanese jungle to clear the land, construct a few buildings and generally make it habitable for about a thousand people, Jones returned to the United States to prepare his flock. They listened and decided to go.

And so, after packing some key belongings, around a thousand men, women and children followed Jim Jones and his wife to Guyana. When the group arrived in Jonestown (the name Jim had given to their new jungle commune), they quickly realised it was nothing like California. For a start, it was hot and sticky, plus it was full of bugs, snakes and mosquitoes. There was no electricity and the only entertainment was cards, dominoes and mind control. When they moved into their cramped living quarters, getting used to Jim Jones' perpetual sermons through loudspeakers, they settled down and did what most misguided cult members do: they switched off their common sense buttons and allowed themselves to be brainwashed. This set the scene for part two of the whole sorry debacle.

8

Safely embedded within his paranoid South American community, Jim Jones donned his shades and told his flock that the CIA hated them. They would soon be parachuting in, he told them, gleefully torturing their children as they destroyed their camp. After sowing the seeds of this potential CIA terror, Jones told his people that he had come up with a plan. He had talked with the leaders of the Soviet Union and they had graciously agreed to let them live there. Meanwhile, some of Jones' most trusted disciples secretly began smuggling cyanide into Jonestown.

While some people of the commune eyed the sky with trepidation, others may have noticed something odd. Their leader didn't seem as sprightly as he once had been. He had a terrible cough, too. Perhaps jungle life was getting to him, they possibly surmised. When he summoned his congregation and told them that he was dying of lung cancer, they were grief-stricken. In fact, Jim Jones did not have cancer and simply had a bad chest infection (probably from the log-burning going on around the camp), but the reaction from his worshippers was exactly what he wanted: sympathy for what was to happen next.

In November 1978, a US congressman called Leo Ryan flew to Guyana. Congressman Ryan had heard rumours and reports about Jonestown, mainly from worried relatives of the commune. So, with a delegation of eighteen people, including reporters and legal advisors, the congressman turned up at the camp to investigate. Jones knew about the visit and, instead of shooing the delegation away, he welcomed them with open arms. First, he took them to a communal building and made them watch a musical interlude. When it had finished, he showed them around the camp, allowing the delegates to chat to anyone they came across. Everyone the congressman met seemed healthy and happy to live in Jonestown. But, beneath the veneer of friendliness and conviviality, Jim Jones was conniving and manipulating events to suit his purpose. He had instructed everyone to say good things about the camp. Anyone who didn't do this would be sorry. Nevertheless, as the delegates trooped around Jonestown, shaking hands and accepting small gifts, one of them received a note. The owner had passed it skilfully so that no one had seen a thing. The note asked for assistance in escaping from Jonestown.

Things happened quickly after this.

When Congressman Ryan read the note, he asked Jim Jones to gather the whole congregation together so he could address them. Far from refusing to adhere to this request, Jim Jones got on his loudspeaker and summoned his flock. When they were all there, Ryan plainly asked if anyone wanted to leave Jonestown. While most people shuffled their feet or stared blankly into space, some families tentatively stepped forward. All eyes swivelled to Jim. His expression was unreadable, but after a moment, he was seen conferring with a confidant. Then Jim asked the congressman whether he could speak. After taking the microphone, Jones told his people that if any of them they wanted to leave Jonestown, then they were free to leave without repercussion. After a few moments of nervous silence, a few more people shuffled forward. Jim Jones smiled at them. They could leave with Leo Ryan and his delegates.

That was what they did, and Jones did nothing to stop them.

Mood in the camp soured.

As Congressman Ryan's party made their way to the little airstrip that served as a hopping point to the Guyanese capital, Jim Jones paced and hollered. He would not allow anyone to return to their dwellings because he had an important announcement to give them soon. Meanwhile, over at the airstrip, Ryan's group arrived. As two light aircraft began to fill up with passengers, one of the defecting passengers produced a gun and began shooting. He turned out to be one of Jones' most trusted lieutenants. At the same time, a tractor driven by other Jonestown henchmen careened across the runway with more guns. Carnage ensued as bullets struck both planes, shattering windows and fuselages. One plane managed to take off, the other remained on the runway, too damaged to fly. By the time the shooting ended, five people were dead and eleven seriously injured. One of the dead was Congressman Ryan. More than twenty bullet wounds peppered his body.

Back in camp, Jim Jones heard the news and addressed the crowd. After spinning a yarn about forces beyond his control causing the congressman's death, he told his people that the Soviet Union would no longer allow them to move there. He then added that CIA parachutists were on their way and would soon be dropping over Jonestown with knives. There was only one way out, he claimed: revolutionary suicide.

A group of Jones' minions dragged a large metal drum before them. Inside this vast urn was a cocktail of cyanide and valium, mixed with a sedative and a fruity drink to mask the taste. Next to the drum was a table. On it was a collection of plastic cups and syringes. The congregation eyed it with trepidation: they knew exactly what it was.

Jones asked for volunteers.

9

When the first temple member walked up to the metal drum, everyone watched with interest. Her name was Ruletta Paul, a young black mother who was carrying a baby. With a stoic expression, she squirted cyanide into her baby's mouth; then, before she could change her mind, picked up a plastic cup and drank a measure herself. Then some members of the group led her to a quiet place well away from the others. It was good job; if they had heard the resulting screams, some may have thought twice.

Next, a father and his young daughter walked up to the table. At the last second, the girl decided she didn't want to have any cyanide but her father forced some poison into her mouth and held his hand over the girl's lips so she had to swallow. He took his cupful and off they went to the quiet place to die. More people made their way to the table

With so many people taking the deadly mixture, the quiet place was quickly overrun and so people had to sit on the grass to wait out their deaths. This was when people really saw the effects of cyanide positioning. As it took hold, people were crying out, attempting to fight off burgeoning seizures. Breathing difficulties and cardiac arrest soon followed. Dying from cyanide was not a quiet, painless affair. All the same, even with people convulsing on the ground around their feet, the congregation still queued to get their poison, and, if anyone faltered at the final moments, burly men were on hand to forcibly assist them.

Near the end, Jim Jones' wife took her life. As Jim Jones regarded her prone body, surveying the other 919 people who lay dead (including 276 children), would he have felt relief? Did he feel nothing? Did he believe, as he had told his followers, that everyone would meet up on the other side? Whatever he felt, Jones ended his life by shooting himself in the head.

When news of the mass suicide broke, investigators and reporters from around the world rushed to Jonestown, horrified to find the ground littered with bodies, side by side, on top of one another, infants, adults, the elderly: all of them dead in the worst single loss of American civilian life until 11 September 2001.

Today, should anyone want to visit the site of the Jonestown Massacre, they would find it next to impossible. After a fire burned down much of the complex in the mid-80s, the jungle eventually reclaimed everything apart from a few oil drums, a mill and a rusting tractor. The only way to see these items would be to fly over the exact spot and look directly down. And who in their right mind would want to do that?

10

The next morning, I threw back the curtains and took in the view again. The Caribbean Sea was still the same dirty brown colour, the pool was still empty and the only movement I could discern came from a lonely fisherman sitting at the far end of a concrete pier. It looked as if he wasn't catching much.

A small blue-and-white boat powered its way around the turn of the coastal wall, bobbed past the pier and fisherman before stopping near the shore, more or less opposite my hotel window. Though tricky to see clearly, I could make out six men in the boat; while I watched, one jumped into the surf. After feeling about in the water, swishing it this way and that, he came up with something wrapped in black plastic. It was about the size of a football.

Was I witnessing a drug pick-up? Was it something to do with fishing? The men didn't seem like fishermen, even ones who hunted for lobsters, but what did I know? The deck of their boat was devoid of anything notable apart from a few coils of rope and some ominous white sacks that might have been pillows but probably weren't. If it was a drug pick-up, the men were being brazen about it, doing it in front of a hotel. The man in the water passed the package up to the men in the boat, deftly jumped back aboard and shook himself down. Then the boat turned around and returned from where it came.

I looked back at the fisherman sitting at the end of the pier. He was taking no notice of the boat as it passed the tip of the pier. I looked upwards from him. The sky was a hazy blue colour, with not a cloud in sight from left to right. It was a Caribbean morning that promised hot sun. Before it kept that promise, I decided to see if I could find a way to the pier. Perhaps there would be a good view of the city from its extended position.

In hindsight, I should've stayed in my room.

11

I left the hotel, my camera thrust deep inside my trouser pocket. Instead of heading towards the lighthouse, I turned right, passing the other side of the Forestry Commission, then a few warehouses protected by fences and barbed wire. From somewhere came the sound of heavy machinery and men's work voices. And then I came to a large metal fence that blocked further movement. Beyond it was Georgetown's mammoth sea wall.

I spied a thin path of weeds to my right. On one side of the path was the sea; on the other side was a warehouse. The path disappeared around a corner just past the warehouse. I reckoned it was the only route to the pier, unless I wanted to scale the fence and negotiate the sea wall. I walked along the path and a minute later was rewarded: the fence ended just past the corner. Instead, thick bushes formed a natural barrier. I ambled along until the trail took another turn back to the sea. It was then that I noticed a white wading bird sitting on one of the rocks that made up the sea wall. I left the path, crouched down and aimed my camera.

"What'yu doin'?" said a voice.

Startled, I turned to see a young man wearing a white T-shirt and dirty jeans. He was standing on the pathway. He must have come up behind me. Where he stood now blocked my passage back to the trail.

"Taking a photo of this bird," I said jovially. I stood and smiled. The young man just glared. Undeterred, I stepped towards him, watching him warily. He didn't say anything as I approached, but refused to move over to allow me passage. I could either push him out of the way or meander around him. I chose the latter. A few steps later, he shouted something. I didn't hear it and wasn't bothered anyway; I carried on walking. Ahead of me was another turn in the trail; I just hoped that access to the pier and maybe the beach lay soon after.

"I talkin' to you, white man!" shouted the youth. I turned to face him. He was still standing in the same spot, but now looked furious. "Why you here?" he snarled. Behind me somewhere, I could still hear the clickety-clack of heavy machinery. "Why you here, white man? We kill white men here." He spoke the last sentence with a snarl.

My thoughts raced. Adrenaline flowed. Had I heard him right? I looked to see whether the youth had any sort of weapon. I couldn't be sure. Maybe he had a gun in his back pocket. I looked for an escape route.

"Why you kill the black man? The innocent black man? Why you do that, eh?"

Finally, I responded. "I don't know what you're talking about. I'm just a British tourist looking around your great city."

"You people kill black people, we kill fuckin' white people." He remained in his spot, but he was getting more agitated. His arms were pointing, thrusting; one hand was a fist.

I decided that speaking to him further would only inflame the situation so turned and made for the corner at speed, wondering what would happen if the man followed me. Around the turn, I scoured the ground for a small rock and found one. Picking it up, I ran through some thin bushes until I came to a dead end. Except it wasn't a dead end – it was a chest-height wall of concrete that told me to keep off. Fully expecting the youth to appear around the corner at any moment, I hoisted myself (using muscles I'd not used in a decade) and clambered upwards. It was then I discovered it wasn't a wall but a short concrete platform backing onto a warehouse. At the other end of the platform was a drop to the sea wall and pier. If I got onto the pier, I would have access to the beach. From there, if I needed to, I could make my escape.

Still with no sign of the man in the white T-shirt, I considered the drop. It was perhaps three feet, but the landing would be rough. Uneven concrete spilled off towards the sea wall, eventually forming the pier I'd seen from my hotel window. The fisherman was still at the far end, I noted, unaware of the drama going on behind him. For a second, I considered retracing my steps; after all, the man in the white T-shirt was nowhere to be seen. But what if he was still there? What if a few friends had joined him? I decided to jump rather than return. With my camera still in my hand, I stepped off the ledge.

The next few minutes are a blur.

12

One second I was standing on the lip of the platform, the next I was on the ground, my camera flying free of my grip. I saw it bounce over the edge of the concrete path and down into the boulders of the sea wall. At the same time, the vision in my left eye clouded and I felt thick liquid oozing down my face. Instinctively, I reached up. My hand came away red, dripping red. And then I noticed fat spots of blood falling onto the concrete beneath me. Blood was coating my shoe. I tried to get to my feet, but felt so woozy, I only managed to get to my knees. Instead, with no coherent thought forming, I absently wiped blood away from my left eye and momentarily saw light. Then wet darkness took over as blood streamed down. At least I wasn't blind.

Men's voices sounded but I didn't care. I was broken and hurt and my main concern was the bleeding. The horrid dark red puddle beneath me looked bad. Streams of red were flowing from it towards the sea wall. It looked like something from a horror film. What I couldn't understand was why there was no pain. Perhaps adrenaline was keeping it at bay. Even when I saw four young black men running towards me, all I could focus on was the blood. It was dripping over my shirt, pooling on my knees; it coated both hands and I realised that didn't care whether I was going to be robbed. Then the men were upon me.

One man checked my wound. Another poured water over it, sluicing away a waterfall of red, then pink, liquid. A third young man poured water over my hands. The fourth was peering down into the rocks of the sea wall, presumably looking for my stricken camera. I allowed myself to fall utterly into their hands.

"Man, that was some fall," one of the men said. "I saw you from the window over there in the warehouse. As soon as you landed, I knew it was bad. I saw your camera fly into the rocks."

"You need sutures," his pal said, using the American word for stitches. He poured some more water over my wound. Light flickered back into my eye, and now it was starting to hurt. And the second I felt the pain, I felt more. Suddenly, it rose to a crescendo of stinging, with my left elbow joining in with the orchestra of agony. Someone passed me a large leaf and told me to press it hard against my wound. And then, the man by the sea wall said something and all four jumped down into the rocks of the sea wall. A minute later, one came up with my camera. They passed it to me and I slurred a thank you. Its lens was twisted, its bodywork scratched and chipped. When I turned it on, it whirred and buzzed, but these were its death throes. A second later, it was still, the screen blank. I knew how it felt.

"You need to go to hospital," one of the men with the water said. "You're going to have a black eye." My wound was still bleeding, and more blood was running down my face. I touched the wound and immediately wished I hadn't.

"Where you stayin'?" one of the men asked.

I told him.

"Good. It's not far. You need to go back to your hotel and tell them you need to go to hospital for sutures. You understand?"

I nodded.

Two men lifted me to my feet. The exertion of this caused a fresh wave of blood to stream down my left side of my face. More water was poured; another leaf was produced and the men guided me towards a small track that led parallel to the beach behind the hotel. When I told them, I would be fine from there, they looked unconvinced.

"I really am okay," I said, though I felt anything but. "I'll be at the hotel in five minutes. And thanks for helping me. I truly mean that. And thanks for finding my camera." I could not believe how helpful they had been. If they hadn't stepped in to help, who knows what I'd have done. Maybe I would have got up, staggered around and fallen onto the rocks. It didn't bear thinking about.

"Take care, man," the man who had found my camera said. "And get those sutures done."

In hindsight, I wish I had given them some money, but with the pain, my clouded vision and the general shock of what had just happened, it didn't even enter my head. Feeling about as sorry for myself as I ever had, I lumbered towards the hotel, quite literally a broken man

13

I somehow entered the hotel, walked to the lift and escaped to my room without anyone noticing me. Or if they had, then I'd been in too much pain to care. I stood in front of the bathroom mirror, wincing from the pain in my head. Blood smeared the whole of my left face. More was still joining it, trickling from a flap of open skin just above my left eyebrow. I looked like someone had attacked me with a knife. My unbloodied skin was ashen, my eyes sunken: I looked a wreck.

I grabbed a handful of tissue paper and pressed it against the wound, gritting my teeth from the fierce agony. Then I lay on the bed wondering what to do. I probably did need stitches, but couldn't face dealing with this at that precise moment. Instead, I looked at my watch. It was a smashed circle of metal, the glass covering gone, the mechanism broken beyond repair. Then I noticed my knuckles –

they were bloodied and raw. I moved my left arm and winced at the terrible pain in the elbow. It felt like no other pain I'd experienced and I concluded I'd broken something. I lay still for moment, taking stock.

For ten minutes I didn't move. I didn't dare. One thing was for sure, though: I was not going on my afternoon sightseeing trip around Georgetown – not with a bleeding head and potentially broken arm. The only positives I could see were that my mobile phone had survived the fall and so had my wallet. Both lay on the bed beside me. And it could've been worse. I could have been stabbed to death by the white-T-shirt-wearing youth. I could've knocked myself unconscious. I could have fallen into the sea. But I could take little solace in this and so started berating myself for going out on a walk when I should have remained in the hotel.

Thirty minutes later, the bleeding had slowed to a trickle. With a wad of tissue at hand, I washed my face and decided my arm was now the primary focus. I could not stretch it out. If I tried, then pure white agony shot down through my elbow. Something was definitely wrong. I found the room telephone and called reception.

"Hi," I croaked into the receiver. "I need a doctor or someone. I fell over and my head won't stop bleeding. Also, I think I've broken my arm, but I'm not sure."

The receptionist didn't say anything for a moment. Then she processed the urgency of the matter and told me that there was no doctor available, but there was a member of staff trained in emergency first aid. She would send him straight up.

The young man arrived two minutes later. He had a little bag of medical supplies. After walking me to the bathroom, he washed my wound and then dabbed it with iodine. The pain was horrendous and immediate. It was so bad that I instinctively reached up with my left arm, causing a sickening slice of pain to erupt along my left-hand side.

"You need to go to hospital," the first aider told me gravely, still dabbing at the wound. "This needs sutures. It won't stop bleeding without them. They can check your arm, too." When he found out I had a tour booked in fifteen minutes' time, he said that they should take me to a hospital. It would save organising a taxi.

I nodded. This whole thing was turning into a disaster. But then I thought of something else. "How long will the hospital take? I have a flight to Suriname tonight at 10pm."

The man looked at his watch and shrugged. "If you go to the public hospital, it will take . . . maybe eight, nine hours. If you go to a private one, maybe two hours. I really can't say."

"How much will a private hospital cost?"

The man looked apologetic. "I don't know. It depends on what treatment you have. But I do know this: if you don't get to a hospital, the wound might get infected. You don't want that to happen."

I nodded wearily. The day had turned into the nightmare – a nightmare of my own making.

14

Somehow, and I do not know how, I managed to remove my bloodied shirt and pull a clean one over my body. I wiped the blood from my shoes and then shuffled my way down to the lobby. A tour guide was already waiting for me. The hotel staff had clearly briefed her because as soon as the young woman saw the state I was in, she sprang into action. After talking with the hotel first-aider for a moment, Lucy introduced herself and led me out to the van and driver. When I climbed into the back, she had to help me up the step, telling me that a private hospital was about ten minutes' drive away. I tried to sit as still as I could, feeling utterly miserable.

From the outside, the hospital looked very unlike a hospital. There were no ambulances and no large red crosses, and I was slightly disappointed not to see a stretcher and a couple of nurses waiting for me. After we parked, Lucy helped me onto the pavement and towards the door. Not knowing what to expect from a Guyanese private medical establishment, I followed her inside.

It was chaos. People were queuing up, shuffling about or sitting down with pained expressions. Orderlies rushed past, nurses swept through and I stood in the centre of the whirlwind, not knowing what to do or where to start. A woman, cradling a bleeding face far worse than mine, was sitting slumped upon a chair. Without Lucy, I may have given up and died, but somehow she found a way to register me so I could see a doctor. I thanked her profusely as a slip of paper came my way. The woman behind the Perspex counter wanted me to sign it; because I was left-handed, I couldn't write a thing. Instead, I scrawled something with my right hand and passed it Lucy, who handed it to the woman behind the desk. Money changed hands and then I had to wait.

Lucy and I found some spare seats, which gave me chance to look around. One section of the waiting room was set aside for collecting medicines, another for people waiting to pay. Around a corner was a little area for x-rays, and, by the door, a parking area for wheelchairs. The wheelchairs, I noted, grimly, were not the metal contraptions seen in UK hospitals: no, these were simpler things. Basically, they were white plastic chairs stuck onto go-kart wheels.

We waited for fifteen minutes until, finally, a doctor was ready to see me. While Lucy remained in the waiting room – going above the call of duty for a tour guide, I genuinely felt – an orderly led me to a side room containing a bed, a long glass cabinet containing medical bottles, and a fire extinguisher. The orderly told me to sit on the bed and then left. A few moments later, a doctor appeared. Instead of a white lab coat, the young man sported a black T-shirt, jeans and designer stubble. He looked more like a gangsta-rapper than a physician, even with the stethoscope around his neck.

He regarded my wounds. "What happened?"

I told him and he nodded. "You need sutures. But you are a lucky man. I'm Georgetown's master at suturing, and, when I'm done, there will not be a scar." He then examined my arm, asking me to curl my fingers, bend my wrist and move my elbow. I did all of these, but the elbow caused me the most pain. It was like a knife slicing away at my joint. It made my eyes water. "We'll have to do an X-ray," he said. "I suspect a fracture. I'll get that arranged for you. In the meantime, let's sort out your head."

While he sewed me up, I asked the doctor whether he ever had to deal with any serious incidents at the hospital.

"We sometimes get gunshot wounds. Once, a police officer was rushed in with a serious wound to his right eye. A bullet had gone straight through it. We couldn't deal with that one and so we transferred him to the specialist hospital. I went with him and, in surgery; we removed a bullet from his brain. He was a lucky man."

"So he survived being shot through the eye?" I could not imagine such as thing.

"Yeah. We saved his eye too."

At that moment, a needle was tugging on my skin, and I could feel it pulling upwards towards the ceiling. I cried out involuntarily.

"I'll tell you one thing we do have a problem with in Guyana," said the doctor, ignoring my pathetic whimpering. "Suicides and suicide attempts. I think we might have one the highest suicide rates in the world. Alcohol, poverty, mental illness, a lack of clinical psychologists – it all contributes. We see suicide attempts in here a lot."

With my stitches finished, the doctor produced a mirror, the same way a hairdresser might. I regarded his handiwork and gave a satisfied nod. Then he placed a huge white plaster over my wound. It was the biggest plaster I'd seen outside of a medical drama. Satisfied I was in good hands, I retired to the waiting area again. It was time for part two of the patch-up.

15

While Lucy and I waited, an emergency came in. A young woman, slumped unconscious in a wheelchair, was rushed through the doors. Blood dripped from beneath the large towel draped across her prone body. As she was wheeled away, tracks of blood were left in her wake.

"What do you think happened to her?" I asked Lucy. She looked as shocked as I did.

Lucy shook her head. "Maybe she's been stabbed."

Whatever the cause, it put my stitches firmly into perspective. I sat back, trying to get my head around what I'd just seen. And then, barely a minute after the blood had been mopped up, another emergency came in – this time an older woman. She was also in a plastic wheelchair, unconscious and slack, with a drip attached. The people with her, presumably her family, were beside themselves, screaming and crying and spinning around in panicked circles. "Help her!" one woman screamed. "She's dyin'!" Some orderlies dragged the group away towards a second emergency room.

The upshot of the double emergencies, apart from shocked awe, was there were no more doctors available. I waited for close to two hours until an orderly appeared, and when he did, everyone pounced upon him, wanting to know when it would be their turn. I remained seated, nursing my arm as best I could.

"Jason Smart," shouted a voice. It was another orderly. He led me to the X-ray room where a torturer awaited. Even though I had a suspected broken arm, he manhandled my limb onto a plate so he could take his photographs. It was agonising, especially when he made me repeat the process because he'd messed up the first shots, but when he was done, the X-ray plates confirmed what I already knew: my arm was fractured just near the elbow joint.

Three hours after arriving at the hospital, I was ready to leave. My head was in stitches, my arm was in plaster, and my wallet had been emptied of over 35,000 Guyanese dollars, which equated to almost two hundred US dollars. With some painkillers in my gullet, the worst of the pain would hopefully be kept at bay. And, as we walked back to the minivan, Lucy gave me a choice. Either, we could go back to the hotel or we could have an abridged tour of the city. "I would hate you to leave Georgetown without seeing what it has to offer."

I considered this. "Is there time?"

"If we're quick. The way I see it is this: you paid for a tour and you have not had a tour, unless you think visiting a hospital counts as one."

I gingerly raised my left arm a little. A ripe strip of pain bolted along my arm and into my brain. But at least it was protected as it could be. If I went back to my hotel, I would only feel sorry for myself. But did I want to go out and see the city with a newly broken arm? I decided I did.

16

On the way to central Georgetown, I finally had time to think. Though I was looking forward to seeing something of the Guyanese capital, I wasn't looking forward to what would happen after that. When I got back to the hotel, I would have to pack my suitcase, drag it around an airport and then manhandle it into a Suriname Airways' overhead bin, all with one arm. What about eating? There was no way I could eat using a knife and fork, at least not simultaneously. And what about getting undressed? Going to the toilet? Opening a bottle of water? Filling in immigration forms? The list of things that I needed two hands for was long. And the more I thought about it, the more morose I grew. I tried moving my arm a centimetre. A sickening shot of pain was my reward. I stared out of the window, catching sight of the ridiculously oversized plaster on my head. I looked like I'd had a lobotomy.

We stopped near a large area of green where a group of teenagers were playing football. Lucy told me it used to be called the Parade Ground. "It's now Independence Park. If you look in the centre – and I know it's hard to see – there is a memorial. It's for the Demerara Revolt. You heard of this?"

I shook my head.

"Demerara was an old Dutch colony that included Georgetown. The sugar they made in the plantations is where the famous Demerara brand of sugar comes from. I'm sure you've heard of it. Anyway, in 1823, thousands of slaves rebelled against their masters – the British by this time. The slaves took over the plantations, tied up a few white men, even killed a few, but mostly the protest was peaceful. In return, the British killed a couple of hundred slaves and then brought a few to this Parade Ground. They tied them up and lashed them – lashed them until they bled. But the ringleaders got worse. They were shot and decapitated, their heads nailed to posts and their bodies left hanging for months, rotting away so everyone could see."

"That's horrible."

"As it happened, though, the Demerara Rebellion was a turning point. People in England already wanted to end slavery, and this was the final straw. A decade later, the British abolished slavery."

We headed further into the city.

17

Georgetown's most famous sight is the magnificent cathedral. Striking in its gothic design, the cathedral towers over an otherwise lacklustre district of the capital, gleaming with its painted white sections and tall pointed steeple. St George's Anglican Cathedral is all the more remarkable because it is made entirely of wood: one of the world's tallest wooden structures, in fact. First unveiled to awestruck Georgetown residents in 1892, the builders promised that their new wooden place of worship was not only capable of withstanding the ravages of Guyana's tropical heat and rain, but it could also resist the hardiest of wood-loving insects. What about fire, someone asked? Don't worry, the designers hollered. The cathedral is fireproof, too. And so it was proved, because it is still standing 124 years later.

Up close, it didn't look quite as splendiferous. In places, the white paint is peeling, and some of the wooden panels look like they needed replacing. But, to stand for so long without burning down, falling down or blowing down is testament to the skills and forethought of the designers. I mentally tipped my hat to them and took a one-handed photo with my phone.

Further into Georgetown, we arrived at its busy and sun-drenched central core. Trees, with their lower trunks painted white, lined the streets. Fetching, old colonial-style buildings lay behind them. People wandered hither and thither, often hidden under sun parasols. No one rushed, though. Caribbean time was strictly enforced in Guyana.

The centre of Georgetown was a hotbed of fruit stalls, hat shops, lottery sellers and cigarette stands. With my wounds temporarily forgotten, Lucy and I wandered a pathway towards City Hall, avoiding the drainage ditches and Dutch-built canals. We found City Hall on a hectic intersection between two of Georgetown's most picturesque streets, the aptly named Regent Street and the grand sounding Avenue of the Republic, both brimming with old architecture. City Hall was one of the best of these buildings, described by some as Georgetown's most handsome construction. It was a stately, three-storey white mansion of grand wide verandas, ostentatious arches and, in keeping with the Cathedral, gothic spires. Unfortunately, garbage littered its grounds, some of it piled up into heaps. It was like a gorgeous cream gateau standing in a rubbish bin.

I asked Lucy about the litter.

"It's because the building is closed off. No one is allowed beyond the fence, and so people think they can toss garbage over. I think it's so sad they do this."

"Why is it closed off?"

"It's sinking. There are sinkholes beneath City Hall's foundations. One of the buildings across the road – I think it was a shop that sold car parts – was pulled down a few years ago because of the sinkhole. Then City Hall started to sink, too. So they closed it off. It's been like this for a while now – thus the garbage. No one seems to care."

I couldn't believe that the city chiefs had not done something to rectify the situation, especially since such a beautiful and important building was possibly under threat. They needed to get structural engineers to look at the ground and add reinforcements. I asked Lucy why this was not happening.

"Money. It's always about money."

18

We stopped by another canal. Deep water stirred within its inky depths. "When the Dutch settled here," Lucy told me, "they knew the ground was below sea level and so would flood. That's why they built the canals. When it rained, water collected in the canals and did not flood the city, even when the tide was in. When the tide went out, special wooden gates called *kokers* – you can see them all over Georgetown – were raised to let the rainwater escape into the sea. Their system worked for two centuries."

I nodded at the forethought and intelligence of the Dutch, wondering whether they had built Amsterdam's canals for the same reason.

"But now when it rains," Lucy added reflectively, "we sometimes have floods. And the reason is simple: some of the canals have been filled in, with roads built over them. The rainwater has nowhere to go and so it floods the city. You should've seen it this time last year. You couldn't see the roads; they were rivers."

Our next stop was Georgetown's second most famous sight – Stabroek Market, named after the old Dutch capital of Demerara. The market is the nation's largest and busiest place of vending, peddling, bartering and thieving. If I were going to be robbed anywhere in Georgetown, then Stabroek Market would be it. Lucy told me to keep my phone in my pocket and one hand around my wallet.

If I were blind, I'd have still known I was at the market. The clattering of carts, the hubbub of street selling, the beeping of the minibuses – it was all part of the cacophony that made Stabroek so noticeable. But I wasn't blind, and I stared up at the market's famous clock – a glorious burgundy-and-white, Victorian-style tower made from cast iron. An impressive red spike jutted from the very top. Sloping away from the clock was the equally dazzling zigzag-roof, forming the cover of possibly the oldest structure in the city. The market itself spilled beyond the building's walls, forming a tight jumble of stalls selling everything from cuddly toys and cheap jewellery to aluminium cooking pots. Cars were parked haphazardly; people wandered around with fans of lottery tickets; even the bedraggled were there, wandering aimlessly or washing clothes in the drains around the edge of the market. Vying for attention with the visual spectacle was the smell. As we approached the main building, the dripping odour of sun-cooked fruit and garbage assaulted my nostrils.

Once inside, my eyes were plunged into near darkness. But once they had adjusted, there was not much to see beyond a tight huddle of stalls selling mangos, chillies and pineapples, and another stall selling sunglasses. Once through the other side of the market building, Lucy and I found ourselves beside a small but ridiculously busy harbour. Small boats were powering towards the jetty, unloading sets of passengers, collecting more, and then speeding away into the Demerara River. As soon as they were gone, other vessels replaced them. For 100 Guyanese dollars (about 40p), I could've taken a trip to the other side of the river. As it was, I wiped my brow, being mindful of my head wound, and then followed Lucy back through the crowds towards the van.

19

With time sadly lacking, we had to skip the botanical gardens, the zoo, the Roth Museum of Anthropology and, worst of all, the Steel

Pan Museum. Instead, we headed straight to one of the most inappropriate statues I have ever clapped eyes upon.

I did a double take at the strange figure standing atop the pedestal. Whoever had cast him had done so with a perverted mind, for it showed an open-mouthed and oversized-headed man masturbating. His facial expression looked like he was saying 'Ooooh!' I couldn't believe a thing existed, especially in such close proximity to the Arch of Independence. It was only when the angle altered that I saw my terrible mistake. The figure was not up to anything untoward, and was in fact, holding a small animal.

"This is Cuffy," Lucy told me. Behind her, a fat ochre sun was sinking below the horizon, meaning that darkness would soon be upon us. "It was put here in 1976 to celebrate ten years of Guyanese independence. Cuffy was a West African slave who led a rebellion in 1763. He and his men took over some white-owned plantations. He even took the wife of one of the plantation owners as his wife. I can only imagine what her husband thought of this."

"Was she agreeable to this arrangement?"

Lucy admitted that she did not know.

"What are the things in his hands?" Now I was up close to the statue, I could see that Cuffy had something in both hands.

"One is a piglet, the other is a dog. He is squeezing them to death. They are symbolic, of course. The pig means ignorance; the dog, greed. Cuffy is ridding Guyana of both."

"What happened to him?"

"After the rebellion, he killed himself."

"Why?"

"I'm not sure."

I peered up at the identified objects. Neither looked like a pig or a dog, or any type of animal for that matter. In fact, they looked like large sausage rolls. Whatever they were, Cuffy looked a man not to trifle with, especially if you were walking with a pet piglet; after one final look at his open mouth, we retired to the van. My brief tour of

Georgetown was over and it was time to return to the hotel so I could prepare myself for an evening of misery.

20

I don't know how, but somehow I managed to pack my bag and haul it to the lobby with one arm. Now that the painkillers had worn off, the pain in my arm was merciless. Every time I moved my elbow – even a millimetre – a bolt of pure white pain struck me. As I checked out, the lady behind the counter looked at my plaster, then my arm. "Is it broken?" she asked, concerned.

I nodded miserably. The evening was going to be a long one. First I had to get a taxi to Cheddi Jagan International, the city's main, but distant, airport, check in, wait for my flight and then travel to Suriname to repeat the process in reverse. It didn't bear thinking about how I would manage all that with a broken arm.

"I saw you earlier," the receptionist added, "when you were with your guide. I had no idea you had broken your arm, though. You must be so brave. If that were me, I'd have been screaming the hotel down. You're a man of steel."

The woman looked sincere with not a hint of jest about her. I mumbled a thank you and then slunk off with my luggage to find a taxi. But what she had said made me feel a little better. Perhaps not a man of steel, but I was definitely a brave little soldier. All I needed was my mummy to tuck me up in bed and I'd be happy.

My taxi driver was a young Indian-Guyanese man called Kamal, recently divorced, he told me. "I can't stand her, man. Nag, nag, nag, you know. Don't do this, don't do that. Don't go there – I had enough. We've got two young kids, but it's better for them I'm gone. They're not bothered anyway." He seemed to dwell upon this theory for a moment before switching back to his ex-wife. "She was just too bossy, that was the problem. Actually, no, her bossiness was just one of the problems."

As we left the by now darkened city, we began a drive along what looked like a rural road with only the occasional street light or porch lantern offering any illumination. Then the conversation turned to cricket. “I love the game,” Kamal told me. “As a young boy, all I ever wanted was to be a professional cricket player. It almost happened, too.”

“What went wrong?”

“The usual – work, wife, kids. But I’m only twenty-eight and I still play. My average is forty, which isn’t bad, you know. Who knows? Maybe there’s still time for me.”

“I’ll look out for you on TV when the West Indies play England.”

“You do that, man,” he laughed. “But I doubt it will happen. For one thing, cricket in Guyana is dying out. Kids prefer football these days. Plus, West Indies cricket is not as good as it used to be. Not enough funding, not enough training, too much favouritism.”

By the time we reached the airport forty-five minutes later, Kamal and I had broached wide-ranging topics from Islamic extremism to poor driving habits in Guyana. When we pulled up outside the departure terminal, he passed me his card. “If you’re ever back in Guyana, give me a call.”

I told him I would do just that. Then I shuffled off to catch my flight to Suriname, the final country of my Caribbean misadventure.

Clockwise from top left: Stabroek Clock Tower; Georgetown Cathedral – one of the largest wooden structures in the world; Georgetown's old lighthouse; Cuffy Monument – it's not what it looks like; The corner of Regent Street and Avenue of the Republic; Broken and battered in Guyana; The view of Georgetown from the Marriott

Chapter 10. Finally, Suriname!

I could not recall a single time when I felt sorrier for myself. Despite all the rational thoughts I'd had since leaving hospital (that it could have been so much worse and that at least I still had an arm – in Georgetown, I had seen a man with only a stump), I was utterly miserable. And, even though people at the airport had gone out of their way to help me – carrying my luggage, filling in my immigration forms and helping me to negotiate security – all I wanted was to be at home in bed.

Certainly, I had no wish to see anything in Suriname, and my plan when I got there was to stay in the hotel, lick my wounds and feel even sorrier for myself until my flight back to Europe. And that was another thing: almost ten hours to Amsterdam, followed by another hour to Manchester – a torturous journey in ordinary circumstances, horrendous with a broken arm. So in the departure lounge of Guyana's small international airport, I found some Wi-Fi and did something utterly ridiculous. I upgraded my Suriname Airways economy ticket to business class. It was expensive, and I almost backed out at the last second, but when it was all done, I actually felt better. A reclining seat to while away a ten-hour flight to Europe would give me something to look forward to at the end of the nightmare.

I looked at the clock on the wall and brooded. Then I winced when my left arm moved. Then I shifted in my side and brooded some more. The brooding highlight was when an announcement told me my flight was delayed. It was already eleven pm. At this rate, I would be at the hotel by 2am. Brood, brood, brood.

Two minutes to midnight, we took off. Thankfully, a friendly member of the cabin crew put my luggage in the overhead bin (almost breaking her own arm with the weight of the thing) and then helped me get my seatbelt on. So this is what it feels like to be an invalid, I thought morosely. *There, there, Mr Smart, you have a nice nap now.*

Forty minutes later, we landed in Suriname, but I took no enjoyment in this. The thunderstorms on approach had jolted the cabin sufficiently for me to knock my left arm against the seat rest a couple of times. The throbbing was agonising.

At Surinamese immigration, I handed my passport to a man in uniform. He flipped it to the information page, studied it and then studied me. "This is not your passport," he stated, thin lipped and humourless.

I opened my mouth, then closed it again.

The man examined me. "The photo does not match your appearance."

"It is me!" I stuttered, feeling ridiculous to be even saying it. "I'm Jason Smart!"

The immigration officer tapped my passport. "This man does not have an eye-patch." He then laughed raucously at his own joke, stamped my passport and handed it back. "Welcome to Suriname, Mr Smart."

2

Because I was staying at the Marriott, the hotel arranged a van to transport me there. Sharing it was a thin, fifty-something man wearing a dark suit. When he saw me struggling with the seat belt, he offered to help. I gladly accepted and we introduced ourselves. His name was Simon, a Trinidadian businessman. I could tell he was looking at my wounds.

"I fell," I said, by way of an explanation.

"It looks like you've been fighting."

"No, I fell – honestly! I was taking a photo whe—"

Simon smiled. "Don't worry; I'm only joking with you. Does it hurt?"

"A little," I lied. It was hurting like mad.

As we set off, Simon told me he worked for the Trinidad government, in the Ministry of Energy. "You know who Patrick Manning is?" he asked.

I nodded and said, "The former president of Trinidad and Tobago. He died last week."

"That's right. Though he was the former prime minister, not the president. Let me tell you a story about Patrick Manning. Back when I was twenty-one, starting out as a new petroleum engineer, he was Trinidad's energy secretary: my boss. In my first week, he came into the tiny room where I worked and sat down. I can remember how he put his feet on my desk, crossed them over and said, 'Let's chat'. I have no idea what we talked about, but I do remember this: whenever I spoke, he listened intently. I was terrified of saying the wrong thing, but he had this knack of putting me – a lowly officer junior just out of school – at ease. Even back then, though, Manning *oozed* power. I wasn't surprised when he became prime minister." Simon paused. "He let himself down in the end, though. During his final two terms, the power got to him. When he made his wife the Education Minister, I knew the end was coming. He thought he was above the law. But when he died, I was still sad."

Our Marriott minivan was traversing dark countryside towards the capital, Paramaribo. Anything beyond the roadside verge was impossible to make out in the gloom. I asked Simon whether he had been to Suriname before.

"Many times, and let me tell you this: Suriname is one of my favourite places in which to do business. Unlike Guyana, and even Trinidad and Tobago, Suriname is perfectly safe. I have never felt any element of danger on my visits. And another thing I respect about the Surinamese is their cosmopolitan attitude. They embrace every faith, every creed, every belief and culture. If you look around the city, you will see Chinese stores next to local coffee shops next to African souvenir stores. And that is why Suriname is doing so much better than Guyana. It's a forward-thinking country, a melting pot of ideas, a mini-world, if you like, quite unlike your country, the United Kingdom."

He stopped speaking. "I'm sorry to offend; I have many fond memories of living in London, but the vote to leave the European Union is one of the worst decisions your people have ever made. The UK is a leader in commerce and education. It has rich natural resources and a stable government. Trade flows in and out of the country and yet you have stepped back from that. The UK wants to close its borders? Utter madness. Take Venezuela: another country accepting the backwards step. They closed their borders with Colombia, thinking they did not need outside help because of their vast quantities of oil. But look what at what's happened. The economy has nose-dived, and now its citizens are sneaking across the border to buy medicines for their children. The Venezuelan government are slowly realising the error of their judgement, but it has taken them a long time." Simon shook his head. "Let me tell you this, Jason: eventually the people of your country will realise the error of their ways and will go back to the EU with their cap in hand. It will be painful, but there will be no other way. If a country wants to survive – no, survive is not the right word – if a country wants to *succeed*, then it needs to embrace different cultures and different ways of thinking. It's the only way forward. No country on Earth can avoid globalisation; any that does will fail."

Wow. The conversation had turned heavy, but then again, Simon was a politician, and a clever one to boot. To change the subject from the stupidity of the British voter, I asked him about his time living in London.

Simon smiled. "My petroleum company moved me to London with my wife and daughters. It was funny, though; my neighbour turned out to be a wealthy South African gentleman. He was a bigot and a racist, and he made no bones about it. Whenever he saw me, or a member of my family, he would call us racist names. I later found out he had been a landowner during apartheid, and had fled to London to escape the black men taking over his nation. This is why he hated us, a black family from the colonies living next door to him; he couldn't stand it. But we didn't actually live next door; we lived above him, in the penthouse apartment. I used to smile to myself every time I unlocked the door and walked across his ceiling. He was living below a black man, in every way possible."

I smiled at the thought of this. Just deserts came to mind.

Simon asked me of my impressions of Guyana.

"Well, apart from breaking my arm, it was quite nice. There are some great buildings and some interesting hospitals." I told him about the youth who had inadvertently contributed to my fall.

"There are many disenfranchised young people in Georgetown. But do you know what? Things could change soon. Guyana had just discovered oil. During the next decade, things will change dramatically for them. The country will have money and lots of it. Then, the people will suffer for a while; it always happens when a country discovers oil. They call this phenomenon *Dutch Disease*. Have you heard of this?"

I shook my head.

"The name comes from the 1970s when Dutch engineers found a huge gas field in the Netherlands that brought in massive amounts of money. Almost overnight, their economy changed. Dutch exports became massively expensive due to the rise in value of the guilder and so manufacturing industries went bust. Conversely, their inflated guilder was able to buy foreign goods at reduced prices. Food became cheaper for the Dutch, so did electronics. To them, it was boom time, but beneath the surface, things were rotten. When the gas ran out, and with no export industry to fall back on, the country was in trouble. It took them a while to get back on their feet. I think the only oil country to avoid Dutch Disease is Norway."

By now we were driving through the dark streets of Paramaribo. Along one semi-lit street, a trio of prostitutes were plying their trade and, when we passed them, a line of neon-lit bars signalled we were nearing the centre. Ten minutes later, we pulled up outside the Marriott, where Simon and I alighted. In the lobby, we shook hands.

"Well, Jason, it's been a pleasure chatting to you. I hope you enjoy your stay in Paramaribo and I wish you a speedy recovery."

3

I awoke with the sun streaming through the partially opened curtains. I was fully clothed. With an arm in a sling, I had been unable to undress myself. I couldn't even remove my socks. In the end, I had simply lain on the bed, above the covers, keeping as still as possible. At 2.30am, I truly believed that sleep would be impossible; yet here I was, seven hours later, after having slept like a baby.

I realised my arm was not hurting. I moved it, and then it did; a maddening assault that flared along the entire arm, from the shoulder to the tip of my fingers. It was if someone had my arm in a wrench and had just yanked. The pain almost made me want to throw up. With my flight at 10.20 that evening, I intended to remain in bed until I had to go to the airport.

An hour later, hunger took over. I'd not eaten anything substantial since before my fall. I supposed I could have ordered some room service, but I decided I was a little bit bored and so decided get up, carefully slipping my legs over the edge of the bed to stand up. Then I lumbered to the bathroom to regard my sorry self in the mirror. What a way to end my trip around the Caribbean, I lamented as I stared at the stubble-ridden face, the dry, cracked lips and the stupid patch above my eye. Speaking of which, I decided to lift a corner of the plaster to look at the damage beneath. I did so and was surprised when the whole patch came away in my hand, revealing an angry set of stitches and the beginnings of a bad black eye. I put the patch back over then removed it, comparing both looks. I decided au naturel was the lesser of two evils. Then I decided to have a shower. But this needed some planning.

I returned to the bed and removed my socks. It took an eternity. Each sock took about ten minutes of stretching, contorting and swearing. Then I started on my trousers. Removing a belt and flicking a button open with one hand meant using dexterity I hitherto never thought I possessed, but somehow I managed it, and swung my hips until the trouser legs were down by my ankles. After twisting out of them, I was sweating like mad and so decided to save the T-shirt for later. Pulling it over my cast and head would require a superhuman skill I doubted I had.

To regain a semblance of sanity, I walked over to the curtains and fully opened them. From my top floor room, I gazed out at Paramaribo. The Surinamese capital looked pleasingly tropical, with a thick wash of trees receding towards the distance, edged by a straight strip of road on one side and a sweeping blue line of the Suriname River on the other. Maybe after some food, I could go for a little walk. I would wait and see.

When I felt ready to tackle my T-shirt, I returned to the bed. For the next hellish ten minutes, I twisted and turned, stretching the fabric over the cast and then looped it over my head. By the time I was free, I was in agony and ready to give up again. But I was starving and the thought of having to order room service, and then answering the door wearing only a sling and a smile made me carry on to the bathroom where I had a shower with my left arm sticking out the door. Still, it was the cleanest I'd felt in a long time.

Grappling with a towel built for two-handed use was fun. But things were about to get a whole lot worse. As bad as undressing myself had been, doing it in reverse was harder. The socks were the easiest things, and they took fifteen minutes. Thinking that a button-up shirt would be easier to manipulate than a T-shirt, I spent close to thirty minutes doing the buttons up, all with one hand, only to find I'd done them one button out of sync every time. I shouted at the window, at Suriname, at Guyana, at anyone who had slighted me in the last few days. I could not do this anymore! I didn't have the strength, patience or dexterity! In absolute frustration, I lay down on the bed and closed my eyes. Then, when I realised that no one was going to help me but myself, I got up and undid them, redid them and then checked my watch. Since awakening, almost two hours had elapsed, and all I had achieved was getting dressed.

4

After a cheese and ham sandwich in the hotel café, washed down with a strong coffee, I felt a lot better – so much so that I decided I would see some of the city. Instead of going for walk, I would get the hotel to find me a taxi. Ten minutes later, one of their airport vans turned up. With a reasonable price quoted for a three-hour sightseeing trip, I felt better than I had since before my dramatic collapse in Guyana.

Keith, the hotel driver, was professional enough not to ask about my arm, head and knuckles. But I told him anyway, explaining in detail about the lead-up to the event.

Keith whistled. "I do not know what I would have done in that situation. He sounded like a bad guy, especially for you as an American."

I corrected him, which brought about a swift apology. "Oh sorry, man. It's just that we don't get many English guys here. Most white guys are Dutch, but when you spoke English, I just assumed…"

We were driving along a thin road into the centre of the town. Apart from the fine quality of the road surface, the other thing that struck me was how clean and orderly the Surinamese capital looked compared to Georgetown, and most of the other Caribbean capitals I'd visited. Its modern buildings, its flat pavements, the sophisticated street lighting: Paramaribo could've been in Europe, perhaps Holland. Dutch was still the official language of the country, and, as we drove along, I caught snippets of Dutch writing splashed upon storefronts, street signs and advertisements.

Because Keith had a free rein on what to show me, he decided I might be interested in a hotel just down the road. I wasn't interested at all but, because Keith seemed so keen, I allowed him to lead me into the Royal Torarica, a huge green-roofed hotel.

"This is the lobby," he said, stating the obvious. "And this, in here," he said, pointing at a door which said CASINO on the front, "is the casino."

He opened the door and invited me to peer inside. I blinked at the harsh lights, at the slot machines, at the whizzing and whirring and the people sitting at blackjack tables. Keith, ever helpful, suggested I take a photo, which I did, though for no other reason except to appease him, which brought a harried gentleman in a suit rushing towards us. His raised his hand, palm facing me. "No photos," he barked.

Thanks Keith, I thought. Getting me into trouble for nothing, but he was already gone. He was chatting to a hotel worker behind me. A moment later, Keith bounded over. "Don't worry, I've smoothed things over. You can take a photo of the casino. No one will stop you."

I told him I was fine, but he insisted. This time, with the hotel manager (if that's who he was) in tow, I took a photo of a roulette table. The man in the suit nodded in acquiescence. Finally, we could leave the damned casino to see the rear of the hotel.

The Royal Torarica's expansive pool area was packed, each face as white as my own. It was as if I had stumbled through a portal and had arrived in Spain or Greece. Kids played in the shallow end of the pool, teenagers tried to look cool at the deep end. Couples sunbathed on gaudy loungers while wrinkly pensioners sipped cocktails. There was a man in charge of the music, blasting out tinny Euro-pop while his head bobbed to the beat. Another man flipped burgers on a large barbecue. I shook my head to dismiss the image, but it was still there. Europe had come to Suriname in the form of Dutch holidaymakers.

"You like it?" asked Keith, grinning. "This is more fun than the Marriott. The Marriott is for business, the Torarica is for pleasure." He grinned at me.

More like for decadence, I thought. Suddenly Keith had a great idea. “Pass me your phone, I’ll take a photo!” I told him he didn’t have to. “I insist. Stand by the pool. It’ll be a great shot.”

I pulled a face.

“Come on, sir! And don’t forget to smile!”

I took a step towards the pool and posed in my sling. Keith counted to three them took the snap. A few people watched this as they slurped from their bottles of Parbo Bier, the local ale. Then he made me pose on a grassy trail nearby. The resulting image depicted a man who wished to be elsewhere. Keith didn’t see this. “Great photo, man. You will remember this.” He was right.

5

Our next stop was not another hotel, but an old military installation called Fort Zeelandia. Its collection of old buildings, fortifications and cannons bordered the banks of the River Suriname, offering the chance to ponder colonial barracks one minute and huge cargo ships the next.

Keith was content to let me wander the grounds alone, preferring to rest against the bonnet of the car while he checked his phone. Away from the main buildings, almost hidden in undergrowth, was an information placard. It informed me the Dutch had given the fort its jaunty moniker of Zeelandia after one of their homeland provinces. When they moved in, they were probably rubbing their hands with glee. To secure this little parcel of tropical land, they had swapped a troublesome colony to the north with the British. They were glad to be rid of New Amsterdam, though, because now they could pour all their energy into Suriname and its sugar. Later, they came to regret this decision. The British renamed New Amsterdam New York; the rest is history.

The Dutch, like all the other colonial powers in the region, utilised local manpower as slaves. When the population proved inadequate, they shipped thousands over from Africa. After the abolition of slavery, men from the Dutch East Indies (now Indonesia), China, India and even parts of the Middle East arrived in Suriname to toil in the sugar, tobacco, cotton, cocoa and coffee plantations. Due to this influx of different cultures, Suriname became one of the world's most ethnically diverse countries in the world. It still is.

Following the discovery of Bauxite, gold and oil, the country has done okay for itself. According to figures released by the International Monetary Fund in 2015, Suriname is classed as a mid-ranking economy, coming in at number 73, lumped around countries such as Brazil, Thailand, Barbados and Iran. Compare this to its neighbour, Guyana, which languishes at a lowly 117, around places such as Angola, the Republic of Congo and the Philippines. With their wealth, the Surinamese government has funded new roads, schools and hotels. No wonder holidaymakers from cold and rainy Rotterdam journey to this often forgotten outpost of Dutch colonial history to lap up a piece of Caribbean tranquillity. If I were them, I'd be doing exactly the same thing.

I walked to the sea wall where two small children were watching the passage of a huge white vessel called *Seatrade*. This large cargo ship was ponderously chugging its way inland. Once clear of the city limits, water is the only way for anyone to travel around Suriname. Beyond Paramaribo, the country is an expanse of rainforest, savannah and floodplains. Anacondas, anteaters, vampire bats, armadillos and piranha fish live there.

To finish my short tour of Zeelandia Fort, I circled a grand statue of Queen Wilhelmina, an old Dutch monarch. Wilhelmina looked a little weather-beaten, and all the birds that had roosted upon her head had stained her face a little, but she still looked royally poised, staring at the river in her expansive gown. All around her were pleasant Dutch-style town houses standing in freshly-mowed gardens. If I squinted my eyes and ignored the palms, I could have been on a leafy, nineteenth-century Amsterdam street.

6

Suriname in the early 1980s was not the peaceful, prosperous nation we now know and love. A military coup, led by thirty-five-year-old Desiré Delano Bouterse, had just overthrown the government and had installed itself in Fort Zeelandia. With strict curfews and even stricter press controls in place, people left in droves to seek new lives in the Netherlands. Those who stayed lived in fear for their lives. When a group of prominent intellectuals – lecturers, lawyers, journalists and the like – tried to speak out about the new regime, Bouterse's cronies rounded them up and delivered them to a mock courtroom in Fort Zeelandia. Needless to say, they were all found guilty and shot to death, two of them, allegedly, killed by the great leader himself; the killings were known as the December Murders. The Netherlands asked Bouterse to explain the deaths; Bouterse claimed the men had tried to escape and had therefore forced his men to take such drastic action. The Dutch government didn't believe this outrageous lie, especially as one of the victims was found with a swollen face (in keeping with being repeatedly struck), a broken arm and eighteen bullet wounds in his chest. If this man had been escaping, then he was running backwards while punching himself in the face. The Netherlands ceased all aid to its former colony.

As for Bouterse, he eventually got sick of everyone pointing at him, whispering that he was a crazed dictator, and allowed national elections. He didn't win, but was pacified with a new job as head of the army. Away from the public spotlight, he turned his talents to drug smuggling. He was good at it. After trading weapons for cocaine with Colombian drug barons, he set up an efficient smuggling operation that transported narcotics to the Netherlands. When the Dutch authorities discovered his little, but highly-lucrative, sideline they convicted Bouterse, in absentia, of drug trafficking. They said that if he ever set foot in Europe, he would end up in a Dutch prison for eleven years. Bouterse, of course, denied the charges, claiming his total innocence. Nevertheless, being prudent, he decided it would be best not to leave Suriname for the time being.

Things, meanwhile, were hotting up at home for Bouterse. After intense lobbying by the Dutch, the Surinamese government decided to find out exactly what happened during the December Murders and so Bouterse and a few of his henchmen were summoned to explain themselves in court. On the day of the trail, Bouterse didn't bother turning up, claiming the trail was a farce. He didn't turn up the next day, or the one after that. Then things did indeed turn farcical when a political act was rushed through the Surinamese parliament stating that all the suspects in the December Murders trial should receive total amnesty from the charges. Inexplicably, it passed and all court proceedings immediately halted.

The Netherlands shook its collective head and halted the 20 million euros it was about to send to Suriname as part of an aid package. Bouterse, however, cheered and began plotting his most audacious move yet. In 2010, in the biggest flip of the finger possible to the Dutch, the people of Suriname elected Bouterse as their new president. The man who had started a bloody coup, had allegedly overseen a kangaroo court and had smuggled drugs into Europe was now President of Suriname!

One of the first things he did was award a few of his fellow coup pals a Yellow Star, the highest honour in the country. He then declared the date of his coup a national holiday. Most controversially, he pardoned a murderer. This made the headlines for two reasons: one, because it was the first time in history that a Surinamese president had ever pardoned anyone convicted of murder, and two, the young man turned out to be Bouterse's foster son.

As the current president of Suriname, Bouterse enjoys total immunity from any crime he may or may not have committed; however due to the international arrest warrants out on him, he rarely leaves his little slice of South America.

7

Behind Fort Zeelandia is a collection of streets with names such as Kleine Waterstraat, Henck Arronstraat and the almost unpronounceable Onafhankelijkheidsplein, all of them sounding deliciously Dutch. A wide expanse of green called Independence Square separates the streets, while a series of grand, governmental buildings, including the National Assembly and the palatial Presidential Palace, form a pleasing backdrop. I walked past the latter, hoping to catch sight of President Bouterse, but his domicile was too distant to see anything of note. Instead, I walked towards a large statue of a portly gentleman. The placard told me his name was Johan Adolf Pengel.

Keith joined me underneath the statue of the former Surinamese president. "Was he a good man?" I asked.

"Very good. A people's president. He made Suriname the country it is now."

"Better than the current president?"

Keith shuffled his feet. "No comment."

Close to Independence Square is the finest part of Paramaribo – its inner, historically intact, central core, deemed so authentic that when a group of bigwigs from UNESCO visited, they nodded their collective heads, conferred for a minute and immediately added it their list of places that must never be destroyed.

Keith and I took an ambling walk along some of the grid-like streets, all of which were full to bursting with seventeenth- and eighteenth-century wooden houses that the Dutch had built so masterfully. I found it remarkable that the white verandas, the fancy wooden doorways and the dark-brown, gabled roofs could still be enjoyed today. True, some looked like they needed a lick of paint, or a few wooden panels replacing, but, by and large, the 250 or so UNESCO-protected buildings looked great, evoking a time when horses and carts traversed the streets instead of cars and tourists with broken arms and mobile phones.

I asked Keith why so many of the original buildings had survived the ravages of time, especially since most capital cities in the word had torn down their old buildings in the face of modernisation.

"It's simple. For the last forty years, Paramaribo hasn't changed. So it's not as if we kept them on purpose, they are just here. Mind you, I think the government is worried about them catching fire – because of all the wood – but I think they'll be okay. The government won't want them to go because the tourists like them."

Before returning to the car, Keith and I strolled to the nearby waterfront area, a place of empty cafés, moored boats and even more old wooden houses. Possibly due to their proximity to the river, the buildings were in pretty bad shape. One was so bad that scaffolding crisscrossed its front facade and a corrugated metal fence guarded its broken entrance.

Suddenly there was an almighty splash. We turned in time to see something big disappear into the water. Involuntarily, we moved back from the water's edge.

"What was that?"

Keith laughed nervously. "I don't know. Maybe a fish?"

"Maybe a caiman."

"No, caimans only live in freshwater."

"I thought this was a river?"

Keith moved back a few centimetres. "Oh yeah, you're right."

8

Keith wanted to show me the other side of the river, which meant traversing a long concrete span called the Jules Wijdenbosch Bridge, named after another former president of Suriname. As we descended back to ground level on the opposite side, Keith asked me whether I'd ever tried banana chips.

"Banana chips? Like French fries, but made from bananas?"

"No, banana chips, like in a bag. A bag of chips made from bananas."

"Oh, you mean banana crisps?"

"Crisps? Chips? Yeah, the same thing. Have you tried them?"

I admitted I hadn't, but didn't add that I was thankful for that. Deep fried slivers of banana sounded like a snack manufactured by devils. Just then, a strange sight caught my eye. It was a young man holding a large lizard up to passing motorists. I couldn't tell whether the reptile was alive or dead. Further along was another man holding the same type of long iguana. It was about four feet long and the lizard was definitely dead. I asked Keith what was going on.

"They're selling them for food."

"People eat them?" It sounded horrific. Maybe they sprinkled banana chips on top of them.

Keith nodded. "They cook them first, though; they don't just eat them raw." He found this thought immensely funny and laughed heartily. His laughter was infectious, and soon we were both sniggering like loons.

There was nothing much on the other side of the river except for some fruit stalls and convenience stores. Keith pulled up outside one of the latter, telling me he was going to buy some water. While I waited, I watched a couple of dogs sniffing around an empty box lying outside the store. One was a puppy, the other its mother. After deciding the box was not worth his time, the puppy decided he wanted to play. He jumped up at his mother's tail and then sprang up on her back. Mum threw him off and regarded her puppy for a moment, then decided to humour him, carefully grabbing his leg and tipping him over. The young dog loved the new game and it was a joy to watch their antics.

Keith returned with two bottles of water and two bags of banana chips. He me passed a bottle of water and then one of the packets of chips. Thanking him, I said I'd save them for later.

"No, try them now." Keith was already opening his. The banana chips were long and yellow and looked like strips of plastic. Keith munched away on his strip, gesturing that I should do the same. To be polite, I opened the clear plastic wrapping, pulled out a greasy strip of deep fried banana and bit off a chunk. To be honest, it didn't taste as bad as I expected and was like a normal British crisp, except with a vaguely banana taste. "Mmm!" I lied, taking another bite for good measure. "Delicious."

Before I could do anything more, Keith dashed back into the supermarket and returned with two more bags. "Save these for later," he told me with a wink.

Fifteen minutes later, we were back in the centre of Paramaribo. It was almost time to return to the hotel. As we made our way through the city centre, we passed a great-looking, almost chocolate-box pretty, orange-and-blue church. Not far from it was a brightly painted mosque. Then we drove by the Chi Min Restaurant and, further on, a tiny little café called the Caribbean Delight, its name painted in vivid colours. Paramaribo was indeed a country embracing its different ethnic cultures.

At the Marriott, I thanked Keith for his impromptu tour-guiding skills, and climbed out of his car. "Sir," he shouted after me. "You forgot these." He was holding the bags of banana chips I'd stuffed into the armrest.

9

Sitting aboard a Suriname Airways Airbus en-route to Amsterdam, some nine hours distant, I manoeuvred myself into the most comfortable position I could find. Thank God I was in business class otherwise I might have considered drinking myself to oblivion to escape the pain, even though my painkillers stated that no alcohol must be taken with them.

Ignoring the warnings, I'd already had a glass of wine with my meal, and was now on my second. I'd even had a snifter of champagne just before take-off, relishing it as I tried to get my money's worth from the seat. Feeling slightly light-headed, I managed to open my laptop with one hand and began to look through the photos I'd taken on my trip. There I was in Barbados having a bottle of Banks Beer in a tiny outdoor bar. I smiled at the memory, thinking of how tired I had been and how a traffic jam near Manchester Airport had almost derailed me being there. I flicked to some photos from Trinidad: a hummingbird, a view of Port of Spain, a black cannon poking over a hilltop fort wall – all great memories, then skipped to snaps taken in Grenada, St Vincent and St Lucia. In one photo, I was standing beside a city-centre park with two good arms. If only I had known that a week later, I would be sitting inside a Guyanese hospital. Antigua, St Kitts and Dominica came next, followed by Guyana and Suriname, whose photos were on my phone. And despite my broken arm and broken camera, I realised how lucky I was to have visited all these different countries. And special thanks needed to go to Liat Airlines, too. Much maligned for their delays and cancellations, they had nevertheless delivered me to seven of them. Without Liat Airlines, I would not have seen them at all.

But one thing was for sure: it was time to go home. I was ready for some rest and recuperation. For now, I closed the laptop, pressed a button on my expensive seat to recline it almost horizontally and then closed my eyes as we coursed over the Atlantic Ocean towards Europe.

Clockwise from top left: Historically intact Dutch buildings in Paramaribo (these two are in particularly bad shape); Me posing for Keith. Note the happy expression; Portly statue of Johan Adolf Pengel, former president of Suriname; Strolling by the River Suriname; Saint Peter and Paul Cathedral, downtown Paramaribo; Surinamese dollars – I especially like the square coin!

Message from Jason

Thanks for reading about my travels around the Caribbean. If you enjoyed it, I would really appreciate a review on Amazon. Just a few lines will do. Small-time authors such as me rely on word of mouth exposure. Just find my book on Amazon and click review.

If you have enjoyed this book by Jason Smart, then perhaps you will also like his other books, which are all available from Amazon.

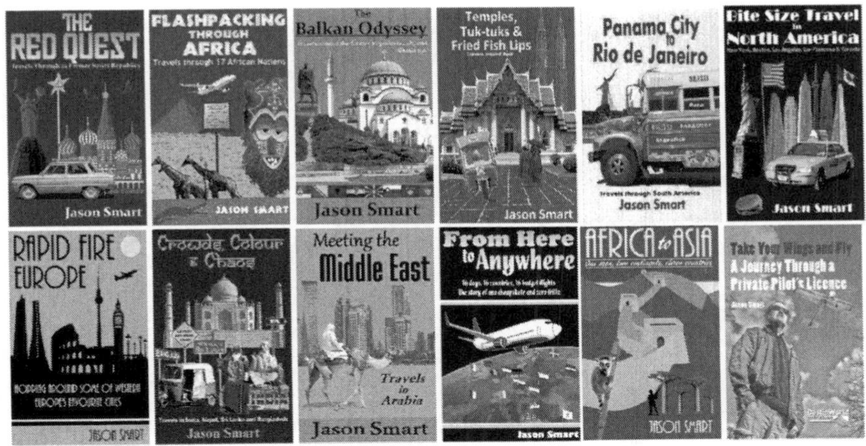

The Red Quest
Flashpacking through Africa
The Balkan Odyssey
Temples, Tuk-tuks and Fried Fish Lips
Panama City to Rio de Janeiro
Bite Size Travel in North America
Crowds, Colour, Chaos
Rapid Fire Europe
Meeting the Middle East
From Here to Anywhere
Africa to Asia
An Accidental Tourist
Take Your Wings and Fly

Visit his website **www.theredquest.com** for more details.

Printed in Poland
by Amazon Fulfillment
Poland Sp. z o.o., Wrocław